NAPA *at* LAST LIGHT

America's Eden in an Age of Calamity

JAMES CONAWAY

Simon & Schuster

New York   London   Toronto   Sydney   New Delhi

Simon & Schuster
1230 Avenue of the Americas
New York, NY 10020

First Simon & Schuster hardcover edition February 2018

SIMON & SCHUSTER and colophon are registered trademarks of Simon & Schuster, Inc.

For information about special discounts for bulk purchases, please contact Simon & Schuster Special Sales at 1-866-506-1949 or business@simonandschuster.com.

The Simon & Schuster Speakers Bureau can bring authors to your live event. For more information or to book an event, contact the Simon & Schuster Speakers Bureau at 1-866-248-3049 or visit our website at www.simonspeakers.com.

Interior design by Carly Loman

Manufactured in the United States of America

10   9   8   7   6   5   4   3   2   1

Library of Congress Cataloging-in-Publication Data is available.

ISBN 978-1-5011-2845-5
ISBN 978-1-5011-2847-9 (ebook)

For beloved Brooklyn and Cooper

To love, and bear; to hope till Hope creates
From its own wreck the thing it contemplates.

—Percy Bysshe Shelley
Prometheus Unbound

They's comin' a thing that's gonna change the whole country.

—John Steinbeck
The Grapes of Wrath

TABLE OF CONTENTS

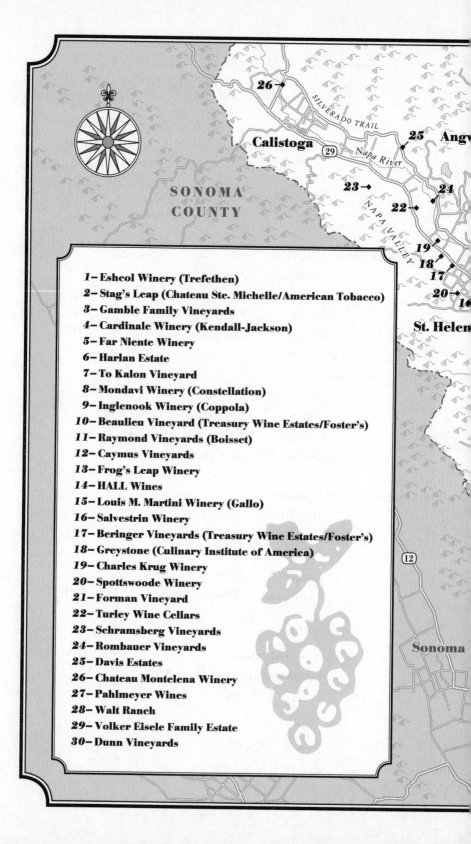

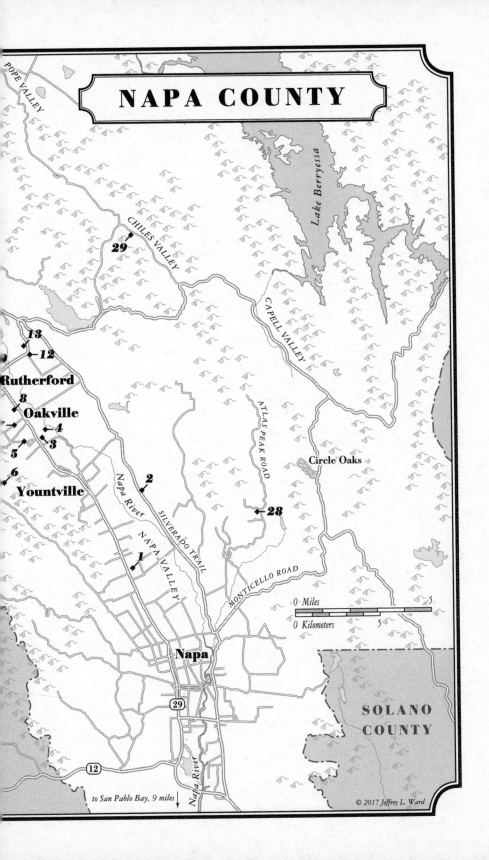

NAPA COUNTY

POPE VALLEY

Lake Berryessa

CHILES VALLEY

29

CAPELL VALLEY

13

12

Rutherford

8

Oakville

4

3

5

6

Yountville

ATLAS PEAK ROAD

Circle Oaks

Napa River

SILVERADO TRAIL

2

28

NAPA VALLEY

1

MONTICELLO ROAD

0 Miles 5

0 Kilometers 5

Napa

29

SOLANO
COUNTY

12

to San Pablo Bay, 9 miles

Napa River

© 2017 Jeffrey L. Ward

DRAMATIS PERSONAE

Note: The names below all appear in the narrative. A *founder* in most cases made wine at some point, *vintner* is mostly an ornamental title nowadays, and *growers* are often farmers who no longer do the actual work. *Citizens* have become more than bystanders at the twin spectacle of celebrity agriculture and marketing.

Founders:

Jay Corley (Monticello)

Jack and Jamie Davies (Schramsberg)

James and George Goodman (Eschol)

John Benson (Far Niente)

Robert Mondavi (Robert Mondavi Winery)

Gustave Niebaum (Inglenook)

Georges de Latour (Beaulieu)

Tiburcio Parrott (Miravalle)

Jacob and Frederick Beringer (Beringer Vineyards)

Alfred Loving Tubbs (Chateau Montelena)

Peter Newton (Newton Vineyard)

Mike Grgich (Grgich Hills Estate)

Warren Winiarski (Stag's Leap Wine Cellars)

Jack Cakebread (Cakebread Cellars)

Dave Phinney (The Prisoner, Orin Swift Cellars)

Randy Dunn (Dunn Vineyards)

Larry Turley (Turley Wine Cellars)

Delia Viader (Viader Vineyards & Winery)

John Williams (Frog's Leap Winery)

Stu Smith (Smith-Madrone Vineyards & Winery)

David Graves (Saintsbury)

Charlie Wagner (Caymus Vineyards)

Ric Forman (Forman Vineyard)

Joe Heitz (Heitz Wine Cellars)

Volker Eisele (Volker Eisele Family Estate)

Vintners:

Gil Nickel (Far Niente)

Francis Ford Coppola (Niebaum-Coppola, Inglenook)

Mike Robbins (Spring Mountain Vineyard/Miravalle)

Jim Barrett (Chateau Montelena)

Bill Harlan (Harlan Estate, Bond)

Fred Schrader (Schrader Cellars)

Jean-Charles Boisset (Raymond Vineyards, Buena Vista)

Christian Moueix (Dominus)

Koerner Rombauer (Rombauer Vineyards)

Jayson Pahlmeyer (Pahlmeyer Estates)

Craig and Kathryn Hall (Sacrashe Vineyard, HALL Wines)

Garen and Shari Staglin (Staglin Family Vineyard)

Mike Davis (Davis Estates)

Growers:

Andy Pelissa (Pelissa Vineyard)

Tom May (Martha's Vineyard)

Andy Beckstoffer (Beckstoffer To Kalon Vineyard)

Tom Gamble (Gamble Family Vineyards)

Inheritors:

Will Harlan (Harlan Estate, Promontory)

Peter Jr. and Marc Mondavi (Charles Krug Winery)

Bo Barrett (Chateau Montelena)

John Daniel Jr. (Inglenook)

Dramatis Personae

Robin Lail (Lail Vineyards)
Hugh Davies (Schramsberg Vineyards)
Beth Novak Milliken (Spottswoode Estate Vineyard & Winery)
Rich Salvestrin (Salvestrin Winery)
Mike and Kristina Dunn (Dunn Vineyards)
Andrew Hoxsey (Napa Wine Company)

Citizens:

Geoff Ellsworth (Citizens' Voice)
Susan Kenward (Citizens' Voice)
Jim Wilson (Defenders of East Napa Watersheds)
Mike Hackett (Save Rural Angwin)
David and Cindy Heitzman (Circle Oaks Homes Association)
Dan Mufson et al. (Napa Vision 2050)
Chris Malan (Living Rivers Council)
Lois Battuello (Freelance Researcher)

Commentators:

Robert M. Parker Jr.
Elin McCoy
Jon Bonné

FOREWORD

A journalistic foray to California in the early 1980s led me into gorgeous mountains bracketing a narrow valley unlike any place I had ever known. I grew up in the faraway South, yet here on the far side of the same continent were distinct similarities to the place I had left behind. Like the South, many in the Napa Valley were related, they helped each other, shared and traded things as southerners might (equipment, knowledge, wine) and intermarried with a bit less alacrity than in rural Tennessee. But in Napa they raised children to take over what was an odd combination of farming, high craft, and an almost religious belief in the God-given rightness of "the cause"—not states' rights, but their ability to make wine as good as anyone's, anywhere.

The established families were agricultural, and a few of the scions rocketed into roles for which they weren't prepared, like Jett Rink in Edna Ferber's *Giant*, or stories out of William Faulkner's fiction, with sunstruck approximations of the Snopeses. Other accounts read like latter-day narratives from Genesis, such as the brothers Mondavi brawling in the vineyard and the expulsion of Robert, that family's own prodigal son. There were actual southerners, too, including a vineyard owner from Tidewater Virginia who would be an ongoing player in Napa's rapidly unfolding, truly phenomenal success.

The valley I came to know in the 1980s is reflected in my book *Napa: The Story of an American Eden*, a social history comprised of the stories of latter-day founders of great wine estates and those working to perfect their own sometimes idiosyncratic visions. These harkened back to the vineyards of France, Germany, and Italy, and from extended families and the collective experiences of others emerged a critical and financial success of a sort never before seen in America.

As important was the idealism of newcomers whose energy and imagination made the new Napa possible, names like Forman, Winiarski, Heitz, Davies. Crucial to the management of so much success were growers, winemakers, and citizens whose names still ring in the clear, sunlaved air of Northern California: Pelissa, Erskine, Cronk, Eisele, Malan, all pushing for control of the mounting bonanza that now threatens to emulate California's traditional boom-and-bust past best symbolized by the Gold Rush.

The 1960s, '70s, and '80s were in retrospect years of great innocence and promise, the latter soon realized and the former rapidly diminishing. My book's sequel, *The Far Side of Eden*, dealt with the growing conflict between new wealth and individual freedom in the final years of the twentieth century, and many of the same people, older and sometimes wiser, appear in its pages, as do some of their children. Land-use issues loomed large, and still do; so does the phenomenon "lifestyle" vintner, inherent in the conflict between development and the agrarian ideal.

The latter is embodied in the agricultural preserve established in 1968 to prevent the valley from becoming another extended bedroom community and is still a matter of contention. Cautionary tales included that of a maverick whose ambitious vineyard development set off a gargantuan legal struggle with the Sierra Club and a homegrown environmental wunderkind, an epic battle that sharply divided the valley. But the real subject of that book—and of the one in hand—is the valley itself.

This last of the trilogy comes at the end of an era and combines narrative journalism with personal reflection. It is based on three decades of note-taking in a place I came to know and love, and in ways to mourn. Readers of the first two books will recognize many of these characters, but some, like the times, have changed, reemerging in new roles. Burnished by experience, they and the valley are drawn in the harsher light of a long year stretching from the conclusion of a severe drought in 2015 to the eve of the national election of 2016 that ushered in a new era for the nation and the valley.

This book is not about wine but about place and people. The reader doesn't need intimate familiarity with viticulture, or the exclusive world now representing it, to see this as a unique American story with great value in its own right, and a shared relevance. Wine isn't just another example of corporate commercialism, for the traditions it represents have always stood apart. They no longer do. Napa was so blessed that its land and communities should have withstood the excesses of the system, should have survived in their own right even as others passed by in America's ongoing maelstrom of development and greed. But it has not and best serves now as a microcosm of a country where opportunity and the ever-intensifying struggle for financial supremacy have trumped even the most sacrosanct ideas and institutions.

The story begins with a ruminative look at the mysterious subject itself, wine, and its influence beyond social cohesion, money, and sensory appeal. We then move through Napa's once-great wine estates, Brigadoon-like visions that became white elephants and had such influence on the desires of the inheritors. Collectively they and their imitators changed the valley: citizens, laws, vistas, the place itself. Avatars of our time, some positive, some decidedly not, these all reflect more ambition than vision in a place whose fate is unavoidably tied up in theirs.

Not so long ago Napa was thought of in Edenic terms, but today is as closely defined by conflict as by wine. Characters weave in and out of the narrative, for there is no other way to accurately and fairly portray the valley. Key players distinguish themselves by deeds, not properties, and this will leave its own lasting impression on readers.

Two words—*the valley*—denote both the flats laid down through time by the Napa River, and the steep forested hills on either side that are the wellsprings of the valley's water. Here, real lives form a matrix of connections and sensibilities around this precious resource that will ultimately determine how their stories play out. A few characters have been assigned pseudonyms, or in some cases, no name at all, often at their own request.

Five of the seven sections are devoted to specific struggles similar to those all over the country but heightened by Napa's fame and outsized concentration of wealth and notoriety. Complete in themselves but interrelated, these stories are bound together by common fears and common foes, with overlapping casts and, in some cases, common dreams. And deep within them lurks the potential of their unraveling.

Much rides on the outcomes of our latter-day Gilded Age, the enemy personified by abject self-interest—individual and corporate—and by co-opted officials, judges, and representatives of the presumed civic order. Altered lives, captive dreams, the loss of virtue—all reflect like facets on the main character of the book, the valley itself: extraordinarily blessed with natural beauty, globally recognized, relegated now to the vagaries of human ambition.

The struggles are in their way all between profit-driven schemes and the preservation of places and resources. Unless the characters can agree on and effect sustainable development, the things that render life worth living here and elsewhere will disappear and this lovely corner of the earth will become unfit not just for vines but also for people.

The challenge is relevant to the arc of human history going back to the origins of wine itself and, as is true wherever wine is made, place is inseparable from the voices of the people living in it. Their stories, old and new, touch us, whether outlandish or all too human, comingling like lees at the bottom of an old bottle brought up at last into the light, now uncorked.

PROLOGUE:
Monticello West

Those who labor in the earth are the chosen people of God.
—Thomas Jefferson, *Notes on the State of Virginia*

There's no little mountain, just the flat floor of the Napa Valley with a backdrop of dry, distant chaparral. The winery is called Monticello nonetheless and is much like its namesake outside Charlottesville, Virginia, but smaller. None of Jefferson's beloved Chinese Chippendale railing above the faux-Palladian porch, and the geometric wood tiles in the entrance hall are not in Monticello's pattern. "When I saw how long it took the carpenter to lay those tiles," says the owner, a retired National Security Agency linguist named Jay Corley, "I thought, 'My God, I'll go broke.'" But then, spending too much money on your house is very Jeffersonian.

Corley, in khakis and Stanford University windbreaker, bears no resemblance to the third president of the United States, yet his white hair gleams in the refracted autumn sunlight as Jefferson's does in the well-known painting by George Peter Alexander Healy. I interviewed Corley twenty-five years ago for the book I was then writing and remember him sitting at his desk after lunch, nursing a glass of red and discoursing on the challenges of selling what was still considered in some circles an un-American product. I was struck then by how effortlessly a former spy of sorts became a "vintner." But transformation was the hallmark in Napa in the wake of the Paris tasting of 1976 that favorably compared California wines with top-ranking French ones and catapulted the valley and its estate owners into vinous stardom.

Wine has triumphed in Napa, more than two centuries after Thomas Jefferson envisioned something similar taking place on his own turf. I have often wondered what the author of the Declaration of Independence would make of wine's prominence in California's landscapes. It was Jefferson's hope that grapes would provide an alternative to tobacco that had already worn out the commonwealth's soil and that affordable wine would wean the yeoman farmer from hard cider and whiskey and help civilize him. "No nation is drunken," Jefferson wrote plaintively in *Notes on the State of Virginia* in 1781, "where wine is cheap; and none sober, where the dearness of wine substitutes ardent spirits as the common beverage."

Monticello Vineyards west is a relatively modest endeavor by Napa's standards, yet it hardly represents that agrarian ideal. Jefferson considered farmers essential to the survival of democracy because they were tied to the land by living on and working it; the discreet planted parcel was the farmer's preserver and the farmer, by virtue of his devotion to the land, the preserver of the nation.

Working in vineyards—which could also be done by women and children—was an essential part of that vision. But here such labor is done by outsiders—many of them undocumented immigrants—and the aspirations of the vintner class are much more akin to those of the aristocracy that Jefferson deplored even though he belonged to it.

Jay Corley's prosperous children run what amounts to an upscale roadside attraction offering well-made but expensive wine while the paterfamilias expounds on things Jeffersonian. "The proportions of the dining room are about right," he says, showing me around. "Jefferson would come in early and sit and read until the rest of the family gathered for dinner."

There's no signature dumbwaiter, and the wine cellar below, with its temperature controls and plush decor, is full of New World cabernet sauvignon and chardonnay that didn't exist in Jefferson's time, rather than the wines of Bordeaux, Burgundy, Germany, and northern Italy that Jefferson prized.

"Jefferson was all about quality," Corley says, which is true of what Jefferson drank. Wine was a fact of daily life at the real Monticello, but usually consumed after a meal. Though Jefferson liked his Latours and Haut-Brions, paragons of structure and depth, his precise tastes are unclear. Of a wine he encountered on his European pilgrimage in 1787 outside Turin, he wrote: "There is a red wine of Nebiule made in this neighborhood which is very singular. It is about as sweet as the silky Madeira, as astringent on the palate as Bordeaux, and as brisk as Champagne."

He imported two dozen varieties of *Vitis vinifera* from Europe and had them planted on a single acre on the south slope of Monticello. Filippo Mazzei was brought over from Tuscany for the purpose, but Jefferson lost interest in the enterprise and never spent a moment actually working in the vineyard, so he's not a good example of his own agrarian ideal, either. But his ultimate wish was not "dear" wine, but the sort most people could afford, and the high prices and high octane of Napa's cabernet sauvignon ("rocket juice"), often pushing 16 percent alcohol, would have shocked him.

So this is—and is not—Monticello, like the enduring paradox of the man himself. His life, thought, and aesthetics inspire in his spiritual descendants, real and feigned, as many contradictions as virtues. Jefferson wanted to prove viticulture not just possible in America, but viable. His vineyard was to serve as an incubator and an example, proving that grapes could be grown and wine made in America. But as with many things, he was distracted by affairs of state, family, and travel. The vines, planted on overlays of clay that don't drain well, did poorly and were often neglected, the grapes eaten by animals and slaves. His winemaker lacked the knowledge and the science available today, and in this endeavor Jefferson failed.

Joseph Ellis wrote in *American Sphinx*, "Jefferson provided a sanction for youthful hopes and illusions, planted squarely in what turned out to be the founding document of the American republic. The American dream . . . is the Jeffersonian dream writ large."

Wine is part of that dream, and nowhere in America has it been realized sooner or more completely than in California. Here vines—and wine—flourish in all terrains, from wild to heavily populated, not just a commodity and a measure of wealth but also a cultural artifact. Paradoxically, wine has less and less to do with agriculture and more to do with a vague but persistent force running off like rows of comely vines. They terminate in viridian mountain views and a prescribed way of life quite separate from the real lives left behind.

Three million tourists spend more than a billion dollars a year in Napa Valley, but the total economy built around wine is estimated to be as high as $18 billion. Yet close to half the population lives at or below the poverty line. Housing is difficult to find and prohibitively expensive, the roads crowded, cancer rates high, and the glaring disparity between incomes growing. The valley may represent the apotheosis of the American family farm, with what was until recently the most valuable legal crop anywhere, but not in the way Jefferson imagined. The twenty-first-century manifestation of his vision is fraught with the desires, impulses, and material delights of our time; it has become unrecognizable even to those who have spent their lives in the shadows of the Howell and Mayacamas Mountains.

I.

THIS EARTH
IS THEIRS

*The phenomenon of wine explored; the
glorious past toured; and a secretive
paragon of the vintner class well met.*

CHAPTER ONE:

Master and Slave

Wine has an animal life.
—William Younger, *Gods, Men and Wine*

1.

What beverage is so freighted with myth and fortune as to radically alter whole landscapes and minds, yet lacks nourishment and the life-sustaining quality of water, requires protracted physical effort to cultivate, is prone to loss and spoilage, is costly to produce and store, serves no practical purpose beyond temporary euphoria, and helps sustain kings, poets, politicians, priests, lovers, idealists, the sick, the stricken, and all manner of rascals throughout the human moment?

Wine, none other. And in the age of global warming it also underlies the destruction of woodlands and the enrichment of corporations at community expense, creates delusions of grandeur, occasionally deranges (in recent years Napa Valley has experienced a bizarre murder in the vineyard, financial scams, and—in 2005—a multimillion-dollar inferno, all in wine's name), burnishes fortunes based on little more than style, and in its veneration lie unspoken desires and motives, noble and base.

Despite its sublime nature and lasting appeal, wine's true cost is occurring to more and more people in places abounding in it at the outset of the new century. Everyone once loved it without qualification, but to many it has now become an adversary, even a grotesque one. Many fear its effects beyond showiness and profit, and they band together in geographical tribes named for creeks and slopes where they live, "ordinary" citizens in the parlance of the industry. They pick at the beast with sharpened spears, determined to bring it back to its old docility, and some to bring it down.

Back in the 1980s, in the sun-baked groves of academe in the town of Davis, in Northern California, an august professor of enology speculated about how wine might first have come into contact with the human palate. He imagined a place in the Caucasus Mountains and an early humanoid discovering a rock crevice into which wild grapes had fallen and fermented a delectable drink from *Vitis vinifera* or some evolutionary cousin of that grape, and the discoverer lapped it up.

Human beings never got over the first experience, wherever it took place, and were determined to replicate it. In that dim cognition are the roots of Napa's ascendant glory, and possible undoing. Today artisanal winemakers know all the science and all the provenance, but they're still surprised by small changes in a wine and occasionally stunned by an apotheosis that, as one Napa Valley vintner was fond of saying, could drop you to your knees.

The Davis professor was no fabulist. He had endured hardship in his quest for knowledge, flying to Afghanistan half a century before to search for such a rock crevice, figuratively speaking. The car in which he and his fellow scientists traveled had to be leveraged with tree trunks across a river, a challenge that apparently diverted the natives from possibly killing the visitors. Real-life Indiana Joneses, the scientists drove on with an enhanced appreciation of chance and the dangers, as well as the romance, of wine.

Alcohol had a lot to do with that early humanoid's reaction. Transcendence of the human condition, post-Eden, meant shedding for a time the yoke of toil, uncertainty, and suffering. The first sipper must have felt godlike, and mightn't wine have been an element in the conversion from a nomadic to a place-based existence, a notion of terroir before *terroir* was a word?

By the second decade of the twenty-first century, wine, by nature traditional, was anything but. Millions upon millions of cases were out there, from the most basic to legendary Petrus and Haut-Brion. Learning about and selling it had become complex with the radical shrinkage of distributorships and was loaded with scientific speculation and political association. More than ever wine was an ideal vessel in which to view the broader society, and never before had there been so much available.

The search for "the best" was widespread and ardent, a manifest reflection of the celebrity-driven age. The stuck fermentation of wine criticism had changed radically, too; the big developments being the 100-point rating scale, and later the exuberant Internet bloom of wine opinion. The meager choices had left many drinkers unhappy with both the small, insular group of critics who announced what was good and assigned numbers seemingly arbitrary and inflated, like the prices of the wines themselves, and with the energetic if polyglot democracy of oenophiles often engaged in Internet warfare that was as much about personality as it was wine.

One of the former band of critics, a Maryland lawyer named Robert Parker, had created America's collecting tier back in the 1980s by introducing the 100-point scale in his homey mailer *The Wine Advocate*. He is important because he altered not only the way wine is sold but also how it is made and seen, and—inadvertently—its overall effect on people and place.

The Wine Advocate appealed to the new money elite rising with the fortunes of the new president, Ronald Reagan, and eager for proof of sophistication. Close behind it was the *Wine Spectator*, a glossy appropriator of Parker's point system but one heavily augmented with additional tasting heads and "lifestyle" features—lavish ads, soft-focus profiles of vintners, wine destinations, and wealthy investors. These two leviathans, one serious, the other overwrought, should have been archrivals but in fact offered each other tacit support by persisting with a flawed rating system that amplified small, expensive differences among wines.

Of the two, Parker was the most respected, yet over time all 100-point critics would come to be criticized as narrow, elitist, and often unreliable. But wine bloggers had proved so diverse and divisive that their early promise of becoming major movers of brand wasn't realized, the result being a broad reassessment of the way wine was evaluated and presented to the fast-growing number of wine drinkers.

A common fable has Marvin Shanken, publisher of the *Wine Spectator*, envying Parker his nimbus of rectitude and wishing that Parker would one day run ads in *The Wine Advocate*, as the *Wine Spectator* did, let others do the tasting, and sell controlling interest to investors in Asia, all of which would cost Parker his sanctity.

Then one day Shanken woke up to discover that all this had more or less happened. Parker made a lot of money by selling controlling interest in *The Wine Advocate*, allowing stand-in tasters—one of whom was accused of accepting bribes, and becoming involved in a legal dispute with another contributor. The *Wine Spectator* then cast itself as the ne plus ultra of the 100-point duet, while Parker struggled to heave his considerable bulk back onto its pedestal, meanwhile denouncing "jihadists"—bloggers and younger critics who considered his favored style of wine unbalanced and his views hopelessly old-fashioned.

Parker remains a figure of speculation, particularly in Napa Valley, where those who knew him back when remember a friendly young man with remarkable olfactory abilities pushing a newsletter published in Baltimore. Parker hustled it in liquor stores most critics wouldn't have bothered visiting, and told amusing stories of being forced in Bordeaux to conceal himself so Baron Philippe de Rothschild of the sacrosanct Mouton Rothschild, passing in his limousine, wouldn't have to look at this American, and having a dog tear at his cuff after being released by a vintner outraged by a Parker review of his wine.

But Parker's true loyalties are a mystery. In Napa, wines were made to emulate those he favored, particularly the soft 1982 Bordeauxs. Never tolerant of criticism, his ambition seems to have been shaped by a blue-collar upbringing. He didn't taste wine for the first time until in his twenties, traveling with his girlfriend in Alsace, and he never got over the experience.

So, an enophiliac by revelation, with no one to emulate and "no one to explain to Bob as a child what power is," says his biographer, Elin McCoy, who chronicled his extraordinary rise in *The Emperor of Wine: The Rise of*

Robert M. Parker, Jr. and the Reign of American Taste, "or how to manage it. Bob always denied that people made wine just to please him, even when examples were provided. He also never felt comfortable with people who, for want of a better word, were of a higher class. And yet he would use others' claims that money was a huge influence in the world of wine as an excuse to denounce the whole notion of favoritism. He's a paradox," just like his subject. "In the process The Wine Advocate went from a personal brand to a thoroughly corporate one."

Parker made friends among vintners in Bordeaux on the scruffier right bank of the Gironde, McCoy adds, "and championed some at the expense of the higher-class representatives across in the Médoc." In Napa, he was a major force behind the success of the decidedly blue-collar vineyard developer Dave Abreu, and Parker also greatly enhanced the reputation of the wines of Bill Harlan, latter-day advocate of wine dynasties whose father had been a meat cutter, as we shall see.

The question of wine's effect on the California landscape—Kendall-Jackson's deforestation on the Central Coast, the radical alteration of Napa's hillsides by Abreu and developers like him—seems never to have occurred to Parker. Anyone reading his newsletter would infer that the notion of an "environment" was of little interest to him and that the owners of the labels he praised should be encouraged to do with their land whatever they desired. He, like *The Wine Advocate*, was so influential after hard-selling the 1982 Bordeauxs that they shaped not only America's newly endowed palates but also the hillsides and flatlands of Napa and other lovely, vulnerable climes.

2.

The 100-point critical scale ignores most of the world's wines and is, in essence, a 20-point scale concentrated on those at the presumptive top of the heap. Many of the dominant so-called cult wines made famous by Parker and the *Wine Spectator* are lush, the sometimes freakish offspring of deliberately over-ripened grapes whose enhanced power derives from greater concentrations of sugar. Their fruity, alcoholic "assault" overwhelms the palate and the finish goes on and on, but not necessarily pleasantly. Others are so dense as to defy evaluation, their impenetrability due more to the persistent, concentrated taste of ripeness than to too much tannin, the old culprit that once made cellaring of expensive bottles mandatory.

Most cabernet sauvignons blessed by *The Wine Advocate* and the *Wine Spectator* didn't complement food and often competed with it. As expensive as they were out of balance, they served as appropriate metaphors for a valley with wide social imbalance and loudly contending voices, all asking what were the rights and proper roles of wineries, agriculture, and citizens, and how much of a once-traditional culture could possibly survive triumphal extremes of modern capitalism.

Where vines were planted was still important to some winemakers and critics, but terroir now had a parallel universe that lurked in sales catalogues of "enhancers" that could legally be mixed with wine to alter its appearance, smell, taste, and feel. Expensive machines could literally dismantle a wine and put it back together again, minus the flaws and, in many cases, the personality. Such lobotomized potions were one reason oenophiles began to focus on "context": viticultural, environmental, artisanal, social. Increasingly they found the 100-point system irrelevant and the wines divorced from the places where the grapes are grown. But many winemakers continued to look on terroir as a quaint anachronism.

As more cerebral, historically minded, socially conscious drinkers slipped away from the 100-point scale, new wealth in China, Russia, and India helped fill their shoes. High-scoring wines were made with foreign nationals in mind who might need the same simplistic scale Parker provided his countrymen back in the 1980s. And Americans wanting trophy wines for important dinner parties continued buying them as well.

Wine critics and more knowledgeable drinkers meanwhile questioned how good these wines really were. "The vintners are on autopilot," wrote Jon Bonné in 2013 in the *San Francisco Chronicle*. "The playing field's crowded with those who evolved in the era of big flavor." Winemakers' reactions over the years had become "Pavlovian," Bonné added. "They just keep doing the same thing over and over again, for the score and money that automatically comes with it."

The author Wendell Berry famously wrote that eating is an agricultural act. So is drinking wine. It's also an environmental one. Greenwashing to shield wineries from the fact of their Roundup dependency, and reliance on certain critics to vouch for them, turned off drinkers of all ages. And those promoting Pavlovian wines were no more secure than those making them. Changing course at a late date, as is now the tendency, and abandoning proclamations of the supremacy of over-ripe fruit is as difficult for a publication as it is for a winemaker, as well as embarrassing.

William Younger's assertion in *Gods, Men and Wine* that wine has an animal life referred to specific stages of existence—birth, youth, maturity, old age—but implicit in that comparison is appetite. This was one of the traits cited by Aristotle for animals and vegetables alike, distinguishing them from minerals, but wine is in a singular category, incorporating the sublime effects of grapes, environment, craft, and sensibility, all in concert.

Can solastalgia—that existential distress caused by environmental loss—be mirrored in a glass of wine? Can someone both adore and resent it? Wine's exalted position in corporate history is fairly recent, reflecting the usual concern with money first and product second, the former almost always detracting from the quality of the latter. Wine thus becomes a prime example of the difficulty of maintaining high standards when these don't produce the highest income, the very notion of "branding" an inadvertent acknowledgment of trending mediocrity.

The essence of a thing that by virtue of excellence testifies to an aspirational ethos promptly loses it by embracing brand, which is primarily the assertion that one has arrived, whether or not one really has. Such capitulation destroys the vision and creates something else entirely, while independent winemakers who come in at the bottom are sucked upstairs and then blown out the other end, their fortunes made but their wines soon "masstiged" (high prices maintained while quality is abandoned) and their reputations, too.

Wine's thread in the contemporary corporate fabric, ironic and potentially tragic, is now ensnared in Napa in real estate and tourism as well; profiteers who once followed the conquering army and are now poised to lead it.

The one material aspect of wine likely to endure as long as there's water are the vines themselves. Never has a plant species done better for itself than *Vitis vinifera*, reigning in Napa between the Mayacamas and Howell ranges and on top, the fruit pampered beyond the dreams of Turkish pashas, the study of their happy lineage the life's work of human servants at their computer screens.

Vines' planting and upkeep are accomplished at the expenditure of money that would be the envy of regal scions of old. Vines now occupy the best ground, have the best views, are catered to at every turn, their progeny lovingly delivered and tended with near-maniacal concern. What their fruit is turned into isn't just a valuable liquid for consumption, but one imbued with human and, according to savants through time, divine attributes: transcendence, the magic carpet effect, an ineffable quality that ultimately defies definition even as the grapes' manifestation is drawn reverentially from the blackest depths of the birthing barrel.

But is this newborn slave or master?

CHAPTER TWO:
White Elephants

1.

Back in the mid-1960s, when newcomers to Napa Valley like Warren Winiarski—a future winner of the pivotal Paris Wine Tasting—Ric Forman, Jack and Jamie Davies, and others were still in their "what if" moments, the Davieses used to drive up near-deserted Highway 29 expecting a revelation. As Jamie told me much later, "We didn't want one of those Victorian piles built in homage to Europe, with too many rooms and too much view . . . and strange names like Chateau Montelena, Chateau Chevalier, Freemark Abbey—white elephants all, and all for sale, with weeds in the yards and blank windows staring back into the illusions of their founders."

A white elephant is, by definition, "a possession that is useless or troublesome, especially one that is expensive to maintain or difficult to dispose of." The latter is no longer true, but those windows still stare into illusions, not those of the founders but the quarterly reports of private and multinational corporations, for it is these that now own what most Americans think still belong to the illustrious families of old.

A tour of the white elephants serves as a reminder of the transitory nature of families and their enterprises, however grand, and their role in shaping the valley. Remembering the names is less important than registering the collective force of those abandoned dreams. Highway 29 is still the main corridor splitting the valley south to north, where Mount St. Helena glows in the distance and the setting sun turns the ridgeline of the Mayacamas into a bejeweled saw edge. Best settle back as the highway sheds the city of Napa and planes across vineyard land, past ghostly eucalyptus trees pinkish in the evening light. On the right stands a stylish frame barn with air shafts on the roof and overall a sense of optimism from the century before, known then as Eshcol ("a cluster of grapes"). Just beyond Yountville is another grand illusion, Far Niente ("without a care"), nestled in the foothills. Both wineries are owned not by their founders but by inheritors in the modern era of derivative wealth.

The Spanish colonial archway over the entrance to the Robert Mondavi Winery nearby, provocative in the 1960s, looks old-fashioned today. Owned by corporate giant Constellation, the winery as a whole represents the valley's most striking loss of family control of recent times, and a shelter for yet another alien corporation. But the most impressive white elephant of all stands outside the hamlet of Rutherford and is known as Inglenook.

Purchased by Heublein in the Aquarian 1960s, Inglenook was built in the 1880s by the Vermonter Hamden McIntyre in conjunction with William Mooser, and reflected the vision of its owner, Gustave Niebaum, Finnish trader in furs from the Pribilof Islands and a disciple of the wines of Bordeaux. McIntyre's skill would defy all attempts by subsequent owners to impose their own ideas on it, including those of the current one, Francis Ford Coppola, who added a wall and installed a gate on the road leading in from Highway 29. In Niebaum's time, and that of his great-nephew and successor John Daniel Jr., trees lined the driveway, the bases painted white, and beyond them were vines still head-trained and spur-pruned in the antediluvian fifties. Scenes from *This Earth Is Mine* were shot here by the director, Henry King, starring a wistful Jean Simmons and a forceful Rock Hudson. The cinematic conflict was—and still is today—between honor and profit.

The winery's towering, creeper-covered stone mass remains an architectural touchstone, the added pergola and outsized, ever-flowing fountain mere clutter, as are tables set in the gravel for tourists eating bread, cheese, and sausage purchased in the winery. This would have maddened old Niebaum, a student of Pasteur, who used to stroll through the winery in white gloves, testing for grime while wine flowed down from the upper stories into huge casks.

Some of these casks still stood in the interior gloom when Heublein bought the place in 1969. Gone now, along with the magic of suggestion, they were replaced with a grandiose staircase built with South American timber shortly after Coppola acquired Inglenook's edifice in 1975. The thriving trade in boutique clothing and other impulse items persists, and up the stairway the museum pays homage to film and to Coppola, featuring a Tucker sedan left over from his movie about car-making like an unwrapped mummy from the temple of cellulose.

In the beginning Coppola attempted to attach his name to Niebaum's, as if the two shared something more than real estate, but Inglenook remained itself despite everything Coppola and his staff could do to it. Shades of Niebaum and his great-nephew still hang about the magnificent representation of Northern European architecture and an altogether different sensibility from the faux-Mediterranean additions. As the late John Daniel Jr.'s youngest daughter, the poet Marcia "Marky" Smith, wrote years ago:

Father, your ghost still comes—
So thin in the thickening afternoon

Inglenook ushered the first big corporation into the valley, to the dismay of the natives. Then Heublein/née Inglenook opened its mouth and out stepped a corporate wunderkind the likes of which the valley hadn't seen, who would become one of the most influential arrivistes in the pivotal mid-twentieth-century invasion of opportunists and agrarian utopians, but again we're getting ahead of the story.

Wandering in the woods above Inglenook, I once came across the gunboat used in Coppola's *Apocalypse Now* stashed amid runty live oaks—a cinematic prop and a reminder of the monumental loss of this property by its original family owners.

Someone who knows Coppola well says the film director paid as much in 2011 to acquire the Inglenook trademark as he paid for the entire property almost forty years before: "I think Francis was trying to heal the past."

Attempts to equate Niebaum and Coppola were abandoned, but even then the place wasn't whole, as if sentient wine resisted the best latter-day efforts and Niebaum-Coppola was unable to produce a truly distinctive bottle. Ironically, it wasn't until Coppola finally hired the assistant wine-maker from Château Margaux in Bordeaux that Inglenook began its long journey back to a traditional red wine made from grapes picked early enough to show distinctive but restrained fruit, relatively low alcohol (for Napa), and a hint of the local "Rutherford dust" smell and taste that would have, at last, made old Niebaum happy.

2.

Just across Highway 29, the second-most-influential Napa winery, Beaulieu Vineyard, lacks Inglenook's regal air. It fed the needs of crafty old Georges de Latour, who had made money at the turn of the twenti-eth century in cream of tartar, a by-product of winemaking. He sailed prosperously through Prohibition selling wine to California's Catholic archdioceses. The only notable de Latour architecture is the residence at the end of a long allée of plane trees where the brilliant, diminutive winemaker André Tchelistcheff was brought from Paris in the thirties and de Latour served him a trout dipped from a cold stream on the property.

As late as the early 1990s you could still drive up the lane to the lovely frame structure, all windows and old-world assurance. Even then, no one unexpected would have dared knock unbidden on that august door. De Latour's daughter, the supremely privileged Madame de Pins, and her titled husband drove her anointed winemaker to distraction producing quality cabernet out of a Dickensian winery. The de Pinses left Beaulieu to their daughter, Dagmar, no match for her American husband addicted to the ease of selling real estate in mid-twentieth-century California. He brokered off Beaulieu behind the backs of wife and mother-in-law in one of the more dubious real estate deals in the valley's history, the first being the sale of Inglenook.

Heublein acquired Beaulieu, too, and inflicted on the wines a formula that to many destroyed their distinctiveness. Then the next corporate overlord, Diageo, whose first love was spirits, sold off Beaulieu's precious vineyards so it could lease them back again and not have to bother with farming, not so long before the point of it all.

In St. Helena, farther north, is another foundling now in the corporate embrace, Beringer, owned by an offshoot of Foster's, the Brobdingnagian Australian brewers. Beringer is a prime example of what can happen to a historic property when it goes through enough sanitizing corporate makeovers. Inspired by Tiburcio Parrott's Miravalle in 1880, Beringer's founders were the enterprising brothers who outdid Parrott with their Rhine House next to beautiful elms embowering the highway. Owned by Nestlé for a time, it's now owned by Treasury, a hamper of brands mostly without vineyards. Beringer possessed good ones and made exceptional wine, before standardization took hold.

Next to Beringer rears old Hamden McIntyre's second triumph, Greystone Cellars, built in 1889 as a grape-growers' cooperative and at one time the largest such structure on earth, as well as a testament to successful communal agriculture. Greystone's lapidary art celebrates the bygone glory of farmers blessed with good terroir and energy who could fill this magnificent hall, once owned by Heublein and the now-defunct Christian Brothers before being picked up by the Culinary Institute of America, far downstream of Greystone's original purpose.

One white elephant to hold out against outside corporate ownership sits on the other side of Highway 29, cradled among ancient Douglas firs, beyond broad green grounds. This shade is eagerly sought by community groups and wedding parties. In silent rebuke of Inglenook, Beaulieu, Robert Mondavi, and Beringer, frumpy old Charles Krug Winery no longer belongs to descendants of nineteenth-century viticulture, but it is still in possession of the family of Cesare Mondavi—the so-called

Mon-day-vees, as opposed to the *Mon-dah-vees*—who bought it a decade after Prohibition.

A bit farther on is Freemark Abbey, which also did well in the famous Paris Tasting of 1976. It was later bought by the Legacy Estate Group, among other investors, which went bankrupt in 2005, and was sold to shape-shifting Jackson Family Wines of the alcoholic, wood-infused chardonnays.

Among other pilgrims of the 1960s was a Los Angeles real estate attorney named Jim Barrett. He looked upon his job as "the equivalent of selling frozen chocolate bananas" and wanted to do something with soul. He and partners bought Chateau Montelana, a towering, spooky tribute to a fortune made during the Gold Rush, not in precious metal but in rope, an essential component in dragging California's first romantic adventure. The first proprietor of Montelena, Alfred Loving Tubbs, bought the land just north of Calistoga, at the foot of Mount St. Helena, after visiting White Sulphur Springs Resort nearby. Tubbs sold Montelena to a Chinese engineer who created a garden and what he called Jade Lake, with a steep footbridge, the whole of it overgrown by the time Barrett came along.

Fantasy has always been a part of the property's allure, but nothing could equal the Paris Tasting of 1976, which delivered a gift to Napa's doorstep from a British wine writer and merchant named Steven Spurrier. Montelena won in the whites category, and the tasting was hailed in *Time*.

The other winner in the Paris Tasting, in the reds category, was Stag's Leap Wine Cellars, a less happy tale in that it no longer belongs to the Winiarskis, who sold it in 2007 for $185 million to Chateau Ste. Michelle of Woodinville, Washington, which is partially owned by the tobacco and food conglomerate Altria (formerly Philip Morris), and to Piero Antinori of Italy. Thus in a single stroke the property that surpassed sacrosanct premier cru Bordeauxs like Château Haut-Brion and Château Mouton Rothschild and did most to assure Napa's international reputation joined the latter-day white elephants.

The collective failure of Napa winemaking families to hold on to hard-won individual reputations and land contrasts starkly with the French examples that so inspired the mid-twentieth-century American idealists. And those wines the Napans narrowly beat in Paris in 1976 are still made by France's same vintner families. Some of those families sold wine to Thomas Jefferson.

CHAPTER THREE:

The Legacy Thing

An object seen in isolation from the whole is not the real thing.
—Masanobu Fukuoka, *The One-Straw Revolution*

1.

Up behind Far Niente, off Oakville Grade Road, which eventually leads
to the Sonoma County line, nestled in the steep foothills of the Mayacamas is what might be the most audacious foray into fast-track canoniza-
tion in the valley's history. The name is H. William Harlan—the H is
for Howard, which doesn't suit—and he already owns an extraordinarily
successful, eponymous vineyard that produces a wine worth a thousand
dollars a bottle, five vintages of which received a 100-point ranking in
Robert Parker's *Wine Advocate*. That is an extraordinary amount of perfec-
tion even for Napa Valley, and Harlan's new vineyard, Promontory, was
being celebrated before any but a few had a chance to view it or taste its
bounty.

Harlan grew up in the same town as Richard Nixon, Whittier, Southern California, and there the story must begin. Whittier's elemental qual-
ities gave both men a powerful desire to get up and out, but how they did
so couldn't have been more different. Sometimes in his aerie Bill Harlan

ponders lessons taught by his hometown, a former outpost of Spanish explorers and later a farming juggernaut totally unlike Napa. Whittier shipped trainloads of oranges and lemons across the country in the days of Steinbeck's *Grapes of Wrath*, and its seemingly endless orchards filled the air with the fragrance of citrus.

Ranks of trees also produced walnuts, and past them ran—starting in 1904—the first of Pacific Electric's Big Red Cars on the trolley line extending all the way to Los Angeles. In its first two decades more than a million passengers rode each year, but the advent of the automobile and an orchestrated campaign by large oil companies killed the Big Red Cars. After World War II many of the orange and walnut trees were cut and subdivisions built to accommodate an influx of aspiring Californians that never really ceased. This was what later happened to the Santa Clara Valley farther north, before the microchip boom, a tragedy that inspired supervisors up in Napa Valley in the 1960s to create the first agricultural preserve.

The writer Garry Wills described Whittier in his biography *Nixon Agonistes*: "I saw little of that agrarian valley remaining as I came down off the throughway and went east out Whittier Boulevard, past the very small buildings and very large signs that trigger America's bottomless lust for hamburgers. . . . Even one day in Whittier, spent imagining the America of Nixon's childhood, is suffocating. That world has a locker-room smell, of spiritual athleticism."

Nixon, "a self-made man," had been the "boy who, listening to trains in the night, became a racing engine of endeavor," as did Bill Harlan in the following generation. Bill's grandfather told him what grandfathers were supposed to tell their grandchildren in mid-twentieth-century America, that there was nothing they couldn't do if they chose. Bill would say in later years, "Some words you hear only once in your life, but you remember them. They're *in there*."

His father worked in a slaughterhouse, which was struck by the Teamsters. The strike hardened his father, and indirectly changed Bill, too, who grew up unencumbered by books, a rangy kid good at sports but with a sense of the aesthetic. He attributes this to color renditions of the world's great artworks he saw on the backs of cards bought by the packet at the five and dime.

He worked in local vegetable gardens to make money, and raced motorcycles through the sunny days of SoCal until he went off to Berkeley, still unsure of what it was he wanted to do. He didn't excel academically, earning spending money by playing poker in the basement of a fraternity house. And, he says, when union members struck a soft drink bottling plant in nearby east Oakland, Bill told people, "I'm going to work as a scab," an exceptionally gutsy move. But *in there* was an aversion to unions, too, and a visceral imperviousness to the politics of the Age of Aquarius.

Union members followed Bill on his delivery route, and sat next to him in restaurants while he ate lunch, announcing to other diners, "This guy's a scab."

He stuck it out, being single and without worry about the effects of the strike on a family. Some union members, he claims, followed other workers home, hassled their wives, put nails in their car tires. "And they could level a mom-and-pop shop in three minutes, tipping over shelves and leaving broken bottles all over the place." He would never forget it.

Harlan was considered the least likely to succeed in his graduating class. His next step involved another motorcycle, as well as trains and buses, and the continent of Africa, which he claims to have traversed north to south under the influence of Alan Moorehead's *The Blue Nile*. He had at last been induced to read because he found himself alone so much, in more or less constant motion. "To travel far," he likes to say, "you have to travel fast."

But he can't name another book that had a profound effect on him. Another favorite during the African trip dealt with visions—"a really wild piece of psycho-pictography"—but that title, too, is lost. Likewise the specifics of conversations he had with stars and luminaries in San Francisco where he ended up—the actor Sterling Hayden, Zen sage Alan Watts, fading Beats still hanging out at City Lights bookshop in North Beach. Not memory loss, just the effects of continued speed and distance covered, his upward trajectory transcending real visions just as it transcended the politics of the 1960s.

He learned to fly and then, typically, figured out how to make money selling airplanes. He bought a sailboat and plied the Pacific, lived on a houseboat in Sausalito, including one named the Taj Mahal, and turned that experience, too, to profit, taking advantage of the last unregulated housing in Northern California. Along the way he earned a reputation for intelligence, guile, charm, and occasional ruthlessness. But his rarest quality in the rising real estate tide was imagination and the ability to massage a vision of a particular place into something extraordinary.

He bought a little country club in a lovely valley—Napa—not yet maxed out on real estate development, envisioning even then, he says, someday producing a wine of his own that would in ways be comparable to a Bordeaux, maybe even to Richard Nixon's beloved Château Margaux that the president drank surreptitiously while in the White House. But Bill was the anti-Nixon: adventurous, joyful, effective in the freewheeling entrepreneurial mode. If Nixon had hung around with someone like him in the old days there would have been no Nixon presidency and no Watergate, but no Environmental Protection Agency, either. Over and over again Bill would remind people of how well this country accommodates material ambition when it's combined with the genuine ability to dream.

2.

His assistant's instructions are precise: arrive at 9:30 A.M. and wait in what's known as the office but looks more like a monastery in Provence or Tuscany. Bill will descend from the oak-shaded house higher on the property, she adds, though exactly where he will alight isn't specified.

The narrow courtyard opens onto a low stone wall underlining the sweeping view of the valley floor and the distant Howell and Vaca Mountain ranges to the east. The foreground's brushed verdant corduroy studded with distant houses, and the long ribbon of Highway 29 is pinned to coveted Napa terroir by wineries, more houses, and the Oakville Grocery. All is in proper scale, all seemingly subject to the gorgeous supremacy of agriculture and nature.

The stone building to the right is Bill's office: deep-set shadow-box windows through which furniture's visible, vaguely reminiscent of California's nineteenth-century heritage. Except for the exquisitely restored black-and-white Matchless (AJS) motorcycle, the feeling's more like an old assay or railway office, or some other romanticized enterprise in the early pursuit of Manifest Destiny.

Suddenly Bill's there, a lean presence like a drawn bow: swept-back mostly white hair, wire-rim spectacles, a thin white goatee, the ur-Californian in signature blue jeans, high-topped suede shoes, and an earth-toned shirt with a high thread count, its blousy sleeves buttoned at the wrists. From one angle he looks broad-shouldered and robust, from another frail. This shape-shifter is dominated by cold blue eyes that are often commented on in the press; their hold on their subject can be disquieting.

Asked about his choice of site for this lovely complex and big house slotted among oaks, he smiles, the gaze softening as he takes up an impressionistic narrative that at this point seems preordained. There's a fabulous quality to almost everything he says, much of which isn't readily verifiable, truth and imagination locked in a tale that rarely fails to mesmerize, even when it doesn't convince.

"Winegrowing has a real aesthetic. You have to look at the earth as a three-dimensional canvas, though instead of using a brush you have a bulldozer. Follow the contours like an animal moving across the land, so it looks and feels right. It's the same with architecture. Don't let it overpower the landscape. And vice versa."

By the time Bill arrived on this hillside he had made a fortune as a builder of condos, commercial properties, and mansions from Tahoe to Big Sur. He was one of three controlling partners of Pacific Union of San Francisco, a multibillion-dollar developer, and he turned little Meadowood into the hallowed locus of the Auction Napa Valley, annually bringing together billionaires to buy unimaginably costly lots and acquire a very particular sort of bragging rights. Yet Bill first came to Napa, he says, "to get away from development. And this seemed the last best place able to be saved."

It's a confounding statement, but then paradox is essentially Harlan. He was considered for a time a possible successor to Robert Mondavi, who told him of the virtues of Bordeaux and, Bill says, took him to visit great estates there, giving him "a whole different perspective" and an epiphany of sorts, this "vision of something that would last, that had to start with great land."

Bordeaux led him to Burgundy, where he was enchanted by the concept of the clos—small, discreet vineyards of great value, inseparable from a long tradition. The Burgundians told of carrying soil back up the hills that had washed down during storms, an element in his education. He took such impressions back to Napa, where he walked vineyards with Ric Forman, the maverick vintner who never joined the expansionists or the sellouts and who told Bill, in essence, *Do it carefully and do it right.*

Bill didn't become the next Robert Mondavi and had more to gain as wine country's éminence grise. He commercially developed the south end of St. Helena before residents saw it coming, and as a New World *négociant* gathered together choice growers to create Bond, based on the Bordeaux example, a less expensive but still pricey second line that generated sufficient profits, he says, to finance the very expensive first line, Harland Estate.

He also built something called The Napa Valley Reserve near the entrance to Meadowood, a high-end wine country tease one needs an appointment to enter and $150,000 to join. Once in, the six hundred–odd members may acquire a handful of choice vines and have a special wine made from them. They may also buy luxury goods, like Bentleys. The Reserve brought about the sale of so many of those that the manufacturer, Bill says, gave him a seafoam-green Bentley all his own.

Travel faster, go farther. By now what matters most to Bill is staying put with his "legacy," a word imbued with the sanctity that has launched many an idea and property. His legacy is less American than Bordelais, harkening back to the left bank of the Gironde where he saw for the first time family succession epitomized by first-growth properties like Latour and Lafite. Now seventy-six years old, Bill has proven to his own satisfaction that wine can be made on the slopes of the Mayacamas about as well as it can be made in the Médoc.

He wants his estate passed on to his son and daughter in a fractious, uncertain future where a vinous Shangri-la might best withstand the challenges. Hence Promontory, an 860-acre property first seen by him back in the 1980s, with volcanic soils mixed with ancient seabeds and metamorphic rock. A retired geologist from Stanford University was brought in to explain the promontory itself, which had been separated from the main mélange by plate tectonics and the shifting of the San Andreas Fault.

Also brought in were silent partners, signatures of a Harlan deal, one of whom owns professional sports teams—always a ready source of cash, another a former candidate for a governorship in flyover America. Bill won't say how much he paid, but undeveloped land on the slopes of the Mayacamas is worth at least $25,000 an acre and as much as $175,000, all part of "the two-hundred-year plan," though it's less of a plan than a notion, the two-hundred-year time span chosen because "we can live almost a hundred years now, and your first memory goes back almost that far."

Bill Harlan's first memory is of his maternal grandmother telling stories of her childhood, and through her he could figuratively touch the nineteenth century and pass some of those impressions down to his children who can do the same for theirs. "With the stories you feel connected to the distant past. And you can look almost that far into the future," an elegant concept, if hardly original. He believes it will be determined by three things: land, family, and debt—that is, its absence. "Land provides a cradle for the family, which in turn provides culture. And virtual lack of debt means you can make it through crashes, droughts, and pestilence."

Debt has probably driven more personal wealth, including his, than any other experience in America and California, and wrecked a lot as well. The tradition of heady real estate debt goes back to the days of the pioneer West, and without it Bill would never have achieved what he did. It's true his heavily diversified Pacific Union rarely puts up more than 10 percent of capital for projects, depending instead on outside investors, but real estate development remains the backbone of his fortune, a fact he doesn't like to be reminded of.

"It wasn't flattering to call somebody a developer," he says, of the 1980s and '90s, and it still isn't. Development for him and many of his peers belongs to that past rinsed clean by wine and the salutary honor "vintner," though development is still a primary driver of investment in hundreds of new wineries from Canada to Mexico, and certainly in Napa County.

Few have traveled faster or farther than Harlan Estate. Its understated tastefulness and sense of shadowboxed history is near-impossible to resist, the lovely, costly surrounds as seductive as the wine itself. Visitors—even journalists—should be forgiven some enthrallment, but not all.

3.

The two-hundred-year plan has been glowingly featured in various publications and duly accredited by wine evaluators like Parker and Antonio Galloni, who accepted an invitation to an initial private, limited tasting of early vintages of Promontory, as the wine is called, before any was released. They praised it, a remarkable bit of promotion and image control few but Bill Harlan could have brought off. This might have raised eyebrows in the past, but so incestuous has the world of fine wine appreciation become that the difference between critics and promoters is sometimes difficult to discern. Mutual accommodation is considered proper, and the tacit assumption is that an owner's past is either off-limits or irrelevant.

Wine writers today seem uninterested in the bottomless environmental footprints of Harlan, and the same can be said for the anomalies of his life. Unmentioned are Bill's early, hilarious seat-of-the-pants endeavors, like the time in the 1960s he tried to get a job, bearded and straggly-haired, in finance when he admittedly knew nothing about it, or his decision to instantly become a mortgage banker in the go-go '70s by telephoning insurers and telling them he knew reputable developers who wanted to borrow money, and then calling developers and telling them he had insurance companies wanting to lend. He called this new creation "the New England Mortgage Company" because that sounded most respectable. These stories, once gleefully told, now aren't in keeping with "the vision."

After he was established in Napa Valley he got into an acrimonious dispute with Tom May, owner of Martha's Vineyard, producer of the grapes going into Heitz Wine Cellars' now legendary cabernet sauvignon that had created a sensation. Harlan had bought the property next to May's and a lot line adjustment would gain Harlan additional acreage and bring great consternation to the aging May, according to his own account.

One of Harlan's companies owned a piece of four thousand seven hundred acres up in Pope Valley, behind the Howell Mountains but still in Napa County. He and other owners of the land intended to build ranchettes or the equivalent, some on land too steep and droughty to support it. Investors had tried over the years to build houses or resorts up there using vineyards as cover. This parcel came to be generally known as Juliana and has a long, convoluted history that includes no less a personage than Kermit Roosevelt, Theodore's grandson, uber-patriot and intelligence operative thought to be a front for foreign money. Roosevelt's shadowy company was Buttes Gas & Oil, and another entity, Reunion Industries, reportedly paid a subsidiary of Pacific Union $1.5 million for its piece of Juliana.

Bill says he originally chose Napa Valley because it was "the last best place where development might be avoided," but he developed it nonetheless.

Harlan may be from the wrong side of the tracks, but his political sympathies aren't and never have been. The world changed radically after 1959, now given as the official launch year of Bill's two-hundred-year vision, and since then midlevel American jobs like meat cutters and even managers have become unavailable to people like Bill's father. It was part of capitalism's ruthless expediency that shipped them out of a country no longer bearing much resemblance to the one Bill and his father grew up in.

But those unionists drove Bill so deeply into the ranks of what passes for conservatism in early-twenty-first-century America that his contacts reached into the White House of George W. Bush and Dick Cheney. Bush dined with the Harlans, and slept in a bedroom at Meadowood that was stripped of all its plumbing and electrical work and replaced before the president arrived. One can't help but wonder what he and Bill talked about. By then Harlan was a charter member of, among many other organizations, the Winegrowers of Napa County.

"We have a huge responsibility here," he says, bringing the discussion back to Promontory. "This is more than a mountain, and it still has to evolve to make a lasting contribution to the country and the world." A tall ambition, indeed. Obeisance is paid to the usual suspects: steward-ship of the land, showing "by example rather than preaching the fact that Napa's a national treasure," and the importance of location, the Realtor's absolute. Most pivotal is the close proximity of the San Francisco Bay, its shores providing an inexhaustible source of bodies and revenue drawn by wine and the valley's potent otherness.

"San Francisco's the fulcrum, with life to the south moving at the speed of a microchip, everything virtual. Silicon Valley's about invest-ment, then you come up here and things move at the pace of the seasons. Instead of a return on investment, we have a return on life." There's some truth even in clichés.

"Life in Napa before the baby boomers involved a connection to the land. Eventually the pendulum will swing back again," although he doesn't venture to say when or how. "This is a homogenous community because of the amount of money. As in Jackson Hole and Aspen, we have two different cultures living here"—the rich, and those who work for them. "Here people live with the vagaries of nature, and realize there's a lot we can't control. These people rely on each other, with no one job more important than another. Whatever their skills are, it's noble work because you're connected to the soil. It involves a long perspective, and you want to build on that."

He echoes Mondavi in attempting to equate wine with art: "You move beyond craftsmanship into whatever the chosen endeavor is—music, bal-let, sports, wine. It's only one-half of one percent that can do this." Free as-sociation is Harlan's wont, and he's now inspired: "First wine was thought of as just a beverage. There was water and wine, then you bypass the mind to a connection with the spirit, or soul, and a glimpse of the sublime."

4.

Early March and raining. El Niño has finally touched down in force, dousing the North Coast so thoroughly that the Napa River threatens for the first time to overtop spillway banks put down in Napa by the Corps of Engineers to prevent additional flooding. Up-valley, moving water glazes the Oakville Grade, and on the Harlan Estate sluices through artfully installed stone gutters—no mortar—that line the driveway, cut by that bulldozer operator he said followed a deer trail.

Bill sits in his office with his back to a view that's gray, cottony, and wet. The sound of running water is alien, and most of this moisture will drift beyond the Howell Mountains and across the Central Valley at an altitude of two thousand feet to the High Sierra, where it will finally be dumped and begin feeding aquifers and reservoirs. Come October, the valley will again be parched.

On one side of Harlan sits his son, Will. Same pale Harlan eyes, and a putty-gray shirt his father might have chosen. But Will's hair is short, dark, and stylish. He has driven up from San Francisco where he lives on Nob Hill, to lead a tour of Promontory, but the rain has canceled that. Across from him sits Harlan Estate's winemaker, Cory Empting, also youthful and dark-haired, wearing a jacket and an expression of infinite patience. It's Cory who sometimes speaks of "the wisdom of the vine," a reference to its natural capacity for adjustment and endurance in the absence of chemicals, fertilizer, and water. Maybe less than a vine whisperer, but he does admire the sort of small farming practiced and written about by the late Japanese rice grower and savant Masanobu Fukuoka.

Talk has been of changes foreseen over the next half-century, notably rising temperatures and water shortages. Predictions are being made of a catastrophic rise in less than a century, and more severe heat in summer than grapes can stand. One popular theory has it that Napa will actually be cooler because intense heat over the inland Central Valley will suck additional cool air in from the Pacific, but that's small comfort and has introduced the most uncomfortable subject yet: climate change.

So far, "crashes, droughts, and pestilence" is as close as Bill has come to uttering the hated phrase *global warming*. Even *climate change* is a stretch for him. Two years before, in 2014, it so annoyed him that his majordomo at Harlan Estate, Don Weaver, had to intervene in a conversation with a journalist. But now Bill says, "I think there's a chance there's something to the idea of global warming," quickly adding that he drives a Tesla instead of a car with an internal combustion engine, and asking pointedly, "Is that good or bad for the environment?" The implication being that everything requires energy, including the building of costly batteries.

Harlan Estate employs solar power, something Bill doesn't advocate because "I don't like the idea of telling people what to do." Organic practices, and some biodynamic, are also followed at Harlan Estate, and up in the Promontory vineyard, to be officially unveiled the next year, along with yet another beautiful winery. Developers are taking precautions, he insists, that will keep all that fine sediment out of the Napa River.

His "forester" selectively cuts trees to guard against ground fires, preserving "the health of a forest" that has thousands fewer trees than it did before the vineyards went in. Bill denies that houses might also eventually go up at Promontory, but from the sound of it the infrastructure there is extraordinary.

Water use has been reduced, another creep toward dealing with climate change. "Harlan Estate is close to being dry-farmed," Bill adds, finally conceding that "the Earth's getting a little warmer. The oceans are going to rise—but just a little bit." Then the climate deniers' familiar saw, "We need to do more research," which is true, but then it always is, as climate change is real and already long known.

Will reveals nothing. If he has learned anything from his father it is that you never tip your hand. "It's moot at this point," he ventures. "The real question is, 'Where are *we* coming from?' " meaning his and Cory's generation. "We have to limit man's imprint, so what's *our* role in lessening its effect on the planet?"

But he leaves his own question unanswered.

II.

CARRYING
THE DEFECT

*A deserter of the corporate boardroom triumphs
in the vineyard; a charmer from Burgundy pushes
the entertainment envelope; and a member of a
family that has farmed the valley for a century
battles the scuttling of a sacred rule.*

The Velvet Rope

The hotel's anonymity—blond floor-to-ceiling panels—is the antithesis of what's being discussed: how to build a tasting room so distinctive that visitors will pay dearly for the experience.

Those in the audience are in the hospitality business and have paid well for advice on creating the perfect tasting room. The basics have already been dispensed with: Add curves to prevent the space from seeming masculine; figure out wind and sun patterns; make sure visitors are comfortable at all times. Take an anthropological approach to retail sales because wine buyers are a "tribe." Remember that people instinctively turn right when entering a confined space and refuse to buy anything if they're too close to other tribal members.

They also won't buy if the floor's not attractive, or the restroom too close to the tasting bar. The pourer on the other side must be less than thirty inches from the taster, or more than forty-two inches. And they must feel sure their limo driver's in a space of his own, watching sports videos and eating free popcorn.

If your customer drives a Tesla, or flies around in a Gulfstream G6, "you have to reflect that in your tasting room." This is an "ultra-premium" experience, adds the young architect with sideburns in a plaid shirt and jeans. It lives in an altogether different dimension, creating what would once have been called aura that's shared by the product. Essentially an evocation of rarity, it offers a fleeting glimpse, and a taste of something more than wine that one may never own.

For such a winery experience, the designer must "go on to the next level," artfully replicating the vintner's life and "vision" with "artifacts" of authenticity—barn boards, traditional-looking objects suggesting provenance, worn finishes on wood and artworks, and objects of feigned spiritual heft. The visitor must feel that these things are somehow his or hers for a moment, and a fleeting bit of the vintner's "life experience," too.

Part of the appeal is that the two will never meet but will share an ersatz intimacy in the transient taste of a wine subjected to the most as-siduous mechanical and chemical alteration in the history of viticulture. "Here we get back to the idea of kings and queens. You have created a yearning to get past the velvet rope" by adapting, staging, controlling. But the rope's still there.

The speaker helped design a tasting room in a winery sold to a billion-aire who wanted his own recognized cult cabernet, as well as the glorified factory in which it is made. But he didn't want people. So there will never be visitors. People still clamor about the property's periphery for a souvenir of this new royalty, which would be an $800 wine instead of, say, a faded rose stolen from the vineyard. "The level of exclusivity is what makes it," the bottle being the ultimate affirmation of brand by virtue of its being utterly unattainable.

CHAPTER FOUR:

American First-Growth

1.

He stands at the end of a hardpan road in Oakville that traverses the most valuable single vineyard in America—possibly on Earth because of its size—as well as America's most famous. It's To Kalon—Greek for "the highest beauty"—and freighted with history as well as highly coveted cabernet sauvignon and other Bordeaux varieties. One of the early, large plots of *Vitis vinifera* in Napa, planted by pioneer Hamilton Crabb in 1868, To Kalon had been preserved by the enormous price its grapes commanded and by its historic provenance.

The late Robert Mondavi once owned a large piece of it, deeding some to Opus One Winery as part of his joint venture with the Baron de Rothschild in 1980. In 1993, Andy Beckstoffer—perhaps the most powerful vineyard owner in the Napa Valley—was able to buy another eighty-nine acres of To Kalon from Mondavi, which he placed under a conservation easement that brought him a large tax deduction even though there was little danger of its ever being developed.

Known the length of the valley as Andy, sometimes as Andy B, Beckstoffer is *the* un-vintner, at ease in a suit and also in boots like the ones he's wearing hazed with his own valuable dirt, pressed jeans, and a soft green corduroy shirt. The face is farmer-ruddy, dark thinning hair neatly combed, and when he talks his eyes dance under long lashes.

"We replanted in 1994, 1996, and 1997"—lingering Tidewater vowels struggle to keep up—"with four Bordeaux clones, but no Malbec. They use it in France for filler." Merlot, too, was later deemed unsuited to the heat, and pulled. Ditto the petit verdot because winemakers didn't like the taste, and Andy B doesn't like the yield. "We wanted to show terroir, but also to add complexity that reflects the winemaker's personality. That means vineyard designation, the old 'spice box' concept," providing a rack of flavors among which winemakers may delve.

"It's not just terroir, man has to be part of it, too." Gender is everywhere in this metaphor. "If a wine was a model with a chipped tooth, you'd have to give her something to compensate with. If she needs better shoulders, better breasts, give her some. But her real charm is in the way she carries the defect."

Martha's Vineyard cabernet may have been the first model with a chipped tooth, back in the 1960s, its mintiness attributed to nearby eucalyptus trees, an Australian invasive, and in those days a selling point. Joe Heitz's Martha's Vineyard cabernet, named for the wife of Tom May who owned the vineyard, fetched a remarkably high price of eight dollars a bottle. The unreconstructed Heitz told people that eucalyptus smelled "like cat piss" to him, but if his wine reminded buyers of eucalyptus, so be it.

"If you're going to preserve these vineyards you have to make them very important." And making this demonstrable on the palate means they're worth more, since gifted winemakers who steadily raise the price of their Bordeaux blends will pay Andy more for To Kalon grapes. A businessman first and foremost, Andy then decided to tie the price of bottles in which his grapes end up to the price the vintners pay him. This has made him unpopular with vintners, particularly those whose continuing success depends on his To Kalon grapes.

"The bottle price is what determines the price of the grapes. But for the vineyard to be considered great, you have to be able to prove the quality empirically." He's walking along a row of manicured vines now, idly pulling leaves and a rare cluster touching another and dropping them. "It's just criminal, but we have to do it to preserve quality." Dropped fruit would fetch, if allowed to mature, a small fortune despite any defects, but dropping fruit on the ground also drives up the price of what remains.

Shade prettily freckles the clusters, the morning's first liberated sunlight lighting up glossy blue-black berries as if from within. The only proof of their quality will be in a narrow black bottle you won't be allowed to purchase unless your name's on a list. Vintners putting "Beckstoffer" and "To Kalon" on their labels must pay him a percentage of the profits, and one customer, Paul Hobbs, makes a To Kalon cabernet for which he charges $400.

But twenty feet from Hobbs's contracted rows are vines under contract to Fred Schrader, who has earned consistent ratings of 100 from the aging drivers of the cult concept, *The Wine Advocate* and the *Wine Spectator*, and yet Schrader charges only $175 a bottle. "I say to him, 'Come on, Fred. What're you waiting for?' " since the more Schrader charges, the more Andy Beckstoffer makes.

In 1969 he was a fresh-faced MBA with dark hair and sideburns departing the Heublein corporation's sequestered compound in far-off Hartford, Connecticut, for a western reconnaissance, an unlikely corporate Meriwether Lewis to an even less likely Thomas Jefferson surrogate. The balding CEO, Stuart Watson, was interested only in the trans-Mississippi as a source of cheap California grapes. He had just bought an unwieldy old showcase called Inglenook in the hopes it would lend Heublein some class. It would have the opposite effect, but meanwhile Beckstoffer played a large role in a momentous midcentury labor struggle, ensconced himself in the valley, and stayed on long after Heublein had slunk away.

No one today will argue with Andy Beckstoffer's success, but some will argue about how he got there and about the nature of his rise. Opinions of him strew the landscape like discarded rifles on the fields of Appomattox. Beckstoffer thought of himself in those days as "just a boy from

Richmond" who knew little about wine and drank milk with meals. The Tidewater Beckstoffers had dealt in lumber, and he had to get out of the South to see the affinity with the land as both a southern strength and a weakness, which is an unappeasable yearning for the past.

He had never seen anything like Inglenook when he first arrived in Napa, nor had he felt a more powerful association with history, not even in the back streets of the capital of the Confederacy. In Rutherford, bottles bearing the labels of legendary Gustave Niebaum, founder of Inglenook, contained more than wine—an inky concentration of another time.

Robin Lail, great-grandniece of the founder, would remember seeing bottles of old Inglenook brought up from the cellar, having been ordered by this brash young Heubleiner. Maybe those cobwebby artifacts were for impressing visiting executives, or big growers whose grapes Heublein wanted for its millions of gallons of cheap stuff—one was named I Love You—or maybe they were bound for his own cellar. Whatever their destination, the provenance was impeccable, their rarity known, their value enormous, and their inspirational power incalculable.

Andy went to the Central Valley to address groups of growers supplying Heublein and was soon dealing with Cesar Chavez, who called the strike by the United Farm Workers of America. It led to the very effective boycott of California lettuce and table grapes nationwide, and when a grower stood up in a hall down in Escalon and asked the visiting Heublein rep, Andy Beckstoffer, why he and other suppliers were being singled out, Andy said, "Because you're not sharing the wealth."

Andy had earlier pledged himself to "going as far into the free enterprise system as possible," and that required adaptation, even to the ways of a labor radical. So he signed a contract with United Farm Workers on top of a television set in a San Jose motel that ended the nationwide boycott, assumed the leadership of Heublein's subsidiary, the Vinifera Development Corporation, and began to manage Heublein's extensive vineyards in Napa, Sonoma, and Mendocino Counties, which he would eventually own.

The story is well known, but not the fact that when Andy left the corporate world he took with him a huge debt. People said Andy B would be cut down to size by the corporation he had once served and that was now

breathing down his neck, but he avoided bankruptcy and emerged trium-
phant. And now, in the second decade of the twenty-first century, Andy
B is talking publicly of corporations being inherently compromised, even
dividing them into "good" corporations and "bad" corporations, of which
the latter are clearly in the ascendency.

2.

Napa's historic wine estates once amounted to an unacknowledged,
Americanized, decidedly unofficial version of France's ranked châteaux
in Bordeaux. Chosen for the 1855 Exposition Universelle de Paris, the
French contenders were winnowed to *Grand Crus Classés* and then down
to a final handful making the most expensive wine, like châteaux Latour
and Margaux, that were designated premier crus. This sanctification by
the federal government would never happen here, but the landscape that
supported the original American premier crus of Napa Valley was, in
Andy's view, occupied by three classes: the processor (winery), the farmer
(vineyardist), and the worker (farmhand).

The latter was most likely Mexican—and still is—though the list of
nationalities is long, running down the spine of the Americas like a tenu-
ous, shadowy conduit akin to the black plastic pipes delivering the source
of life to the vines. But it still provides the human capital without which
the valley would have failed long ago, and in the twenty-first century that
traditional supply is threatened for the first time.

Of all three—processor, farmer, worker—the class that profited least
from Napa's fame was the worker. "When Heublein arrived in California," says Andy, "the workers existed to be exploited. In the Central Valley I saw, firsthand, man's inhumanity to man: paper-thin mattresses,
sewage running in the streets of the labor camps. Those guys were meat,
nothing more."

In corporate eyes, people like Andy were the butchers for the processors—getting the product ready—and that product was the blood of
the vine. But he told his bosses in Connecticut that working conditions
had to be improved with investment—executives refer to this as "unpro-

ductive money"—because Cesar Chavez knew that growers need both the processors *and* the workers, or the crop will rot unpicked. Napa Valley successfully resisted signing with the United Farm Workers, but the contract affecting the Central Valley indirectly forced improvements in Napa, too. This in turn improved many aspects of life from Calistoga to San Pablo Bay, prompting Andy to claim that today he's "honored for things I was condemned for back then."

It was the second class—farmers—that most interested him. He liked them more than he liked the salesmen, and they foreshadowed the path he would take. Meanwhile Heublein was bringing new technical expertise to Inglenook and Beaulieu, as well as cash and nationwide marketing, but the company remained deeply overshadowed by what he calls "corporate attitude"—distant rule rather than local, formulaic rather than adaptive, growth rather than quality—plus obsession with quarterly profits, an abhorrence of long-term commitment, and the use of charitable and political contributions as cover for self-centered activities.

But the most damaging aspect of bad corporate attitude was, in his view, self-interest at the expense of community. Although the claim made vintners writhe, Andy—the newborn farmer—set out to make other farmers realize that they, too, should use "business ways" to succeed: depreciate equipment, determine real costs, treat interest as real money. Make wineries buying grapes cover growers' basic expenditures so farmers don't have to sell their land, as they were forced to do in the 1970s and '80s.

He helped found the Napa Valley Grapegrowers Association, pointing out that grapes are not a commodity but a specialty product. Failing farmers endanger agriculture overall in the valley, since maintaining the high value of Napa grapes is essential to preventing residential development: "Adam Smith was right. If an asset isn't producing revenue, people will move to one that is. Like houses. And we want revenue to come to the land as well as wine."

Bringing growers into the political and social fabric of the valley was essential, an echo of Jefferson's desire to improve the lot of farmers for social cohesion and cultural enhancement. Andy credits the most accomplished salesman of his day, Robert Mondavi, who was also a processor, for nudging Napa onto the cusp of international renown that the Paris Tasting later affirmed. "If Bob hadn't said, 'Our wine can be as good as anybody's,' the Napa Valley of today wouldn't exist. But he was also telling farmers, 'I'm your friend.' One day I told him, 'No, you're not. Because you're not sharing the wealth with the farmers.' And Bob said, 'You're right—let's do a bottle price formula.' "

Apocryphal or not, that reasoning eventually led, in 2015, to Andy calling into his office, one by one, his loyal customers. Sitting in his rocker, he told them all that from then on they were going to share more of their wealth. Specifically, $18,000 would be required to purchase a mere ton of To Kalon grapes, when the average price in the valley was under $6,000. Or the vintner could pay Andy one hundred times the bottle price per ton, whichever was higher. The math was more difficult to swallow than to understand, but the price would soon rise again.

Then came the second rule: from now on the minimum price for a bottle of wine allowed to put "Beckstoffer To Kalon" on the label would be $125. That's $25,000 a ton, and a $300 bottle of wine from his grapes would cost the once-unimaginable sum of $30,000 a ton. Andy stressed that "this isn't a commodity, it's a specialty item."

The growers' share of the wineries' total revenue had instantly doubled. The reaction among his clients was outrage, followed by speedy acquiescence, for without To Kalon grapes their bottles might drop into the dreaded less-than-cult status. Beckstoffer had not only raised some growers to equal social status with vintners, he had also brought about the capitulation of some of the most reputable vintners. Grapes were demonstrably worth what he charged if the consumer would pay cult prices and many could and would, for such was the power of brand at the high end.

Engendered was a yearning both counterintuitive and often irresistible, the same impulse compelling the purchase of Rolexes and Teslas when lesser creations serve equally well, and often better. Some To Kalon wines made from grapes picked early were indeed impressive: powerful, flavorful assaults without overpowering alcohol or cooked fruit, full middle palates, and finishes like long, straight-arrow flights trailing cabernet descriptors and a mere hint of costly earth.

People who had known Andy for years laughed at his new pricing strategy that forced clients into luxurious dependency, but others asked why a bona fide Republican, a member of the Young Presidents' Organization, and a supporter of conservative causes, was simultaneously coming out against additional winery development? Why was he praising what he called "the screamers"—Cesar Chavez and local activists like Volker Eisele, even the environmentalist Chris Malan—who caused the vintners such grief? Why was he railing against winery expansion and giving money to protesters like Citizens' Voice in St. Helena, all on the fringe of haute valley life?

One possible answer was that uncontrolled winery expansion sullies life in general in the valley, and Andy's life specifically, as would soon become clear.

3.

Beckstoffer's vineyard operation sprawls next to a lonely stretch of Conn Creek Road in Rutherford. Turn onto the long dusty lane running toward the mountains and enter an outsized diorama of a nineteenth-century farm, except that the vines are trellis-trained. Agriculture's unlovely heavy machines are parked off to the right, and at the far end of the lane sits a precise apparition: a little Victorian similar to the house that's adjacent to Inglenook winery on the other side of the valley: bright yellow clapboards, a porch, and a steep red roof, all in a tourist-free zone.

The structure is a model of the old Chiles House Andy first saw in the late 1960s when he rolled onto Inglenook property from Highway 29. Inside is Beckstoffer's version of Napa's early glory days: walls pierced by inset stained glass suggesting William Morris's light boxes from the Arts and Crafts movement, ill-fitting doors in his second-floor office from architectural salvage down in Berkeley.

"We love history," he says, settling into his wooden rocker. "I don't care if they don't close right." He and his wife, Virginia, borrowed shapes, colors, and designs from various places in the valley. Overall, there's a feeling of space and purpose, with a view of a big barn and outbuildings, unmanicured vistas, with vineyard-making matériel stacked in the staging yard.

Beckstoffer's heavier than when he arrived in the valley in the 1960s, and his face, too, is altered, but the eyes are those of a man who's been involved in legal and environmental disputes and ongoing controversy. There are traces of the twentysomething who helped convince Heublein to invest in Inglenook and other properties and hung on tenaciously until he, in essence, "owned the farm."

What concerns him most in these latter days—and this is exceptional—is the radical alteration brought to the valley by the exponential rise of "hospitality," that euphemism for tourism. "At this point I have to decide what my career's worth," he says, an old man's tacit admission of limitations required of commerce to preserve the world. "Never in the history of mankind has agriculture withstood urban growth long-term, but here we have the best chance. Agriculture's clearly the highest and best use of the land, but whether that will save it I can't say."

He was a force in the creation of the Winery Definition Ordinance, along with Volker Eisele, back in 1990. It required that wines proclaiming themselves of the Napa Valley be made from at least three-quarters Napa grapes—the so-called 75 percent solution. It also served as a price support for Napa grapes, to the benefit of Napa growers generally and most definitely to Andy Beckstoffer.

But the Winery Definition Ordinance also limited what new wineries are allowed to do to sell their wine, preventing the conversion of new wineries into retail shops, conference pods, and de facto restaurants, which take more land out of agricultural production. Such a law was the biggest change concerning the land since the creation of the agricultural preserve in 1968, and it left much social wreckage in its wake.

Winery expansion is again being demanded, despite unprecedented public opposition, some of it promising true civil disobedience. "Scarce water, bad air, and traffic are great threats to the valley, but environmental damage to the land itself is still the greatest. The community as a whole shouldn't have to suffer for the economic viability of a few."

The demand by winery owners for a legal right to build new structures for tourists, otherwise known as "event centers," may sound innocuous to outsiders but it would release a torrent of construction reaching into the remotest corners of a narrow valley already stressed by similar projects. Of the nearly five hundred wineries here already—officially there are close to seven hundred if custom-crush operations and "virtual" wineries are included—many want to expand what they already possess. The collective bite out of the already finite agricultural lands would be enormous and amount to a second crop of food and "events" as valuable—or more so—than the grapes themselves. "The economics of direct sales to tourists overpower all arguments against it, except the ultimate one—that it will destroy the valley."

Wineries have become for the most part self-interested fiefdoms, the opposite of Jefferson's ideal community of yeoman farmers. "I'd hate to go away," says Andy, meaning die, "knowing I didn't fight." Some would take this as atonement for his role in the creation of a collective corporate behemoth in the valley, others as yet another act of pure self-interest.

One day Andy received a phone call from a neighbor on Zinfandel Lane that runs between Highway 29 and the Silverado. Wastewater from the Raymond Vineyards' winery was flowing into Andy's pond, the caller said, and it smelled like hell.

Andy lived nearby and went over to take a look. Yes, it appeared that the weir had allowed Raymond's gray water to flow into Andy's pond, although Raymond never admitted this. And, yes, it stank. Winery outflow is greater and more of a problem than commonly believed, and has been a contentious issue in the valley for decades since some wineries continue to dump into the river. Having it in your face when you're not even generating it was hard to take.

Andy began looking into the problem and in the process discovered something worse: Raymond's new owner, Jean-Charles Boisset, an inheritor of the largest wine-producing estate in Burgundy and the third-largest producer in all France, was involved in other activities Andy found unacceptable.

Boisset's family also owned wineries in other countries and in Northern California, including the historic Buena Vista in Sonoma County. And he intended to increase the number of daily visitors allowed at Raymond—*right behind Andy's house*—to five hundred a day and to increase production from 750,000 gallons of wine a year to 1.5 million gallons, an enormous jump.

Moreover, Boisset had transformed what were originally workspaces in the sprawling, workaday winery into party venues. These, Andy thought, had to be illegal. He had never visited the one called the Red Room, but he had heard much about it: red-flocked wallpaper, velvet settees, comely women pouring wine for a select few in near-darkness, a lavish, clublike Toulouse-Lautrecian fantasy soaked in cabernet sauvignon instead of absinthe.

It was patently outlandish in the middle of the agricultural preserve, Andy thought, and almost as hard to take as the claims he heard that Boisset was the valley's "next Robert Mondavi." Andy had considered Robert a friend, whose death occurred the year before Boisset bought Raymond, a time when the valley was already at odds with itself and lacking even a symbolic leader. Now Boisset was tooling around the valley behind the wheel of an Aston Martin, in a beautifully cut French suit with a jeweled broach attached to the lapel and shoes from a collection said to rival Imelda Marcos's of the Philippines.

Boisset was often seen in the pages of the *Napa Valley Register* receiving civic awards. He made contributions to charity. He even lived in the late Robert Mondavi's house, the one with the swimming pool in the living room. And he had barrels of pinot noir from Burgundy flown over to mix with Russian River pinot, violating the very notion of *terroir*, quite the opposite of Robert's joint venture with the Baron de Rothschild long ago.

"Boisset's a clown," Andy told people. "Robert Mondavi wasn't a clown."

To Andy, Boisset and now Raymond Vineyards epitomized bad corporate attitude, and there were a lot of contenders for that title. Raymond advertised a playpen, even a "dog motel," an example of the event center concept run amok that would serve as a cautionary example if effectively challenged. But Boisset would be a formidable adversary, his net worth estimated to be in the billions and he himself married to Gina Gallo, granddaughter of Julio and an heir to one of the largest wine-producing families on earth.

But something had to be done about more than Raymond's smelly wastewater. And who better to do it than Andy B?

CHAPTER FIVE:

Hands Across the Sea

1.

Yes, red-flocked wallpaper but also red felt on the pool table and red plush on the divan cosseting aspiring revelers, one of whom looks around and says laconically, "Fin de siècle bordello."

Overall, a rosy saturnalian radiance out of a Byronic dream, decidedly France at century's end—the nineteenth, not the twentieth—with a framed quote paying homage to Marcel Proust and an antique armchair delicately sat upon by a demimondaine suitable for a film based on *The Guermantes Way*. Some visitors have come up from Southern California and all are impressed with the opulence. None seems aware that they're enjoying one of the valley's most controversial and, according to Andy and other neighbors, illicit spaces, where the pour is cabernet sauvignon from the old Raymond Winery in whose bowels the Red Room lives.

Formerly owned by the Raymond brothers, stolid farmers who for many years made good wine in the least showy circumstances, Raymond

Vineyards was radically made over by its new owner, whose feet are firmly planted in the two manifestations—French and American—of the opulent, contemporary wine world. Appealing, energetic, skilled—Jean-Charles Boisset remembers names across a broad international spectrum of associates, friends, and hangers-on—he played a prominent role in *Mondovino*, the documentary about globe-girdling wine consulting, more showman than the late Robert Mondavi and, while equally endowed with Mondavi's appetites, also possessed of the European bona fides Mondavi longed for.

The Red Room is available to members of Raymond's wine club, and in fact to anyone willing to pay $500 a year for membership. Like owners of all older Napa wineries, Boisset enjoys grandfathered perks no new vintner could possibly get today—selling things unrelated to wine, serving food to visitors, providing not just a kennel for their dogs and wine with a dog's name on the labels but also a Theater of Nature, where people may stroll among drought-resistant flora, within view of the parking lot.

His critics insist he's in violation of even grandfathering's outsized privileges, but the most obvious affront is the Red Room. He dismisses his critics with Gallic sangfroid: "In France, when we want to act arrogant, we just ignore the little people."

There's Delia Viader, owner of Viader Vineyards on Howell Mountain, in the blazer with the gold buttons. It was her vineyard that two decades earlier inadvertently dumped mud into the Bell Canyon Reservoir, which the city of St. Helena still worries about. Next to her is Mark Pope, agreeable owner of the Bounty Hunter in downtown Napa, bending an elbow after paying thousands just hours before for special lots of cabernet at the valley's trade auction.

The Red Room is packed for Raymond's annual Napa Gras celebration, guests drifting to the adjoining room where wheels of cheese crowd platters of charcuterie. Out on the main floor of the winery a young woman, who for all practical purposes is naked, dangles upside down from a gymnast's rope while pouring Boisset's JCB sparkling wine into eagerly raised flutes. Other, similarly adorned women on the counter pole-dance without poles and arrange themselves on a flight of stairs usually climbed by winemakers and cellar rats to check fermentation in towering steel tanks.

On the far side of the room two women in skeins of dark and white chocolate smile carefully, feathered masks barely concealing their fear that the delicate, artfully applied facades will melt.

Four hours is long for lunch, even in Napa Valley. But there's a lot to be done this afternoon: eat, drink Raymond Vineyards' reserve chardonnay, assess three Raymond cabernet sauvignons from Oakville, Rutherford, and St. Helena vineyards, taste a blend called Generations, and then and only then a bottle of bright, complex pinot noir, part French and part American, called JCB No. 3.

Raymond Vineyards' well-watered, vernal garden sits on the edge of the Rutherford Appellation—a federal geographical designation for discrete winemaking districts—its white Louis Quatorze–style lawn chairs made of soft, weather-defying synthetics, alarmingly white. At table is the woman responsible for making these wines and four men—five if you count the chef, who is neither up nor down for long, two journalists, and Jean-Charles Boisset.

Thin slices of heirloom tomato in pungent olive oil are followed by an all-American medley of succulent protein that includes bison and alligator. The latter's a tribute to the memory of Agoston Haraszthy, the early Hungarian disciple of California wine known also as the Count of Buena Vista. He built that Sonoma winery in 1857 and was later supposedly devoured by a crocodile in Nicaragua. JCB owns DeLoach and Lyeth in Sonoma, as well as Buena Vista, where a production of *A Midsummer Night's Dream* is about to open.

Boisset's overlapping interests provide a keyhole through which to view the global vineyard. Jet propulsion brings wine in all stages of production to various experts on other continents—in this case 60 percent pinot noir from the Côte de Nuits, and 40 percent from the Russian River Valley, the French component loaded in barrels onto a plane and flown here for a cuvée without precedent. The concept is daring if impractical and a vinous antidote to "freedom fries." And if pinot noir can wing in today from Burgundy, cabernet sauvignon can wing in tomorrow from Bordeaux, Chile, or Australia.

His earliest memory, he says, is of the inside of his mother's womb. There being no witnesses, the story must be accepted or rejected based on one's tolerance of the imaginative, as with much of what Jean-Charles says. Listen and you may find yourself transported to Vougeot in the French countryside and a house where doors stand open in season to relatives, friends, neighbors, and nature in every guise: animals, insects, breeze, rain, flowers, wine, and, of course, lunch.

On Sundays it was as lengthy as lunch in Rutherford would be half a century later. Since there was no church in Vougeot, the Boissets had to drive to nearby Flagey-Échezeaux, another iconic Burgundian name where there was a church, and after worship and travel there and back the family was hungry. The conversation at table was unbroken, the rhythm of the whole—place, food, wine, family—so natural it was taken for granted and yearned for in later life.

Most formative for young Jean-Charles was his maternal grandmother, an elementary school teacher and a blend of Wiccan and the Pied Piper, "very good with a pendulum in detecting rhythm and vortex. The kids would all run to her." She taught Jean-Charles to "douse" for springs and to detect "energy" and "mineral flows" by swinging a crystal. She also, he says, practiced some Gallic version of feng shui and introduced him to the telluric arts he describes as "interactions with the Earth, which are the basis of biodynamics and the realization that we all have a purpose." But, most important, she taught him English.

By age nine Jean-Charles thought he "understood the actions of the Earth, sun, and moon. When I discovered Rudolf Steiner"—Austrian founder of the Waldorf school and creator of the concept of biodynamism—"I already knew his principles." His grandmother "had made me see farming as something beyond viticulture, a sense of *why*."

As kids he and his friends "played naked, swam, fished, rode horses. Meanwhile my parents were building the business. They moved to Nuits-Saint-Georges, and the business got bigger. My father was buying and selling, mostly vineyards. He was driven, one of many doing well, and then my grandfather got into exporting. I saw everything in the business, lived it, and besides the practical stuff learned the art of life that is built around wine."

At age eleven he was brought to the United States and then to California, where he decided "this was the only place to be, in the dream of the American way of life," too young to know that many in Northern California dreamed of the Burgundian way of life. "I thought I must be half American, given to me at birth."

He attended the Lycée Rochambeau French International School in Bethesda, Maryland, where he turned into an exceptional soccer player and later considered becoming a professional striker on the French team. But his father said, "You should carry wine barrels instead of doing sports," the beginning of Jean-Charles the entrepreneur who went from "visions of living in the fourteenth and fifteenth centuries, like Marco Polo discovering new worlds" to getting an MBA from UCLA and living in Oil City, Pennsylvania.

To visualize this requires real imagination. The cumulative effect of the steady Latin gaze, mussed blond hair, blue mohair jacket with that heart-shaped, bejeweled gold pin, French cuffs held in place by gold links embellished with red enamel roses, wince-inducing black patent leather shoes with long pointy toes and socks an approximation of Frank Lloyd Wright's Cherokee Red (which you may purchase in replica in Raymond's gift shop) is thoroughly continental and in no way Pennsylvanian. "But there I got into corporate finance. I was interested in derivatives and the art of the deal. I would have been big in it. But my father kept saying 'You should think about wine.' "

So in 1993 Jean-Charles came back to Northern California, looked around Sonoma and Napa, and asked himself, " 'Why would I go any other way?' "

2.

His parents, meanwhile, were pulling out of America. "They thought it was a nightmare. Europeans just don't get the United States—it's too big. Opus One doesn't get it, or Christian Moueix," founder of

Dominus, the estate carved out of land bought from the Daniel sisters in another age. "I do get it, and I told them, 'We should be buying wineries.' Quality in California is great, but Europeans don't realize that, either. And my mother said, 'Well, why don't you do it? If you believe in it.' "

The Boissets had good brands in France. Jean-Charles put together a small team of consultants on a back street in San Francisco, and they all went looking for wineries and distributors, at a time when there were hundreds of the latter. "In 2003 I made my first big step and bought DeLoach, in the Russian River Valley," producer of good pinot noir and chardonnay. "That was a big deal. And I tried many times to buy Buena Vista, until I finally got it. I was magnetized by the experience and decided to bring *savoir-vivre* to America," assuming that Americans had little and would welcome "the osmosis that would make them dizzy, energize them to live the next vision."

If he had managed to buy Buena Vista earlier he probably would not have bought Raymond and built the Red Room, the Theater of Nature, and the dog motel. He certainly would not have had to deal with the leaky wastewater that brought Andy Beckstoffer into *l'affairs de Raymond*, who had no desire to live any vision his new neighbor had in mind. But Raymond possessed lots of vineyard, and wines with the soft, distinctive Rutherford notes first praised by André Tchelistcheff for their redolent, "dusty" character. Jean-Charles thought Raymond could easily be converted to biodynamic farming. Instead of turning to his family for additional financing, he turned to the Japanese, specifically Kirin, yet another Pacific beer company following Foster's of Australia into the historic wilds of Napa that by the twenty-first century were anything but.

Why Kirin responded to a Frenchman's "vision" remains unclear, but respond they did. "I had to go to them because no one else could see what we saw in Raymond," which included a lot of grandfathered rights and utilitarian space waiting to be reinterpreted. One of the Raymond brothers, Walter, and some other old Napa hands, including a veteran of Christian Moueix's Petrus/Dominus domain, helped Jean-Charles pick a winemaker from among thirty under consideration. Meanwhile JCB "was practically living at Raymond, and spending a fortune on French oak. We kept up production, and walked around the old winery trying to decide what color to paint it."

White with gold trim was the choice, "to bring the unique experience I wanted. People would come not as customers, but as guests. I wanted them to *dream.*"

Also to be "educated" by purchasing high-end paraphernalia only tangentially connected to wine appreciation (but not to savoir faire and joie de vivre): Baccarat crystal, Lalique glass, all manner of luxuries that would eventually include gold spit buckets, a $5,000 handmade trolley for wine bottles, and a black lacquered case containing an artful arrangement of women's panties, a black leather whip, and other nonessentials for $25,000. This was so far from anything the Raymond brothers might have imagined that older employees found themselves gape-mouthed.

An array of sniffers are mounted on the wall of the corridor leading to the Red Room, supposedly containing every essence of wine that can be expelled with the push of a button. On busy days while the real thing's being unspectacularly made on the far side of the winery, visitors who have left their dogs in the dog motel and their spouses in the Theater of Nature wander in a miasma of commingling chemical approximations of oak, berries, lavender, and cigar box, uncertain of what to do with this experience, but intrigued.

"I wanted to bring texture and emotion to the journey" with a conflation of wine, desire, and a hint of the illicit. "I'm passionate about the experience—escape, learn—dream! I want my guests to come back, and we're very lucky to have such a product. *Which is art!*"

This is the ultimate justification cited by established vintners all over the valley, and by recent arrivals. Good reviews tended to incorporate "art" as an intrinsic good. Robert Mondavi, Jean-Charles's American idol, pushed the notion of wine and art to a disastrous conclusion with the failed art and wine museum Copia, in the city of Napa. Its colossal collapse brought down with it the idea that associations with art will float any scheme, however ill conceived, if sufficient money and vanity are packed into it. But Jean-Charles was coming at it from another direction altogether.

He pays homage to the Surrealists, his favorite artists, but declines to elaborate. Part vinous Barnum, part New Age Haraszthy—a contender for the title of father of California viticulture—Boisset also loves Disney and, like Mondavi, has difficulty saying no to anything. Much of what each of these men leave behind is philosophically incompatible with the agricultural idyll in which their dreams flourish.

Agriculture by definition prohibits commercial activities not related to it, including jazz concerts, retail shops, event centers, the removal of land from agricultural production for parking lots, new roads, storage facilities, and other activities industrial by nature. Wineries cause the same problems for communities as do factories, which in reality is what wineries have become: accelerated water consumption, waste, emissions, noise, increased car and truck traffic, and a daily invasion and exodus of workers and visitors who leave money behind, but at a cost. All fuel growth and tourism at the expense of cropland and a traditional notion of agriculture from the Greeks down through Jefferson, Emerson, and Thoreau to the present. But those things are all good for corporations, and Raymond, too, had become nothing if not corporate.

3.

While Jean-Charles was "living the dream, traveling the world, and adoring women enormously as a bachelor," he met a Gallo rep in San Francisco's Tenderloin district, the city's toughest sell. It had been assigned to Gina Gallo because, Jean-Charles says, "she was tough." Also tall, personable, unaffected, and the granddaughter of Gallo's cofounder, Julio.

In 2003 they met again at Vinexpo, in Bordeaux, at a table of international wine celebrities, "and she stands up and looks at me with those beautiful blue eyes and *boom!*" She was headed to Paris the next day, and so was Jean-Charles. He said, "So let's go out," and she said, "Can I bring my sister?"

He invited a dozen male friends to join them, to distract the other granddaughter of Julio Gallo. Later, he and Gina "had a kiss at one of the clubs," then in Santa Rosa they "had another kiss and—*bada boom!*—I was in love."

The account is touching—two sophisticated products of hugely successful wine dynasties married in San Francisco. A diagnosis of breast cancer for Gina, Jean-Charles says, soon made him "start thinking about the meaning of life," and kept him in California most of the time, though he was then running things for his family in France as well. Gina recovered, and though children were not supposed to be a possibility, she gave birth to twin girls in 2011.

Margrit Biever Mondavi, Robert's widow, told Jean-Charles at a chance meeting that the house in the hills behind Yountville, designed by Cliff May so that Robert could swim daily in the living room, "should be your home."

He expressed interest, got a call from an agent, then one from Robert's son, Michael. Clearly the house had become a burden for them, if a valuable one. "Michael asked how soon I could decide," recalls Jean-Charles, who won't reveal the price. He called his father, who asked, "What are you waiting for?"

Discussion became de facto negotiation, though Gina knew nothing of this. Jean-Charles and Michael haggled for two days on two continents—he in Burgundy, Michael in the Napa Valley. Finally Jean-Charles faxed him an offer, and Michael called to say, "Done."

When Jean-Charles got back to Napa he drove his wife up to the house, where an agent was waiting. "I told Gina, 'We can go in and look at it—or we can just have it.' Neither of us had been inside, but in life you sometimes just do things in a lucky moment, and this house had the highest amount of energy of anyplace in the valley. It fit so well with my love of history and Napa, architecture and California's indoor/outdoor living." So they just *did* it.

A photograph taken in the now Boisset-Gallo house graced a Christmas card a few years later. It showed Gina and Jean-Charles in formal attire on each side of little girls dressed in brilliant white dresses. Jean-Charles stands slightly apart, smiling ambiguously, as inclusive of the viewer as he is of his wife and daughters. He seems to be saying, *Now isn't this something?*

In late 2015 Boisset received a copy of a letter that had been sent to the county board of supervisors by the white-shoe San Francisco law firm Shute, Mihaly & Weinberger. It regarded the Napa County Code enforcement action against Raymond Vineyards and read, in part, "This firm represents Beckstoffer Vineyards in matters related to the repeated, flagrant, and longstanding violations of Napa County land use regulations by Raymond Vineyards . . . Over the past four years, Raymond has profited tremendously from its unlawful actions, to the detriment of the County's law-abiding residents and business. Thus far, however, the County has all but ignored these violations."

The law firm urged the county "to take prompt and effective enforcement action against Raymond . . . 'Red Tag' and require Raymond to remove the unauthorized improvements it made to convert over 10,000 square feet of office and production space into four accessory hospitality and tasting rooms." In short, the county should enforce its own rules. "We recognize that Raymond is not the only winery that has violated County regulations or permit requirements. . . . [T]here is nothing punitive or unfair about the County simply requiring a property owner to comply with the law or preventing those who violate the law from unjustly enriching themselves at the public's expense. . . . [I]t appears that, following their purchase of the facility in 2009, Raymond's new owners made a series of deliberate decisions not to follow those rules—and to see if they could get away with it."

Jean-Charles told journalists—over lunch, naturally—"There's always someone trying to bring you down. You can't let the little people stop you. They're like mosquitoes—they bite you, and then they die."

But Andy B wasn't likely to oblige. Instead, he sat back and waited for the county to move against Raymond, assuming that the county government now had no choice and that the fight would soon break out into the open.

CHAPTER SIX:

Orwell's Plow

Political language . . . is designed to make lies sound truthful.
—George Orwell, "Politics and the English Language"

1.

Napa's place in the global wine market is by definition small, like the valley itself, but its worldwide reputation is outsized, based on more than a century and a half of producing good wine, the Paris Tasting of 1976, climate and soils that produce predictably good cabernet, and a concentrated opulence rarely encountered elsewhere. This displayed wealth, including corporate, is used by those possessing it—or their designates—to sell themselves and to sell the valley as a unique, well-contained, convenient venue for monied travelers. That is how the world sees Napa.

The consequences of so-called high-end tourism are increased traffic, glamorized winemaking and farming, clashes between winemakers and neighbors, and staged programs and events at hundreds of wineries that threaten to overpower all else. Shrinkage in the number of national distributors contributed mightily to this trend, but this neither explains nor excuses it. Wineries selling directly to customers may eliminate fees and generally double their money, a near-irresistible dynamic.

But the engine driving customers to wineries is tourism by definition, and catering to and feeding the human element in this newfound bonanza changed the valley. It now threatens to permanently debase it.

Not so many years ago, agriculture was not only considered the highest and best use of the land, but laws regulating tourism were strictly enforced. Experiences like those at Raymond were practically nonexistent. Today Jean-Charles Boisset is far from alone, just better than his competitors at providing entertainment that draws revelers-cum-buyers through doors thrown wide by the heterodox associations of wine. The phenomenon had many contributors, but none more important than an obscure committee—there's always a committee—seeking in 2006 not to explicitly weaken the long-established law limiting promotion by any means but to do so under the guise of making the valley "better."

The committee's stated object was to "reconsider" existing county laws and perhaps to tweak (read: subvert) them in the direction of events and concomitant profits. This meant inserting words seemingly innocuous so wine would flow around the sainted agricultural preserve's rigidity and find its way to more lips and satisfy more unrequited desires, including the desire for more profits.

Tom Gamble no longer wears the ten-gallon hat he had on when elected to the Farm Bureau's Land Use Committee at the annual picnic back in 2000. It was held at the Charles Krug Winery, and Tom's hat reminded people that he ran a small line of organic "beeves" up in the east hills, a sentimental connection to Napa's mixed agriculture that is now almost entirely gone. The Gamble family had farmed in Napa County for eighty-four years, and that included Tom's vines planted on broad riverine flats in the middle of the valley.

Tom was now wearing a flat-crowned straw instead of the ten gallon, reminding the same people—grape growers, family, friends—of the hat worn by Andy Hoxsey, who had also inherited big, historic vineyards nearby that had belonged to Andy's grandfather, Andy Pelissa. There were several Andys among the agricultural preserve's early supporters, as well as a rich assortment of newcomers and future stars passionately opposed to development. These included Jack and Jamie Davies.

Such is the complex overlay of personality, topography, politics, and society embodied by descendants of another age still seen in St. Helena, Yountville, and Napa, ambulatory vessels of history known to fewer and fewer people. They are, for the most part, still faithful to agriculture, at a time when money and notoriety seem to trump all else, and in 2006 Tom Gamble became one of twenty-four people named to a citizens board charged with reviewing the county's General Plan. .

The assignment sounded like work to him, which it proved to be, calling on him to drive regularly from his farm office just north of Yountville—the one with an old movie poster on the wall showing a grinning Ernest Borgnine in *Abilene*—down to the city of Napa and then east into Coombsville. Each time, he passed the Napa State Hospital (formerly known as Napa Insane Asylum) and would come to think of this as a fitting prelude to what followed.

The committee met in a school that provided space for the meetings and was chaired by the county planning director at the time, Hillary Gitelman, a trained professional in land use in a perennial blue blazer. Tom's fellow members were a varied lot: retired teachers, a couple of architects, a winery heir, a sales rep for a steel supplier, some older longtime valley residents, a vineyard developer, and the executive director of the Winegrowers of Napa County, the only paid advocate on the committee.

Her name was Debra Dommen, and she was self-assured, outspoken, and pregnant. Soon Dommen was telling the group that every time Tom spoke, the baby kicked her.

The Bush economic downturn began and would soon be a recession, but for the moment the General Plan had to be updated, and it seemed to Tom that both Gitelman and Dommen were in favor of relaxing conservation safeguards built into the existing plan. The lagging economy had increased pressure on the county government to grant permits to wineries wanting to do things not allowed under the old rules, including serve food. It wasn't called that initially, however; instead, it was euphemistically referred to as "wine pairings," and cast as an essential part of selling wine although wine had been successfully sold to visitors without food in Napa for a century and a half.

Tom was aware that he straddled two worlds here. First and foremost, he was a farmer. But he also owned a small ten-thousand-case winery like a number of other growers, because the economics of grapes had changed. There were not a lot of Andy Beckstoffers out there, and most growers generally needed an extra source of income. Selling your own wine, even with most of your grapes going to other wineries, made an appreciable difference. And you didn't need "tastings" to do it, just good wine to offer drop-ins interested in sampling the products of the land—in Tom's case, a sprawling vineyard he had inherited split by the Napa River and lines of big old trees.

And if a farmer grew grapes sustainably, he also needed capital to replant, another argument in favor of selling some wine to improve return on investment. It helped keep the family business rolling and paid inheritance taxes and some other expenses. But Tom had no interest in entertaining tourists, an activity he considered antithetical to farming.

Wineries that bought most of their grapes from growers were pushing for building concessions that took land out of production. This was not in the spirit of agriculture, but still they clambered to put up more structures that sold directly to visitors, even though this created a dissonance in what had been a tight alliance of growers. Some wanted in on the tourism bonanza in a bigger way, and the Farm Bureau felt the heat of these demands within its ranks.

The citizens meeting in the school went through each element of land use in the General Plan—goals and definitions—and discussed what might be changed and what might be added. Usually such committees tightened up rules to assure the continuance of historic practices—in Napa's case, farming as the highest and best use of the land—but for some reason pressure was this time being brought to loosen them. Very quickly, it seemed to Tom, the definition of agriculture in the General Plan was raised, along with the possibility of changing the wording to include something about tastings.

Neither Gitelman nor Dommen tried to argue that preparing and serving food could actually be defined as agriculture, which was preposterous. But implied was the notion that some mention of food service should be included to help those struggling. Then, almost immediately, the argument was being made that no new wineries could succeed without it.

In retrospect, no one could put a finger on exactly who suggested the change. The planning director seemed to support adding the language, with Dommen adamantly in favor. As a paid advocate for a large, powerful political organization, she regularly sought to affect county elections and get legislation passed that would help the wealthy members of the Winegrowers of Napa County. Critics had pointed out for some time that actions by the Winegrowers led to outcomes good for them but not necessarily for the community. Its proven sympathies were with supervisors favoring development over all else.

Since Jack Cakebread first invited potential members to his "pond house" in the late 1980s and formed the Winegrowers, its membership had been recast by death and incapacity. But its influence had grown and members now included representatives of multinationals as well as prominent family corporations like Trefethen, Far Niente, and Trinchero, and outliers like Craig Hall and Bill Harlan. A significant addition would be Kendall-Jackson, notorious cutter of thousands of oaks along the Central Coast's interstate highway.

Changing the definition of the ageless practice of farming in the county where the first agricultural preserve in the United States was established seemed to Tom Gamble rash and unwarranted. He also thought it odd that Dommen had been allowed on the committee in the first place, since the other members were citizens without apparent links to partisan politics. She was a corporate animal seeking to improve her employers' bottom lines and, he suspected, her résumé as well. Gamble and some other members of the committee were struck by her stridency and the fact that the planning director seemed to openly defer to her.

Tom stuck to his point that the old, narrow definition of agriculture was best because it had endured; it was real. Food service should be excluded from winery activities in part because it wasn't traditional, and forcing it on the process would disturb, in both theory and reality, the valuable but delicate balance between farming and wine.

The existing language was as close as it could get to civic scripture in Napa, but everything was intertwined when it came to grapes, as he knew full well. He had dealt with all the components in the larger equation—farming, making wine, selling it—and the present definition had served the county well since the creation of the agricultural preserve in 1968. It had made the unique American success that was Napa Valley.

Such a change would also create a discrepancy between the rights of older wineries and new ones whose permits allowed them to serve food. Such a change would create new tensions all their own, bringing friction to a system supposedly based on commonality that had been the watchword since the passage of the Winery Definition Ordinance back in 1990.

This had sought to ensure that rampant development was at least consistent, defining a winery as an "agricultural processing facility" in the business of "fermenting and processing grape juice." Wineries were allowed to sell and market wine, too, but marketing activity was an "accessory," clearly subordinate to production. All such accessory uses had to be restricted to less than half a winery's footprint on the land, which was generous enough.

The Winery Definition Ordinance—the passage of which got the former planning director, Jim Hickey, fired before Hillary Gitelman came along—had established the 75 percent rule for Napa grapes in Napa wine, assuring quality while at the same time restricting production. This had angered those wanting to profit maximally from the valley's reputation, since the white elephants and other older wineries were exempt from the rule if they didn't expand. But now what had been new wineries in 1990 would have to ask for permit revisions to allow them food service and so-called eventing, too.

None of this had anything to do with agriculture in the real sense of the word and was in fact antagonistic to it. But food would attract more tourists and sell more wine more profitably, since commissions wouldn't have to be paid to the radically dwindling number of national distributors, and improve the new wineries' relationships with the banks.

It would also cause more conflict with wineries caught between the oldest, with their grandfathered rights, and the newest ones. Farmers and their neighbors all over the valley who had held on to the traditional view of agriculture and land preservation wouldn't be happy with the effects of the changes, but it would be too late to do anything about it.

The whole food service question was a Pandora's box and could prove communally ruinous, Tom argued. And Debra Dommen announced that the baby had just kicked her again.

2.

Since the time of the founding of the agricultural preserve, an interesting new dilemma has arisen: the sheer amount of money required to get into the business. A person has for the most part to be seriously rich to even try, and these types naturally come together to promote their common advantages over lesser competitors and anyone else who gets in the way, as we shall see. That often means neighbors and organizations that, once they object to vintners' demands, are forevermore assigned the role of adversary.

This was the broad perception of corporations in the valley at the outset of the new century, when even concern for the commonweal had become a relic and political positions were intractable. The Winegrowers, once outliers by choice, had gained allies among the Napa Valley Vintners, even among the Grapegrowers who now leaned toward development. All these organizations acted to assuage members' fear of limitations on what they considered their needs and, almost as important, their wants. The enemy, from the corporate perspective, was anyone openly in favor of Measure J, which had subjected any changes in land use by the board of supervisors to a popular vote. When these changes, beneficial to only a few, were put before the public, the public tended to reject them.

Referenda were part of the solution, or a witch's brew, depending on your objectives. Highest among the political stirrers were longtime environmental advocates like Volker Eisele and Chris Malan. The Sierra Club had sued successfully over Jayson Pahlmeyer's hillside vineyard development, but that victory had gone by without a promise being extracted from the county that it wouldn't allow the same thing to happen again later. Now the county was allowing it by simply not acting.

Memories of that fight still strike fear and rage in the vintner class. A proposal for a new initiative to further limit development in the hills would eventually give rise to another group too rough around the edges for Cakebread's loafer-and-blue-blazer crowd, but all those who ignored the rules and wrapped their collective arms around free enterprise at any cost denounced sign-carrying, overeducated, "un-American no-growthers." Thus did the valley reflect a nation whose politics was riven by triumphalism, disinformation, and the base appetite.

Those in the wine business who most feared losing market share, and others who should have been looking after the county—heads of civic organizations, elected and appointed officials, citizens groups—were either overworked, co-opted, or trying to improve their own financial positions. The board of supervisors leaned unapologetically toward development and forgave wineries their transgressions in what amounted to tacitly approved illegality. New structures, water and sewage systems, vineyard expansions, and excess production were overlooked if they occurred at wineries, whereas similar violations by individual citizens were red-tagged and fines levied.

If winery owners wanted to flip their investments, they got illegal modifications approved after the fact. The unstated message was that the valley was no longer primarily about wine, agriculture, or even tourism, but money; how you went about getting it was your business and none of the public's.

Tom Gamble thought, "The big boys are looking for an exit strategy." Large corporations demanded steady grape supplies but lacked the ability to wait for profits, which is the farmer's lot. If it ever came down to a vote on saving the agricultural preserve, Mondavi's alter ego, Harvey Posert Jr., had believed the valley's corporate megafauna would flop for cash and get out. "The big boys can't stand the idea of winning some years and losing others, which are the farmer's odds," Harvey liked to say. "So they institute changes not good for long-term business."

Foreign companies owned a significant percentage of Napa's forty-five thousand acres of vineyard, though it was hard to say exactly how much more. Big publicly traded and privately held companies based in the United States owned thousands more, and collectively their influence was greater than the sum of their parts. This was abetted by smaller homegrown corporations with similar interests, all speaking with a single voice in developmental and environmental matters. They had more money among them to invest in electing candidates and passing laws to achieve those ends, their proven sympathies lying with increased development in the hills and in the ag preserve whenever they could get away with it.

There seemed to be a permanent revolving door for the CEOs, all looking to drive up the price of their winery's stock so they could retire comfortably. They chose masstige over prestige and made fortunes before the public caught on to the fact that quality had disappeared from wine once considered exceptional. This drove up short-term profits, but it diminished the name for the foreseeable future. Beaulieu, Beringer, and Mondavi were good examples. Much more difficult, if not impossible, was the journey back from masstige to prestige, but by then those CEOs would be gone and the winery passing into the next fraying corporate basket.

The old definition of agriculture in Napa County's General Plan had been the law of the land for forty years: "Agriculture is defined as the raising of crops, trees, and livestock; the production and processing of agricultural products." Added to this rudimentary, long-accepted, even hallowed concept was the now accepted "and related marketing, sales and other accessory uses," akin to defining a plow as an implement for parting the soil preparatory to planting *then to be turned on its side and used to serve canapés prepared in the barn for sale to spectators.*

The small change seemed innocuous but was in fact as potent as an aggressively metastasizing cancer cell. The new definition, accommodated almost unanimously by the committee meeting in Coombsville, then had to be approved by the county planning director and the board of supervisors. Clearly at odds with the traditional notion of farming, the new definition alluding to food service and other selling techniques was laughable from most perspectives, but not from that of business. And in the end those able to exploit it didn't care how they did it.

Tom Gamble wasn't the only one bothered by the change. Jim Hickey, when he heard about it, told his monthly Elks Lodge luncheon group, the

Good Guys, "Change the definition of ag, and you change the county's destiny."

Present at that luncheon was the last surviving member of the board of supervisors that had voted in the ag preserve, Don McFarland. He and Hickey both relished their monthly get-togethers, and the rumored change in the definition of agriculture inspired discussion of bygone days. McFarland spoke wistfully of that night in 1968 when "millionaires were jerking on my coat, trying to get me to change my vote, but I wouldn't," a degree of bravery and independence unimaginable on the planning commission or the board of supervisors today.

Now a Napa County planning director in the line descending from Hickey not only didn't question the definition change but would claim a few years later—safely ensconced in her new job down in Palo Alto—that she had no memory of how the subject had come up at the meeting in Coombsville. By then the Napa Valley Vintners, the Farm Bureau, the Grapegrowers, and the Winegrowers of Napa County had all expressed their approval, a damning performance all round. In the new language lay a contagion that would, in the long run, result in the demise of a half-century of protections and high-minded aspirations.

3.

Geoff Ellsworth, an artist living in the town of St. Helena, eventually a co-founder of a Tom Paine–style mailer called *Citizens' Voice*, had a premonition when he first heard about the change in the definition of agriculture. How, he asked himself, had something so important come about in shadow, and who was behind it? He suspected that a master plan existed to increase the advantage of corporations and the larger interests at the expense of farmers and other citizens, and that he would have to look no further than the origins of the change, marveling all the while that such a thing could happen without public debate or even general public knowledge. Why hadn't someone challenged this as a violation of the law and, using the mechanisms outlined in Measure J that prohibited changes to land-use policy unless they were voted on by the people, gotten the question on the ballot?

After the committee on which Tom Gamble sat made its recommendations and the county planning department and the board of supervisors expressed approval, Geoff Ellsworth started watching videos of the meetings of the county planning commission, suspecting that the key to the process was deception by elected officials, wittingly or otherwise. It was a grueling mission, the videos full of bad jokes and complicated parliamentary maneuvers. Geoff had to force himself to sit there, doodling, as sessions came and went like bad footage of creatures swimming in a murky aquarium. Never once did he hear a reference to the definition change.

Then, in a video made in April 2008, he saw the planning director, Hillary Gitelman, sit at a table with her back to the camera and tell the supervisors that the changes proposed for the General Plan were "principally minor," and adding that "We've made this document clearer than it has been historically."

Already watching for the smoking gun, Geoff realized that this was as close as he would get. Mention of the alteration to the definition of agriculture came near the end of her testimony when she said only, "Text change was not the purpose."

Geoff thought, "Well, it was certainly somebody's purpose," a legislative sleight of hand done without proper review under the formidable California Environmental Quality Act and, in his opinion, a moral taint. Changing the definition of a word within a rule to allow what had not been allowed before was deception, pure and simple. It was, by implication, a threat to democracy itself.

The zoning had been changed, too, by allowing every ten-acre plot in the county to have a commercial winery event center, and if you didn't have ten acres, you could do a lot line adjustment and cobble together additional acreage. (Given how often these "adjustments" moved property to the "adjuster," the suspicion that they regularly resulted in the "adjusted" neighbors losing land that was really theirs seems unavoidable.) This plan went to the planning commission and then to the board of supervisors after just a three-month interval, not enough time to analyze the possible impact.

To Geoff's mind, the public had no idea what the changes meant. That a simple Mitigated Negative Declaration could be prepared instead of an Environmental Impact Report (EIR), making a full-blown change to county zoning, was wrong because it meant, presto, intensified commercial use on heretofore sacrosanct agricultural land. All this should have been voted on by the public under Measures J and P, just as the change in the definition of agriculture should have been voted on.

The more Geoff thought about it, the more diabolical the process seemed. Both industry and local government had engaged in what struck him as a conspiracy to put marketing on the same level as farming. That way, when someone complained that an orchard, field, or vineyard got torn out for a paved event center—or, he imagined, a roller coaster like the one down in American Canyon, or nude dancers on a flatbed truck outside a winery—they would be asked, "Didn't you see the law from 2008? Wine marketing is agriculture!"

Wine marketing was now whatever you wanted it to be. It had meant one thing to old Joe Heitz back in the day, and it meant something entirely different to Jean-Charles Boisset and what would surely be a wave of imitators.

Hillary Gitelman soon left Napa for Palo Alto to take advantage of a better opportunity, and one imagines also happy to get out of Dodge ahead of the fallout from the definition change. And Debra Dommen left the Winegrowers to perform pubic relations for Treasury Wine Estates, aka Beringer Vineyards.

The struggle would surface again in 2016, but meanwhile another was shaping up in Geoff Ellsworth's very backyard, the lovely little town of St. Helena. There he essentially reinvented himself as a dedicated—and effective—opponent of development by government fiat, the new bête noire now at large in the Napa Valley.

III.

VILLAGE AND VINE

Development collides with the classic notion of the enduring American small town; a scion of the old order is torn between allegiance to the past and withering market demands; and local citizens rise in unprecedented opposition.

INTERLUDE:

Uber

The drive sweeps steeply upward to a glass and steel amalgam of a house with no apparent entrance beyond the patterned squares of stone set about with low sprawling ground cover that holds all this together visually. There's a metal panel beside a door with a speaker, a dark vertical screen, a cavity that looks like it might be for reading fingerprints, a built-in computer keyboard, and a discreet metal plate bearing the impression of a bell.

I press it, but no response. I take out my cell phone and send the house's owner a text: *I am outside.*

Wind carries up the valley, pushing shrouds of cloud but no rain in this, the biggest fire season ever, 2015. A walk around the outside— one can't easily circumnavigate this house, recently assessed at $100 million—reveals more stone sheathing, glass, a sod roof, and a lower postage-stamp lawn as green as a dream, in deep calm out of the wind. On the higher level are four impervious metal garage doors, but no sign of an entrance or a human being. It's a bit like gazing into a vast, multifaceted aquarium devoid of fish.

I am being hailed. A middle-aged man in a red knit shirt and stocking feet gestures, and I go up to him. We shake hands. "Joe," he says, as if it's my name, not his. His last name is Schoendorf, and he adds, "This is a shoeless house."

Indeed, the sculpture in the entranceway is a brutal composition of fine English leather shoes skewered by sharp wooden spikes, a strong incentive for the visitor to listen to his host. The floors are stone, too, cool even in September, and the house seemingly large enough to wear out a pair of socks if you walk from one end to the other.

We descend stairs to the broad living room beyond which is a southern view of Napa Valley. Joe leads the way into what looks like a cramped metal galley in a ship, though this one has no apparent crew, opens a locker, and takes out a black $100 bottle of Silex, the Pouilly-Fumé from the Upper Loire.

"I don't drink California wines," says Joe. "I asked Aubert de Villaine"—a co-owner of Romanée-Conti—"how old his oldest vines are, and he said fifty-five years. We don't have anything like that here."

The Silex is indeed clean, complex, lively. We sit on separate couches in front of a dead fireplace. Summer's over, winter still a ways off. Joe crosses his legs. His face is long, his dark eyes inquisitive, but he's in a hurry, having, as he put it on the phone, "a hard stop at six twenty" and it's already a quarter to.

Joe came to Napa for the first time in 1966 "and made it a point to get to know the people and to reach out to those who would be my neighbors." Getting his permit for this house took years and required—in his view—digging a cave in the mountain and filling it not with wine but with ten thousand gallons of water, "the basis for all our heating and cooling, all by mother nature. It made no financial sense because of the cost," adding with a laugh, "I belong to the point one percent, and I feel good for being green. But when I'm in board meetings with Al Gore, I get tired of it. I can't count the number of times he says carbonization."

St. Helena was indeed the poster child of California small towns when he decided to build his house just outside the city limits. He also owns a stunning retreat and even better wine cellar on the coast in Big Sur, and other houses in various parts of the world, being an early rider of the computer syncline (Hewlett-Packard, Apple, Accel) as it burst through California's cultural crust thirty years ago. Today he belongs to the World Economic Forum, is a regular at Davos, and a man of some global reach and influence, yet in his way indicative of many in little St. Helena.

Joe has lived in the neighborhood for so long that he has, for California, something close to a historical view. The most important local figure in it, in his opinion, is the deceased former mayor Delbert Britton. "Del had one fundamental, fatal belief: He wanted to pour hot wax over the town and preserve it. I told him he could either grow it or shrink it, but it would take magic to keep it the same."

Joe believes St. Helena's fiscal problems are directly related to thwarted growth. "Now the leaders have panicked and are breaking glass," a powerful metaphor in this gorgeous transparency, by which he means officials are trying to open the place for business in any way possible, despite the fact that many of the citizens don't want that.

We are close to the hard stop. The primary concern of the rich at the end of the day seems much the same as that preoccupying their ancestors back in the Pleistocene: not low-income housing or a new police station or repaved streets, but dinner. "The most difficult question to answer in St. Helena is, 'Where are we going to eat?' You have to go down to Yountville or Napa for a really good meal. The only solution to that problem is Uber."

CHAPTER SEVEN:
Bubbly

The smack of California earth shall linger on the palate of your grandson.
—Robert Louis Stevenson, *The Silverado Squatters*, 1883

1.

For more than a year now his mother had been dying. Although no one put it that way, they dealt with the process as if the end was near, as well as unjust, but he wasn't ready. He still thought of her as the younger woman he remembered, she of the broad, beautiful smile and wide, pale eyes, a beacon of encouragement and optimism in a body as slight as a child's, yet retaining iron resolve despite discomfort, and fear.

Her name was Jamie and he loved her and for most of his forty years had believed that her example would carry forward in one of her three sons after she was gone. He, the youngest, wondered if he had his mother's strength. He was no longer sure of the rosy future once seemingly assured a family blessed with a winery of its own, re-created out of a ghostly shell, with international renown and set in a valley once thought inviolable and now racked by dissent at the outset of the new century.

Hugh Davies had, twenty years before and recently out of college, stood before the county board of supervisors and urged them to pass a

77

law that would protect agricultural land. This was a cause his family had long supported, going all the way back to the 1968 law establishing the country's first agricultural preserve in Napa. This allowed land to be assessed on the value of its agriculture, not its speculative real estate value. Hugh had spoken in the time-honored manner of Davies men: a grin full of teeth, his voice flat, the words coming out Gatling-gun style like his father before him, a midwesterner, with a manner genial, assured, correct.

His father, Jack Davies, had been better at this, though, capable both of a daunting retort and gentlemanly deal-making mastered in the gentler boardrooms of the 1950s, and corporate to the core. But something had moved Jack to reject the rigidity of corporate ascendency for the impossible dream of making wine. Hugh knew it had been Jamie who had inspired him, being an artist and the closest thing to a free spirit Jack ever knew.

First Jamie had Bill, then John and finally Hugh, who turned out to be taller than anyone in the family, and given to abrupt, eyebrow-elevating laughter that sometimes caught his listeners unprepared. There had been a lot less of this since Jack passed away ten years earlier and his brothers went off in their own directions, still less as Hugh watched his mother struggle in the grip of advanced Parkinson's disease.

He assumed he still had two years with her, six months at the least. What there was left of the family on the old Schram property south of Calistoga—Jamie, Hugh and his wife, Monique, and their two little boys—had spent two weeks together in Puerto Vallarta with Monique's parents and Jamie's caregiver. Difficult, but they had done it. The day after their return Hugh had gone off to sell wine to fans of Schramsberg in Florida, command performances being the bane of the latter-day vintner, but he had talked by telephone to Jamie and Monique every day, and learned that Jamie was increasingly in pain. Then the nurse called Monique and asked her to come up to the big house, and when she got there Jamie couldn't talk for crying. Monique had crawled into the bed and held Jamie in her arms.

Hugh returned home the next night. The Sunday before Valentine's Day he and Monique left their little house down the hill and walked up to the big one with the boys, dread in their hearts. They passed the old two-storied redwood barn that formed the corner of the Schram settlement where the road came around, through dense forest, from the highway far below, traveled once by Robert Louis Stevenson when he visited what was then the farm of Jacob Schram. At the top of the property the towering Victorian still reared against the sky, the Queen Anne fretwork on the high porch alight with morning, but the barn below still in shadow.

Its cornerstone was engraved with the initials *J.S.* and the year *1884*. As a child Hugh had tried to imagine what stories the old barn might have heard: in German, Chinese, Italian, and Spanish, as well as English, a chronicle of hard work and discovery on the east side of the Mayacamas, named for the Indians. In those times springs and creeks ran year-round and brimmed with trout, salmon, and steelhead; redwoods, Douglas firs, and tanbark oaks formed a canopy so dense it maintained rain that soaked the earth each winter. This moisture spread over the vast web of terrestrial life, nurturing flora and fauna in a beautiful, seemingly endless fecundity, but that, too, had passed.

Built of redwood logged on the property, patched and added to for more than a century, the barn was flanked by ancient coast live and black oaks. After old Jacob Schram was gone various hapless inhabitants had moved in and out, but not the Davieses. They bought the property in the 1960s and used the barn to store earth-working equipment and to house the Mexicans who did the most difficult work.

The barn still had an earthen floor then, dusty in summer, moist in winter, imbued with the scents of a century of activity, animal and human. Upstairs, accessible by the steep wooden staircase and loft doors, were boxes, old furniture, a clutter of the barely useful and long-forgotten where creatures made themselves at home. The men had believed the loft was haunted because in the middle of the night woodrats raced across the old upright piano's keyboard, producing wildly atonal music.

The Davies boys spent a lot of time in that barn. They joined the migrant workers in soccer, baseball, and football games on the open ground between the buildings, long since paved over to accommodate delivery trucks and the rising, ever-present sea of tourists. Some of the workers belonged to a soccer team, and Hugh and his brothers would ride with them down Highway 29 to St. Helena, Yountville, all the way to Napa, to watch them play. Sometimes the flatbed pickup would be stopped by *la migra* (Immigration officers) and the Mexicans would leap from the truck and flee, and over the next few days trickle back through the forest and reassemble in the barn.

Hugh had learned to flip tortillas on the gas burner there. He, Bill, and John had enjoyed many a meal, too, and the odd Friday- and Saturday-night card and checkers games. Workdays began at six o'clock when first light appeared and the wheels were set in motion for another day, before the sun rose over distant Howell Mountain.

Now Hugh and his little family climbed the broad stairs to the house's deep veranda, set with planters and wooden rockers, south-facing in its grand sweep. It had been built in 1889, so Stevenson had not sat in these bentwood rockers to taste Schram's wines, but sometimes the famous novelist's presence does seem to hover there.

Hugh and Monique were surprised to see Jamie waiting at the door. She had rallied, and they, too, felt their spirits lift. Jamie's nurse took the boys upstairs so Hugh, Monique, and Jamie could sit together in the living room and talk by the tall corner window that let so much light into the room with high ceilings and exquisite woodwork. Tall wavy panes overlooked the garden below where Jamie had spent many hours over the last forty-three years, and Hugh was determined that she would continue to do so as long as she was able.

They chatted, the Weber grand piano by the big window part of the conversation. Though fragile, Jamie could still captivate men and women. Her toughness had revealed itself in her grapples with the gorgeous old architectural wreck when in the beginning bats flew down from the attic and animals lived in the walls. Life had since softened, and exponentially expanded. Now Hugh was sure his mother wanted to say something special on this bright February morning and had prepared for it.

It had always been hard for her to get out intimate thoughts and feelings, a paradox in a woman so warm and outgoing. The tremors didn't make this easier. She said at last, "I won't be here much longer, I've come to accept that. And I'm comfortable in the knowledge that you two will be able to carry on just fine without me."

Hugh's father, had he been alive, wouldn't have accepted the suggestion that she was bowing out. A descendant of Welsh coal miners, Jack had passed some of his self-control and determination on to his sons, and Hugh now said, "Mom, you sound like you're throwing in the towel. You have to keep fighting." People were known to live with Parkinson's for twenty years, more, carrying on even when confined to a wheelchair, incapable of speech. But Jamie just smiled. It was a gesture many in the valley knew: She had made up her mind. Unable to breathe comfortably, in need of someone to feed, bathe, and dress her, she was showing another side.

Hugh dug into the chest of comments his parents had shared over the course of his life: Focus on the positive. Embrace the life in front of you. Above all, live. Jamie had five grandchildren and surely more to come; the business was moving forward, performing better than it ever had. Sickness, loss, uncertainty could all be combated. Instinctively, he and Monique moved closer to her, and Monique said, "Jamie, I'm selfish, I'm not ready to let you go."

Hugh never expected someone he loved to say out loud that he or she was simply leaving, foreseeing all that was to happen and having the courage to will an end. He began to talk about all there was to look forward to: the birds Jamie loved to hear singing in the garden, the frogs in the pond croaking at the end of day, the glorious sun that rose each morning. Nature had always been a source of wonder and excitement for her and the whole family, but now even nature wasn't enough.

They sat for a while without speaking. Finally Jamie said, "Let's have some bubbly."

2.

The pine-paneled kitchen was little changed since the 1950s, and there Hugh opened a bottle of Schramsberg Brut Rosé and carefully poured three glasses. He raised his in a silent toast, and the mood shifted. Everybody gazed out at the big-leaf maples in the garden, the old cellar building, and fir-studded hills above. The upper pond visible from the kitchen window had originally been for irrigation and possible fire suppression, and had once served as the family swimming pool, the long rope swing dangling from the big oak on the pond's bank. The rusty iron wheel valve sticking out of the middle of the pond had long since been rendered useless, but it had provided a fine spot to tie up the wooden raft when Hugh and his brothers were boys. They would mount an old metal slide on the raft and glide down, down into cool green water.

The memories were coming fast now. When he was growing up there had always been a dog or two, the Labs—Victor, Pinot, Foxy—excellent swimming companions, but the strongest swimmer of all was Cecil, the golden retriever. With dogs, a rope swing, a raft, a waterslide, and a rowboat, it had been the best imaginable swimming hole.

He gazed around the kitchen. On the wall was the favorite family picture of him, his brothers, and their father all sitting on the edge of the raft. On hot July and August days they would collect pollywogs in glass jars. The ponds were still full of frogs that each night in season conducted croaking choir practice that by late summer was dominated by the bullfrogs' resonant twang.

The lower pond had been renovated by Jamie and the gardeners twenty years before to honor the workers who tended each vintage of Schramsberg during its long life in the caves. She commissioned a sculpture called *The Riddler's Night Out*, depicting a tuxedoed frog balancing on one foot among lily pads, a bottle of J. Schram in one hand and a glass flute raised in the other. In previous winters the lower pond had sometimes frozen, and one year Hugh and his brothers had played ice hockey there using sticks and rocks. The ice gave way beneath Hugh's feet and he plunged into the frigidity below. Bill and John were able to pull him out, a story Jamie now listened to him tell again, and after he was done she said, "I want to go outside and have a look around on such a beautiful winter day."

Hugh went out and brought back the "mule," a green off-road vehicle they used to get up Schramsberg's steep, winding dirt roads. Monique helped bundle Jamie in coat, scarf, and blanket, and they climbed aboard. The sun shone brilliantly against the blue sky as they mounted toward the water tower, and Jamie started talking: about her first ride up in 1965, before the clearing of the forest, when her father got his Jeep stuck.

Hugh remembered how they had all gone up higher as a family before Christmas, a wonderful time at Schramsberg, full of ritual and celebration. They cut a tree a thousand feet above sea level between steep, redwood-flanked canyons. His father, behind the wheel of the beat-up International Scout, would pass the winery, the former Chinese bunkhouse, and vineyards. The view down-valley included Howell Mountain to the east, Pritchard Hill, Stags Leap, and Atlas Peak farther to the south.

The Davieses always chose the Douglas fir with the fullest top, a simple handsaw bringing it down, measuring tape at the ready. Later, the ten-foot tree filled the windowed corner of the living room, with more trimmings taken from the forest festooning the house, veranda railing, and fireplace mantel. A dark corner of the attic was dedicated to Christmas decorations, and these descended piecemeal into the light, with each person in turn hanging ornaments: the pointed star, balls of various shapes and colors, elves, the red Christmas doggy, birds, tinsel.

Hugh drove on with Jamie and Monique beside him, past vineyards infused with these memories though replanted since: chardonnay and pinot noir for Schramsberg's sparkling wines had given way to cabernet sauvignon for the new J. Davies Diamond Mountain wine. High in a dead fir a red-shouldered hawk perched, and they all sat and admired him. The vineyard was dormant this time of year, the vines and surrounding deciduous trees leafless. The hawk launched at last and they watched in silence as he made wide, soaring circles and vanished to the north.

Jamie pointed out the place marked on the blueprint map of the Schram property from 1885 that hung on the Tower Room wall in the winery. Hugh parked and they all got out, Hugh and Monique helping Jamie walk into the steeply pitched forest. Hugh said, "Mom, we can't just charge down there." If they did, he would have to carry her back, and he was afraid he might not be able to.

They drove down, passing the spot where a winter landslide in 1995 took out a dozen fir trees. Volunteer maples had established themselves. They passed Jamie's Block and Jack's Block, named since the replanting, where the wild turkeys were often seen, and circled back along the lane of olive trees that had been there for more than a century.

Jamie seemed happy. Everything looked good—the vineyards' cover crop of clover, vetch, and fescue, the season's accumulated straw scattered for erosion control. She had worked for over forty years to establish and maintain all this. They passed through Jack's Grove, with its new growth of oak saplings, the trees in the middle of the vineyard the site of countless family gatherings and winery functions—birthdays, Fourth of July parties, promotional Camp Schramsberg dinners, cellar club events. Monique and Hugh had been married here on a wet October day four years earlier, and now they swapped memories of friends and family slurping oysters in the rain and raising glasses to the future while the wild Mexican brass dance band played.

Jack's memorial service had been held here, too, in 1998, people lining the vineyard rows all the way up to the forest. One friend after another had recalled his creativity, warmth, and spirit, and the many contributions Jack had made to the valley. Three dogwoods planted not too long before were just flowering.

Farther down, beyond the McEachron house where Monique, Hugh, and the boys lived, they paused beside the pond. It was full of fish, usually impossible to see, but today they came to the surface in a flurry of life Hugh had never seen, as if they had risen from the depths to have a look. The next stop was the rock wall along the creek next to the driveway, repaired with moss-covered rocks untouched for a hundred years.

At the bottom of the road, they took in the view of the valley floor and Hugh realized that this was the last time Jamie would cross the property's edge, that she was here to say good-bye to the world beyond.

Back up at the house, far from public view, Jamie asked for more bubbly, a tacit acknowledgment of the Benedictine monk, Dom Pérignon, who had, according to legend, discovered sparkling wine by chance, centuries before, in Champagne, saying he had tasted "liquid stars" and giving birth to the now ancient tradition in a distant land. Hugh opened a bottle of the Schramsberg Blanc de Blancs, since Jamie rarely expressed a preference and left it to him to decide, just as she had left such decisions to Jack.

Hugh's boys came down the broad front stairs, Jamie taking obvious notice of everything around her. She had become more than a figurehead after Jack's death, to the surprise of many people, in charge of an enterprise with devotees on five continents, selling some 700,000 bottles of sparkling wine a year, filling glass flutes for toasts around the world by presidents and premiers, kings and queens.

Schramsberg was unique, Hugh knew that. But people were asking if the next generation could carry on this fabulous family enterprise in a time of economic and political uncertainty. Was this the end of an era in the valley, and a way of life? The demands of the marketplace were ferocious, and the often conflicting desires of long-term investors who had helped his parents get started were now causing some acrimony, with a substantial estate tax due. Could Hugh hold all this together without the counsel of his beloved parents, with his brothers alternately indifferent and in revolt, the valley itself a welter of success, extravagance, and conflict?

The next morning Hugh received a call from Maria in the big house. She was helping care for Jamie and told Hugh his mother was very uncomfortable. He went over and tried to comfort Jamie, but by afternoon Maria was putting cold towels on her, and Jamie was still in pain. She whispered, "My God, this is terrible."

Hugh touched her forehead, hotter than it had ever been. An hour later things had gotten worse. Two nurses were now with Jamie, who couldn't stop moving. Several medicines had been prescribed, and there were supplements, too, but when the nurses tried to give these to Jamie, she said, "No more."

Her struggle continued into the night. Monique and Hugh walked back to their little house just before midnight and were back at her bedside early the next morning. Jamie had fluid in her lungs and was no longer talking. Hugh's brother Bill and his wife, Gayle, came up from the valley floor, everyone trying to figure out how to help, but by noon things had gotten worse. Hugh thought, "My God, is this it?"

Suddenly she was gone. He wished he had never left her side, the similarity between his parents' deaths striking him hard: They had both died in this bed, in the same manner, ten years apart. Jamie had been Jack's chief nurse, and he had needed a lot of help at the end. Lou Gehrig's disease, with which he was afflicted, involves motor neurons, as does Parkinson's. First it had incapacitated his fingers, then his hands and arms, then his entire upper body. He could walk until the day he died and he could communicate, although breathing had become extremely difficult. Jack had passed away in his sleep, Jamie beside him.

Hugh thought, "We have no idea where the soul is going."

This was frightening, but mostly for the dying themselves. He had seen it in his father's eyes, and Jamie's, too, and was glad both had maintained an affinity with Buddhism, a surprise to many who knew them because it was unorthodox. It hadn't been devotion exactly, more like sympathy with basic precepts, and something Hugh hadn't even noticed as a child. Tibetan monks had come from their sanctuary in Southern California to spend time with Jack during his final weeks, more often toward the end. They had helped the family deal with life in the absence of his father, lifting spirits, directing thoughts and energy, saying, in effect, "Give your love to Jack so he can take it with him."

The next day the monks arrived and surrounded Jamie's body with flowers. The smell of incense infused the big house; the bell outside that had been rung when Hugh had been brought home from the hospital, forty-three years before, now rang again for Jamie, while Schramsberg's workers gathered below the balcony, tears streaking many faces.

In the days that followed people dropped by ceaselessly with flowers and food; there were more monks with bells and incense. Hugh was grateful and thought his mother deserved such an outpouring of love and support. Work went on at Schramsberg as before, while up at the big house Hugh planned the memorial service. Jack's had been a glorious ceremony up in the Grove, and he prepared for a repetition of this while people took turns keeping vigil at the mortuary.

Hugh's brother Bill, the oldest Davies boy, was trying to branch out on his own but had returned to the big house with his wife and their young son. Bill had left the family business years before for what he referred to as "health and lifestyle" reasons. Now he and Hugh drove down together with one of the monks, Lama Gyatso, to prepare for the cremation. This was harder for both brothers than they had anticipated. Standing outside, they watched thermals rise from the chimney, and before Hugh was ready—again—he glimpsed a rising cloud of ash: distant birds taking flight.

3.

Hugh had heard all the stories: on the first day of harvest employees, friends, and family gathered to pick the grapes, load them into wooden boxes, and bring them down to the secondhand press, a hollow cylinder with removable plates. The juice flowed into a steel basin from which it was pumped into a settling tank. Once, the press, after having been filled, wouldn't start. André Tchelistcheff, the Russian-born, Bordeaux-trained former enologist at Beaulieu Vineyard, turned to Jamie and with old-world formality said, "Madame, your duty is clear," and she had removed her shoes, stepped into the press, and began to tread.

There was the story about Aguirre, the Mexican who had saved Hugh's father's life. Aguirre had gone to school in St. Helena when there were only a dozen Spanish-speaking families in the valley. In those days families traveled from town to town in season working the harvest (*la pisca*), picking walnuts, prunes, grapes, apples in Sebastopol, apricots in Fairfield, cotton all the way down in Fresno. Aguirre was only twenty when he arrived at Schramsberg, and thought it a desolate place, but he took the job as foreman because Jack let him move his young family into the old carriage house.

Aguirre helped clean the tanks, a sometimes dangerous job because one had a small opening at the top just large enough for a man, and no manhole at the bottom. After it was cleaned it had to be retouched with epoxy paint, which had a powerful odor. He and Jack took turns going down the rope ladder to do this, and when Jack came out looking tired, Aguirre said, "Why don't you stay out here?"

"Because I'm the boss," said Jack, "and I'm going back down."

He did, and he fell from the effect of the fumes. Aguirre heard and went in after him. With the help of the gardener and two painters working on the house he got Hugh's father back up, but his shoulders lodged in the narrow opening. The Mexican's shout was so loud that it brought others. Jack was extracted at last and laid out on the ground. Hugh saw, with great relief, his father's eyes open.

The doctor later told Jack, "You owe your life to that man."

*   *   *

Hugh's earliest memory was of a man in a silver suit stepping out of a metallic pod. Much later, he learned that this had been Neil Armstrong emerging from the Apollo 11 mission spacecraft on July 21, 1969, on the moon. Hugh had been upstairs with the rest of the family, in what was called the Marshmallow Bedroom because the mattress was lumpy. They were all crowded together on the four-poster, under screened windows blanketed with June bugs, high above the garden and the ponds alive with croaking frogs. Looking from the man in the silver suit to the spreading branches of what he would learn were maples, then to the bright orb against a velvet black sky, joyous excitement coursed through him: the family was a team playing a part in a mystery joining everyone on the planet.

From the beginning the house was the center of things: winery offices, visitors' room, laboratory. But the long oval dining room table by the bay window was the most important place. Business meetings, marketing presentations, wine tastings were held around it, and when Hugh was small the patterns in the Asian carpet provided imaginary courses for him to push his cars along while, above, his parents talked to important people, like André. Friendly, diminutive, bushy-browed, he had brought quality to the valley after Prohibition, to anyone who had needed a hand.

There had been a saxophonist named Marge, and several young winemakers. One of them, Harold, had a technical degree from UC Davis. Buoyant, playful, he drove a Volkswagen van and loved Frank Zappa and wore rubber boots and blue jeans. Behind his beard was a jolly countenance the Davies boys all chased after from the lab to the winery where the big tanks stood amid hoses, pump, filter, and buckets. One day, trailing him, Hugh became fascinated with a tank valve, moved the handle, and wine gushed onto the floor, a terrifying sight.

The dining room may have been the strategic center of Schramsberg, but the basement was the center of winemaking. When Hugh was older he watched his parents in the blending and dosage trials, and listened as they proposed solutions to each other, joined by retailers, writers, winemakers, restaurateurs, all friends, all together at the table. Hugh knew what *camaraderie* meant before he heard the word, and knew what his father had meant when he quoted Robert Mondavi: "If you succeed, we all succeed."

What happened in Napa Valley hadn't happened before in California. Napa wasn't France, Italy, Germany, or Spain, but the "New World," where hope and enthusiasm for making wine was kept alive by the desire to rival the finest of Europe. This hope was met with skepticism outside the valley, and Schramsberg's sparkling wine was doubly risky, and doubly exciting.

Schramsberg dealt with many growers in the valley, their names signposts in time: Carpenter, Pelissa, Frediani, Phair, Collins, Pecota, Draper. Eventually Schramsberg's Blanc de Blancs would be taken to China by President Nixon and used in a toast with the Chinese premier, Zhou Enlai, unbeknownst to the Davieses before a neighbor called and said, "Turn on your television set."

Hugh went to Champagne with his parents and brothers when he was in the first grade and kept a diary. What most impressed him were the grand old châteaux in Champagne—those of the Rousseaus, Louis Roederer, Bollinger, Pol Roger, where he met the families. Years passed, and the sons of these houses came to spend summers at Schramsberg, working in some aspect of winemaking, and Hugh and his brothers did the same in Champagne, Cognac, even Australia, all part of a tradition going back a century or more in Europe but newborn in America.

At home, Hugh and his brothers played in the caves, calling them "the tunnels." Two heavy wooden doors set in stone stood beside the lower pond, shaded by maples, oaks, and manzanitas. Water dripped from the overhanging stone, and during winter rains people passed through, sometimes pushing carts of bottles, a scene out of the distant past.

The tunnels were strange, irresistible, magical. However cold and wet outside, deep underground it was dry; in the furnace of summer, the tunnels were cool. They had been dug by Chinese migrants in the late 1800s, after construction of the First Transcontinental Railroad freed up the laborers. These men made up the early workforce for the burgeoning wine industry, too, before the Mexicans. The caves were the first in the valley and provided darkness and constant coolness required by sparkling wine.

April, May, and June were the busiest, when wine from the prior year's vintage was to be bottled. First some yeast and sugar were added to induce another fermentation in the bottle. The yeast consumed the sugar and produced fine bubbles of carbon dioxide, called beads, then the bottles were set to rest on their sides in stacks, some to stay there as long as seven years, some for twenty-five, while the sugar caramelized.

The boys were attached to crews as they became old enough, and eventually would perform all sorts of jobs. There were dangers. One day Hugh, a teenager now, was setting a bottle in a tub, trying to keep pace with the older workers, when he struck it against another bottle. It exploded and at once he felt a wet, warm sensation. The production foreman jammed a towel into his mouth. Dripping blood, Hugh was led out of the caves to a car and driven to the hospital in St. Helena, where two dozen stitches were needed to hold his lip together.

Music in the tunnels—mariachi, salsa, banda—never ceased when the workers were down there. Soon, though, they would all be wearing gloves and safety masks.

4.

In Schramsberg's gardens some of the old plants from the time of Jacob Schram still flourished. Jamie had refused to alter the character of the place, and when making floral arrangements for special events would use her own flowers from the garden. She walked there, noting what had to be done to make it better, color very important to her because she had once been a painter.

Whenever labels for the bottles had to be altered, Jamie would lay the samples out on the dining room table, and she and Jack would talk about them. Schramsberg was on its way by then, but large questions remained: Which of the boys would pick up the legacy and eventually lead this unlikely enterprise? Jack and Jamie encouraged them all to get involved. "You don't have to," they would say, "but it would be great." Hugh and his brothers could work together like three legs of a stool, each with a distinct function—production, marketing and sales, finance and administration.

They called individual meetings with each boy. These were uncomfortable. Their parents would ask, "What do you want to do with your life?" They would tell the boys individually, "Do well in college. Get good grades. Be a stand-up person—a doer, not a user. Make something of yourself."

Hugh attended Bowdoin College and was accepted as a congressional intern in Washington, DC. He wanted to get into the environmental movement, to do something that made a difference. His parents were environmentalists, after all, though he felt that label never really fit. Environmental regulations made developers unhappy, but Hugh was glad the state and the valley had them and he wished the laws were more restrictive.

His parents had been dedicated to the idea of the agricultural preserve, established back in 1968, in part with their help. That law had prevented houses from being built on parcels of less than forty acres; it had kept Napa Valley from becoming just another bedroom community.

Hugh had shied away from business in the beginning, telling his parents he simply wanted to do things good for the earth, like working in Washington to strengthen the Clean Water Act and the Clean Air Act, and help set aside more pristine areas as wilderness. So he went to work for a public interest research group (or PIRG) as a phone volunteer, soliciting donations. Then he quit and went backpacking on the Pacific Crest Trail, prompting his father to say, "You have to support yourself, son. You don't want to be a basket weaver."

They bartered: After the trip Hugh would come back to the valley, work the harvest season, and spend the winter pruning in Schramsberg's hillside vineyards. He also worked for the Trust for Public Land in San Francisco, but ended up studying chemistry and physics at Santa Rosa

Junior College, his ongoing practical education fairly typical of the scions of winery founders. This penance included working in Champagne and continuing his studies. He was twenty-nine by the time he got his master's degree at UC Davis. In a way he never really stopped studying. By June 1996 he was ready to get back to California to work in earnest. He was not a basket weaver; in some ways his life had been like his father's: rise early, try harder, go further. He had been set back from time to time but the whole had been, if not joyful, pretty cool by comparison with that of others his age. And it had been lonely.

When he got home he was made Schramsberg's enologist—junior winemaker—then assistant winemaker, and finally head winemaker. Life began to take leaps now. His brother Bill, who worked for Schramsberg in sales, resigned and went out on his own. The middle brother, John— good-looking, dismissive of the wine business from early on—left and ended up doing deals in Russia after the fall of the Soviet Union.

Before Jamie died, John had shown up in the Napa Valley in a chauffeured limousine and demanded an early inheritance. The unexpected fight between mother and middle son had made it into the *San Francisco Chronicle*, and Jamie shared her pain with Hugh. He was wounded by what John had done, but there was no escaping family at Schramsberg.

Hugh had met and married a lovely girl named Lily from just down Highway 29, whose family also owned a small winery. They lived together in the little McEachron house but not for long; the split-up amicable, Hugh was once again alone. He served a year as the president of the Napa Valley Vintners, a title that floated annually among the wine estates, large and small. While president he supported environmental actions on behalf of the hillside and viewshed preservation ordinances, and Napa's "green" certification, which brought some reprimand from men who had known his father: "Now, Hugh, aren't you going a little fast here?"

On a trip to Oklahoma City for the Vintners he found himself in the company of a girl from Coombsville, Monique Nelson. He had known her since his UC Davis days, but not well. Now she worked for Joseph Phelps Vineyards, and he noticed that she had eyes the color of jade, dark blond hair, and a manner both proper and friendly. They went off to

Mexico together, then climbed Mount St. Helena, and Hugh took along a ring he had bought through a friend in New York. They were married on a rainy day in October in the Grove, where Monique asked him to sing "Green Eyes."

The ceremony and several nine-liter bottles of sparkling wine behind them, officially man and wife, both wanting kids, they were ready for life to begin.

Their first son, Emrys, was born that year, as joyous an occasion as any. Their second, Nelson, came along fourteen months later, and their third three years after that. They had not intended to name the youngest after Hugh, but did, to be called Huey.

Hugh adopted a single ruling maxim: Take one day at a time. He wanted to move his family into the big house, but initially there was opposition from the board. Some directors, his brother Bill, and an aging shareholder both wanted to use the house to sell more wine to tourists, but traffic already threatened to overwhelm the little road coming up from Highway 29. The logistics of moving people once they got there, from the parking lot to the house and then to the caves, or the other way around, were daunting. But to prevent a schism Hugh deferred that decision, and the big house sat empty while he, Monique, and their brood remained packed like sardines in the little house down the driveway.

In 2010 Schramsberg had sold more wine than it ever had, an indisputable testament to success. The winery was powered by solar panels and had the Napa Green land certification he had earlier pushed for. But Hugh saw that survival meant adapting to the challenges of a never-ending, always different present, and that what had been done in the past wouldn't necessarily be acceptable in the future. The most obvious need was another facility in the neighborhood to help accommodate winemaking, and visitors. Schramsberg had long ago run out of space.

There was another reason for finding a place down the hill, beyond having to thread the needle with more gondolas and flatbeds loaded with grapes, delivery trucks great and small, rental cars, limos, and winery workers. Sparkling white wine and still reds were basically incompatible in the all-important modern world of wine marketing, an assertion going back to Jack's argument opposing the red wine program: such different wines—cabernet and sparkling whites—were for a small quality producer incompatible in terms of marketing and publicity. They were the vinous equivalent of man and woman, church and state, town and gown. But Schramsberg needed an entirely different kind of facility, with better temperature and humidity controls, as well as open-top fermenters and de-stemming and pressing equipment for red grapes.

The search began for a suitable place within striking distance of Schramsberg. Someone mentioned a former car dealership on the south end of St. Helena. It was called Epps and had sold Chevys to St. Helenans for years. It sat empty and unlovely behind the A&W root beer eatery just off Highway 29. For decades the Davieses had argued against building within the agricultural preserve, and here was a facility within town limits where wine could be made and sold without affecting agriculture, within easy reach of delivery trucks, grape gondolas, and tourists. It was, Hugh thought, the perfect place, never dreaming that some people might think otherwise.

CHAPTER EIGHT:

Our Town

1.

Geoff Ellsworth has a round, cherubic face that belies his half-century of existence. Thin straight nose, delicate nostrils, a way of tucking his chin while talking, big aviator glasses parked on his forehead. His new role is at odds with that of painter, which is one of his professions, another being actor in the ancient, antic tradition of traveling performers. Self-transformation's his art, as well as his new avocation: community organizing in the place where he grew up.

Geoff had discovered that he shared the ire felt by a slice of the citizenry. Here it was toward the planning commission of St. Helena, and though no one knew exactly how large that slice was, it had been exposed by an attempt to rewrite the town's regulations for small wineries, similar to the attempt by the county to rewrite the definition of agriculture. The old regs had served the community well for decades, but the proposed changes would allow expanded sales and activities within residential neighborhoods, and Geoff saw this as a potentially destructive force.

For years he had followed—at a distance—environmental politics in the valley, which was about the only kind there was. Then suddenly, it seemed, the issues had all landed in the middle of little St. Helena. Geoff didn't know how to deal with this, so he went online and got access to more videos, these being of the planning commission meetings that had occurred around the time of the changes to the Winery Definition Ordinance. He downloaded them and began to watch, sitting at the dining room table in his mother's house on Sylvaner Avenue and drawing, always drawing, on plain unmarked paper.

Just two doors away lived Peter and Carlene Mennen, the money behind the big lawsuit against the vintner Jayson Pahlmeyer more than a decade before. The Mennens and Chris Malan had been joined by the Sierra Club, and their phenomenal victory had preceded a similar but much larger fight now going on in 2015 in the far east of the county, over a potential development known as Walt Ranch. The Mennens had been criticized and even threatened at the time of the Pahlmeyer fight, and trash thrown from passing cars into their yard that brimmed with unruly native species. The Mennens had withdrawn from personal involvement in the big, vituperative environmental issues of the day, but their foundation was still at work.

Geoff became fascinated with the planning commission meetings and even made a little sketch of the room where the meetings were held, which helped him visualize them as an artist.

Officials in the videos, Geoff thought, behaved as the supervisors had in the earlier videos he watched when the definition of agriculture was being changed. As if in a special box, the planning commissioners made jokes and remarks in what sounded to him like mock-serious discussion of bike paths and stop signs. Then, on April 16, 2013, he found what he considered the smoking gun. In that video one of the commissioners, a young attorney recently elected, was thumbing through papers at the end of the session when he said offhandedly, "I would like to bring something up, if you guys would care to hear it . . ."

Geoff sat up straight and punched the volume key on the computer. "I was going through the small winery definition . . ."—the lawyer read from prepared notes on a yellow legal pad—"and foremost I find this language extremely confusing and some things contradictory . . . I just feel like it needs overall updating . . ."

Geoff felt his pulse quicken. The lawyer was saying, in effect, that wineries in town had to compete with wineries out in the county, "and don't have the ability to market themselves in ways that Napa County wineries are able to do, specially with tourism, tastings, and marketing events . . ."

The other commissioners agreed, and the proposal went on the agenda for the next meeting. Suddenly the commissioners were all acting as if this was a done deal and that the planning commission would pass it on to the city council for a vote, and protection of neighborhoods from winery expansions would disappear.

Geoff replayed the video two more times. "So that's how it's done here," he thought, googling the attorney's name. He discovered that the attorney had launched his legal career not in St. Helena but in Southern California by helping Hollywood wannabes like Chelsea Handler, Tyra Banks, and Rainn Wilson achieve celebrity. Then he had been retained by Francis Ford Coppola to handle the director's purchase of Chateau Souverain in Sonoma County and all the construction that followed. He went on to work for other companies with issues concerning neighbor relations, water, and zoning, and said publicly of his job: "Knowing how to work with the county employees and city officials, I've been able to use the skills I've developed to help my clients achieve what they want," adding that "the county is permitting more wineries. If that continues in the right direction, my firm will grow with my clients."

Geoff Ellsworth thought what had happened in St. Helena was special interest legislation, to him a small-bore, if legal, version of the stock market insider trading he had read about. Certain people seemed to have knowledge of legislative changes before anyone else had it, and that knowledge benefited them. He started to look at connections among all those who had favored—or seemed to favor—changing the winery definition, and soon found himself deep in the interwoven social and political matrix that is small-town America.

2.

He spent his earliest years on the ridge to the west that he could see today from the pavement in front of his mother's house. His father had worked for Mayacamas Vineyards from which flowed cabernets and chardonnays of legendary fortitude, doing some of the winemaking and much else in what was hardscrabble viticulture. By the time Geoff was ten he was sick of winemaking, having witnessed how a vintner and his dependents labor together.

Geoff's father, Robert, an engineer by training, owned no part of Mayacamas Vineyards and so moved down to the valley floor and opened what amounted to a repair shop and outfitter for wine enthusiasts of all ranks. He called it The Compleat Winemaker and he and his wife, Phoebe, became the go-to source for everything from simple parts to a dizzying array of gadgets. She sold while her husband, the itinerant expert, fixed in situ pumps, bottling machines, and so on, and rewired foreign grape presses no one else could. "It was like *All Creatures Great and Small*," Geoff liked to say. "I would tag along, and have to wait around for hours while the job was completed."

When he was older, he and his friends worked the crush every harvest—at Rutherford Hill, Rombauer, Beringer, Domaine Chandon. They made sixteen dollars an hour, good pay, and were required to stay in the vineyards for only eight hours a day, whereas the smaller operations required twelve and even fourteen hours a day. "The truth was that however much time it took, you didn't go home until the job was done." That was fine with Geoff, who saw it as a valuable cultural link between wine and the community. This was agriculture, and agriculture was what the place was all about.

Then, before his last harvest, he and his friends were told they weren't going to get sixteen dollars anymore, they were going to get only nine. "The wineries had realized they could get unskilled outside workers for half price. And they did, even though those of us who lived here had a history and an emotional attachment to the job." After that, all harvest workers came from outside the county, "the beginning of the disconnect between the community and the wine industry. By maximizing profits they lost an important connection. The loyalty was gone, and it never returned."

St. Helena remained a good place to live, though, with "a great zeitgeist," European in feel, as if the good aspects of wine had somehow bled into the social fabric, imbuing it with "a high level of education and interest in culture." St. Helenans went to watch foreign films at the Liberty Theatre run by a man who "brought a new sensibility and willingness to town, opening cultural doors. Afterward, adults and kids would go to Palmer's across the street to get something to eat and talk about the movies. "St. Helena wasn't a luxury marketing platform but still a town, socially and economically mixed." And it was *home*.

He left for the University of Oregon, in Eugene, where he studied languages and art. "I bought some acrylics and started painting a wall, and it was liberating." Color proved to be a "vibrational resource" that would lead to a career, but what he went into as soon as he got out of college was dishwashing. "A friend told me, 'Go to the best restaurant in a city and get a dishwashing job. You'll eat well, stay in shape, and not have to think about the work when you're not there. It's a great job for an artist.' "

He sold inexpensive canvases wherever he could, mostly in Los Angeles, and this continued after he moved back to St. Helena in the 1990s and began to complement his income with acting. He started a one-man show performing historical mini-pageants about cowboys, football, and the last days of the British Raj, and started a band called the Towne Dandies.

Traveling between St. Helena and Southern California, Geoff had success in small venues, and he made something of a name as the unorthodox, imaginative performer using props and sets he fashioned himself. "I was able to survive until 9/11. After that I realized art would no longer be something people would spend money on—ours had become a fear-based economy."

It began to recover somewhat ten years later, "but by then someone had figured out how to monetize the entire Napa Valley." Even harvest parties cost money to attend whereas before they had been open to the community. "And you were charged even more for tastings. Time-honored celebrations, ways of acquainting the public with wine, became commodities in their own right for the simple reason that tourists, it seemed, would pay any amount for almost anything." He wanted to go back to LA, the best market for his work, "but I was afraid that if I stayed away from St. Helena, they'd sell the town."

3.

They were the politicians, council members, planning commissioners, hired staffers and their allies in the wine, hospitality, and development industries. Geoff started going to public meetings attended by a handful of older residents who brought some of the old countercultural élan that was clearly missing among the younger generation. One of these accomplices heard in her yoga class that the city council planned to sell city hall—or lease it—and that the city wouldn't reveal the name of the lessee, widely believed to be a group of investors wanting to build a hotel within the historical shell.

Geoff went to a council meeting and stood up and announced that this wasn't the way business was traditionally done in St. Helena, and that citizens deserved to know what was going on. Afterward, a woman named Sandy Ericson, whose mother had once been the mayor of St. Helena, explained to him the necessity of exposing long-term development plans early. She had lived in Marin County and knew a lot about transparency in local government, and they teamed up as opponents to leasing city hall.

The proposal was withdrawn, again without explanation, but the proposed changes to the winery definition remained. Geoff went to the first public discussion of the changes, held not on city property but at the Montessori School. This, in his view, was the locus of social and political intrigue by those with close ties to developers and people in city government, both elected and appointed, with the tacit support of the monied parents of students enrolled in the school, including Hugh and Monique Davies.

Again Geoff stood up. He reminded everyone that there were 180 agricultural parcels within the city limits, and that a big winery could just move in and radically change the environment. "The wine industry isn't the only stakeholder here," he said. "The other is the homeowners," whose property values could plummet, and their lives, too.

Later, one of the old-timers came up and handed Geoff a book. "You may need this," he said.

The book was *Ballot Box Navigator*, a step-by-step guide to launching referenda like those first sanctioned in Southern California in the 1960s. A referendum was a means of direct citizen involvement in important issues because it allowed specific issues to be placed on the ballot. Citizens could vote it either up or down, and if it passed it was automatically law, without interpretation. All they needed was an acceptable draft of a law, and a lot of citizens behind them.

One such referendum vote, old Proposition 13, had been vilified in the 1970s for drastically reducing property tax revenue going to government, thereby harming the state's university and other systems. But referenda had also been the savior of much of Napa's wooded hillsides. And Measure J had prevented county officials from making land-use changes in the agricultural preserve without a formal vote, stymieing exceptions often granted by clueless or beholden supervisors. This essentially took a lot of development out of the county's hands.

The citizens of St. Helena could put their measure to stop the proposed changes to the winery definition directly on the ballot, but first petitioners like Geoff and Sandy had to collect signatures from 10 percent of registered voters. That meant at least 320 signatures.

He began writing letters to the editor of the *St. Helena Star*. He told people who asked about his sudden interest in civic affairs, "As Churchill said, 'Everything I've done in the past has given me the skills to deal with the problems of the moment.' " He began to listen to self-hypnosis tapes, read novels revolving around the law by John Grisham and other writers, solved Sudoku puzzles to strengthen his mind, and watched more videos of St. Helena government functions at the dining room table.

St. Helena was subject to its own laws and unaffected by those pertaining to the county. It had its own winery ordinances. But Geoff thought St. Helena's attempt to loosen regulation could be replicated beyond its borders, that is, throughout the county. Increasingly, he felt, citizens were being left out of a process that sought to basically change the town. And he and his allies were going to do something about it.

When proposed changes to the ordinance were presented to the public in Vintners Hall, Geoff, Sandy, and others took turns telling the planning commission, in effect, "Don't vote on this." But the commission passed it anyway, with only one dissension, and the next day, "We hit the streets."

They collected signatures outside the post office, at the supermarket, on the street. Their ranks grew. Sandy's website, St. Helena Window, served as an effective, modern-day political pamphlet, laying out the issues and raising objections to the official view. The most stalwart of the objectors talked to anyone who would listen, explaining what had happened, what might happen, and what was at risk—neighborhoods, the town itself. They also collected e-mail addresses and sent each person the website link, a self-generating loop of information and outrage, with voices heard from outside the county, too.

One, in Healdsburg over in Sonoma County, invited them to cross the Mayacamas and learn what they were really up against: "winery centers" with ticketed events financed in residential neighborhoods by outsiders with speculative loans. "Once you let them in," the caller said, "you'll never get them out."

In St. Helena the objectors still didn't really know what they were up against. Branded as "out-of-it types with too much time on their hands," "old-timers," "fringers," and even "nuts," they endured veiled threats about job loss and other retaliation. The stress increased; one ally was hospitalized with heart murmurs, another suffered a shingles attack. But the list of signatories grew until finally they had more than five hundred, far beyond the required number. This stunned the city council, which decided to kill the new ordinance in a midnight vote. But the fight was just getting started.

4.

The Chamber of Commerce occupies an impromptu row of offices set back from Highway 29, its foyer offering brochures promising visitors fun and satisfaction. On the wall behind the desk of its CEO and president, Pam Simpson, is a blow-up photo of the sign that stood on the southern town line when she took the job: ST. HELENA POP. 5,100 ELEVATION 255. It reminds her every day of what she's supposed to be doing, which is "serve business."

Nowadays the population is closer to six thousand. The ranks of city administrators bent on development have been under attack by what she sees as the bane of St. Helena and, by implication, small towns all over: citizens. Specifically, those who bought their houses in the 1970s and 1980s, don't want things to change, and are secure in their way of life. By this she means out of touch and often immovable.

Also susceptible to what Pam calls "fear-mongers. They stand outside supermarkets and tell people they're going to lose their privacy, peace of mind, water—whatever—if development's allowed. Then they write down names and e-mail addresses—if those old-timers have e-mail addresses—and send them blog posts" that further upset them.

Her view through the narrow floor-to-ceiling corner window is of a parking lot, the homely backsides of supply shops, and a long throw to the base of the Mayacamas, where an emerald swatch of Newton Vineyard gleams in the sun. Commerce and nature—the two poles of life in Napa Valley in the twenty-first century—continue to grow further and further apart. Pam has to regularly remind the town that the sometimes shadowy but interconnected, very real force upon which everyone's fate depends is *"business!"* Bring to St. Helena more of its most important ingredient—*"visitors!"*—interested in natural beauty who will spend money to be close to it and, of course, to wineries, so businesses can *make money*.

Sometimes, thinking about all this, absently fingering beads looped around the neck of her knit sheath dress and wearing just enough makeup to look professional, her thoughts take a more philosophical turn. She has two children, a boy in high school and a girl out of college living at home, as are so many young Americans these days. Pam admits she can't imagine a better town than St. Helena in which to raise kids. She loves it and is proud of its ranking as one of the top American towns by *Cities* journal, and wants it to remain more or less as it is. But growth is a paradox, particularly when it's based on tourism, because tourism tends to devour the thing it craves.

Asked if prosperity is possible without exponential growth, she says, "Absolutely!" But that's the voice of the old Chamber, before its leaders in Washington, DC, threw in with the multinationals and essentially left its historic membership to its own dwindling devices. Growth must be gradual, she adds, and cites as an example the Wine Train, whose owners want to be allowed to let ten couples a day off in St. Helena, after they've ridden up-valley from the city of Napa, so they can dine and spend the night here. Presumably these couples would be more or less sober, though one drunk tried to climb atop the picturesque steam engine while it was running.

Suitable off-loads contribute to the town's "TOT," the acronym on every public official's tongue from San Pablo Bay to Calistoga. It stands for transient occupancy tax, which automatically adds a hefty percentage of tax revenue to hotel bills that is passed along to communities. The TOT contributes significantly to the coffers of the city of Napa, big enough to absorb the growing numbers of visitors, and nearby Yountville, which isn't. In three decades of breathless TOT pursuit, Yountville has made itself rich while largely depriving its citizens of a community, and Pam doesn't want St. Helena to turn into another Yountville.

This assertion is common, in its way, all over America. Aspen didn't want to change into what it couldn't even imagine turning into in 1960, but did. Telluride didn't want to turn into another Aspen, but did. Orlando didn't want to turn into another Anaheim, and turned into something even worse.

"Eight out of ten top property taxpayers here are businesses," Pam says. "People say they don't want chains, they want mom-and-pops. Then they won't shop at them because mom-and-pops are too expensive. It's hypocritical."

For decades St. Helena got along without clothing boutiques, specialty jewelers, art galleries, and fancy restaurants. The hardware store, Steves, morphed into a peddler of the most expensive versions of what homeowners need. Citizens used to shop and eat at the local drug store, buy sundries at the five and dime, buy meat and newspapers at the butcher shop, and sometimes get drunk in a bar on Main. People measured their days by something other than acquisition and spectacle, and at night the town took on a somnolence many thought desirable.

"Maybe I shouldn't have said it quite that way," Pam adds. "We're all about authentic charm here. But it's change versus no change, so let's grant more rentals, like B&Bs, because if we don't they'll rent their places out anyway. And we'll lose the transient occupancy tax."

Of the more than three million people who come to Napa Valley every year many "choose not to spend money in St. Helena because of a limited number of hotel rooms, the stores closing early, and restaurants less well-known than those down-valley." No French Laundry, although one eats very well in St. Helena. You see locals in Sunshine Foods Market, also known as Moneyshine Market, and in Model Bakery. But greater opportunities are missed. "A few years ago a lot of city managers and department heads here were part-timers. They weren't watching the store"—mercantile metaphors persist—"and things fell through the cracks big-time. There was a lot of kicking the can."

St. Helena suffered from what she calls "visitor leakage. And we spent money on the library instead of paving the streets."

There's something odd about St. Helena not shared by other towns in America: It's often guided by people who either own vineyards and wineries, or make money directly downstream from the business of wine. At least one member of the city council owned a winery, and so did one a city council member. Pam herself had an interest in a zinfandel vineyard with century-old vines right here in town, bought with her first husband and sold after their divorce. She's still annoyed that they were unable to build a winery on it because it was less than five acres and they did not live on the premises, as required by law.

So she dislikes the protesters and e-mail address collectors. "*Hello!* We're in the Napa Valley! The process is being hijacked." The same charge Geoff Ellsworth makes of the vintners and developers. "There are only a few people doing this. They're saying the wineries will steal your water, using fear tactics. We had eight meetings to explain what the city was trying to do. Three hosted by the Chamber, and then a couple of those people took it to the streets. Well, the way it works here is that everything happens at dinner parties. That's where I first heard about the referendum." She pauses. "The Chamber stuck its neck out, and we made enemies."

*   *   *

Forty percent of houses in St. Helena belong to people who don't live in them. Many owners don't vote here, and they don't join clubs and civic groups. Squabbles like the one over the winery definition don't intrude on their consciousness, nor do they feel bound by the usual restraints of citizenship. According to a shop owner, they view St. Helena as just another stop in a peripatetic, leisurely life and "are often unpleasant. They see everybody else as their enablers."

Stroll along Main Street and you'll find plenty of charm but a dearth of basics. Enterprises not found in other American towns of six thousand souls include a laboratory that analyzes wine and can alter its components and their relationship to one another. On the second floor of an old building facing Main through tall windows is Soutirage, discreet pairer of producers with fine wine collectors like Joe Schoendorf, who is on Soutirage's board.

On the wall hang photographs of bottles of La Tâche and Corton-Charlemagne. Here a supposedly unattainable 2011 Screaming Eagle cabernet can be had for $5,000, a case of 2008 Harlan for $9,000, and a hard-to-come-by bottle like Pappy Van Winkle's Family Reserve 20-Year-Old bourbon for $1,500. "We're concerned with provenance," says an affable young Brit in a black knit sweater who became an oenophile while studying law and philosophy at University College London.

Nearby is the narrow tasting room of Orin Swift Cellars, named for the parents of the former owner, Dave Phinney, who owns a lovely brick fortress across Main that was bought with the proceeds of the sale of his brand The Prisoner. It was just one of several recent spectacular spin-offs involving people in the valley and once unheard-of sums, paid not for quality but to capture thousands of eager drinkers of luscious, alcoholic wines. This historic building, once a monument to small business, now provides space for wines put together by Phinney and his partners from vineyards as far away as France and as close as just down Main Street.

Climb wooden stairs with heavy banisters, pass through a thick-paneled doorway into a room with fourteen-foot ceilings and confront a forest of bottles standing in antique light. The labels are dark and arty, like snippets from a Goya painting. The proprietor dresses younger than he is—boots, checked shirt, John Deere hat, the contemporary agricultural version of the nineteenth-century entrepreneur for whom the building was constructed. Symbolism is important here—Phinney also sells spirits, a brand of denim jeans called Mercury Head ("heads or tails, you stand a fifty percent chance of winning"), and skateboards. He would sell Orin Swift to Gallo, which has a sea of wine to put in bottles with trendy labels, for more than $200 million.

He rises from his desk and comes warily forward. Asked about the successful referendum that thwarted the winery definition change, his gaze narrows. "They got enough signatures, but I don't really understand how that happened. Living here and not wanting wineries is like moving to Aspen and not wanting snow. Those of us who work don't have time to fight, and retired people"—the familiar culprit—"do have the time. I don't like people telling me how to run my business."

While the referendum saga was still unfolding, Schramsberg moved into the former car dealership here in town. This was a commercial site, not a residential one, and therefore untouched by the battle over the residential winery definition. Schramsberg obtained a license from the state's Alcohol Beverage Control Board, as required by law, set up a small fermenting operation within an ungainly hulk that had once been filled with new Chevrolets, and started making the twenty thousand gallons of wine it didn't have room to make up on Diamond Mountain.

After harvest, Hugh and his CFO and others on the winemaking and hospitality teams decided to apply to St. Helena for an expansion of this new facility. They wanted to make many times that amount of wine and have tasting rooms and host as many as 150 visitors a day. It was all legal, if a stretch. Geoff Ellsworth as yet knew little about this project, and Hugh expected city planners to ask Schramsberg to cut back on the numbers, which he was willing to do. He assumed that such a compromise would move things smoothly along.

He was wrong.

CHAPTER NINE:

Alive on Arrival

1.

Susan Kenward passed Geoff Ellsworth on the street one day, and he said, "You have to attend the planning commission hearing today. It's very important and I can't make it."

Geoff was a friend. Susan had seen his one-man plays and her son had made a video of one for a school project. She had even bought some of Geoff's art. She made sure to tune into the planning commission session on television, and what she saw and heard there shocked her.

Susan had the broad vowels left over from a Virginia childhood even though she had lived in St. Helena for decades, as well as the natural assertiveness of a blonde in blonde country. She was married to Tor Kenward, the former head of public relations for Beringer on the north edge of town, back in the 1990s, who now had his own successful boutique wine made in part from To Kalon grapes he bought from Andy Beckstoffer.

Susan hadn't been involved in the referendum drive, although she had given her signature. Now she was reminded that, a year before, Schramsberg had asked to be allowed to make only twenty thousand gallons of wine and now they wanted to make many times that. And have a tasting room, too. Susan thought Schramsberg had planned this huge expansion all along, and by not telling anyone proven themselves disingenuous, which bothered her a lot.

Now she watched, on television, Hugh Davies standing in front of everybody and talking about his family's history in the valley. But he didn't address any of the concerns that were going through her head. Finally she got so mad she drove into town and found, gathered outside the meeting, friends of the late Jack and Jamie Davies. "They were all furious, too," Susan later told her husband. Some of those people gathered at Geoff's house, where a decision was made to officially start a nonprofit, Citizens' Voice, a 501(c)(4) that eventually garnered more than three hundred contributions in amounts varying from $25 to thousands.

When a sympathetic but cautious woman said, "I can't put my name on this," Susan realized that the sensitive nature of the issue cut several ways, with the capacity to offend no matter what tack you took. The Davieses' enduring reputation as a family with deep roots in the valley, always on the right side of the preservation argument, now seemed to have gone in the opposite direction. So Susan came up with a solution, as Susan liked to do: PayPal. It assured anonymity, and it helped significantly with those who wanted to resist anonymously.

More than one lawyer offered to help pro bono. But Citizens' Voice would have to hire its own legal team if the board approved the expansions at the new Davies Vineyards, originally seen as a small production facility without frills. Because by then Citizens' Voice would be challenging both Schramsberg and the town of St. Helena, trying to haul the whole controversy before a judge.

There were so many things to object to about the Schramsberg project, Geoff thought. He had gone to the mayor as soon as he heard about it and told her he wasn't opposed to businesses succeeding, but this new development would have a devastating effect on the town. "St. Helena is the crown jewel of the valley," he said. "We have rules built in that are supposed to protect us from things like this. It's the equivalent of letting free enterprise into Yosemite Valley."

The mayor just laughed. In retrospect that was not the wisest reaction. Geoff went home and delved into files he had amassed about the project. The city had made only a negative declaration, meaning it was found that no adverse environmental effects would result from the winery expansion. Which meant no proper environmental impact study would be done, and the planning commission would vote it in anyway, knowing that high school students would pass by frequently, and that parking was a problem.

He received more phone calls from Sonoma County, where resistance to wineries was now a full-blown movement. It reportedly even had a children's alliance for water conservation. By now Geoff fully understood the warning "Once you let them in, you'll never get them out." St. Helena was facing—for a small town—something entirely new, he thought, a high-speed business model for new wineries using "hospitality"—another way to bait the old tourist trap—to significantly up the ante, the parochial equivalent of the leveraged buyout. The wine industry was in cahoots with banks that loved the idea of wineries with paid-for "occasions" for paying tourists built into their use permits, a great business model: sell wine, wine tastings, food, *and* events, with ever-increasing tourism as the surefire generator of bodies and therefore revenue.

If neighbors objected, according to this argument, they could be ignored because a precedent had been legally set. The objectors, proponents believed, would eventually get fed up with objecting and some would leave town, as some had already done. This was the opposing argument to Joe Schoendorf's, that St. Helena hadn't lost population because it had put restraint on new business; it had lost population because people no longer wanted to live in the wine-country equivalent of *The Truman Show*.

Some people wanted a life that didn't revolve around selling wine, food, and high-end bling to strangers. But many in Napa Valley now wanted to scrub towns clean of those who wanted limits on business, part of the anti-government sentiment across the land. The pro-business cohort sought to install its own elected officials who, in turn, favored proposals from partisans. And these sought to overturn basic rules by which a town persevered. The justification for dismantling government was the tired old Chamber of Commerce clichés about unlimited free enterprise.

Geoff and others had accepted their relegation to an unofficial "complainer class"—geezers, hotheads—but were dismayed by the paucity of youth in their ranks. It felt as if social protest had skipped a generation caught up in the pursuit of money and electronic distraction. The triumphs of the Free Speech Movement—Mario Savio in Berkeley, Martin Luther King and the civil rights movement, anti–Vietnam War unrest, Watergate, the fight over the winery definition—were ancient history and seemed to lack relevance in a fragmented America. Twenty- and thirty-somethings might speak out against cutting redwoods, but they seemed unaware of similar forces cutting away at the ground beneath their feet.

Objectors could be driven out by the proponents of untrammeled commerce. What they would leave behind was a beautiful town ready for a mounting wave of touristic amoebae. That was the way Geoff saw it. And one big, nagging question remained: Whose idea had this been? Somewhere down the line he would find out, he was sure, but meanwhile there was an entirely new kind of harvest in the valley. Wine sold directly to visitors upped profits by half, eliminated the middleman, and greased the skids for changing residential neighborhoods by insiders. Due process had been truncated and the people ignored in a vitally important matter.

Donna Oldford lives in the same middle-class enclave in west St. Helena as Geoff does, the one with streets named for grape varieties and, by coincidence or cosmic design, freighted with land-use issues and the names of those prominent in them: not just Peter and Carlene Mennen and Geoff Ellsworth, but also Stu Smith, the big-bearded co-owner of Smith-Madrone Vineyards & Winery up on Spring Mountain and an avid champion of property rights. Donna's political, too, and proud of the niche she has carved out of the valley's ongoing winery squabbles.

For years she has helped newcomers dream of a wine of their own and navigate complex rules and regulations. These litter the passage through which all aspiring applicants must sail on an Odyssean voyage toward a label of their own. Ask and she will tell you that her record of accomplishments is quite good, thank you very much, as are her associations with the Chamber and other commercial interests in St. Helena. If people also ask—and they do—about the percentage of her successes, Donna Oldford proudly says, "I don't do dead on arrival."

She takes only those new winery applications she deems likely to prevail. Twenty-seven years of involvement have carried her across a political spectrum littered with issues, right and left, some still considered pivotal, some forgotten. In the process she became a confident, well-dressed, sturdy middle-aged woman with a full head of auburn hair who enjoys a glass of good Napa Valley cabernet in the evening.

"The town's government has traditionally helped business," she says. "But there is a big difference today. It's that people who in the past fought against business development individually have decided to link hands. They've formed a daisy chain. Now there's a Chicken Little atmosphere."

She happily embraces clichés, ready tools of big-picture advocacy since they sum up human intercourse while eliminating all subtlety. "The opposition doesn't have any skin in the game, they're activists by nature. They do it for sport, they"—again—"have too much time on their hands."

Potential clients who ask how much it will cost to start even a small winery are told a minimum of a million dollars, "and that's just to get in. Then I ask them, 'What's your dream?' They tell me, and I get to work making those dreams come true."

Her career by definition involves shape-shifting in a place where conservation, free enterprise, citizens' rights, and corporate privilege swim together in a particularly competitive pool, the issues forever malleable. Donna worked back in the 1990s for Jack Davies and Bob Phillips, another patrician, the basso profundo voice behind Vine Hill Ranch and husband to an heir to the Spreckels Hawaiian sugar fortune. Both men embodied Republican values of another age, yet both broke with class and party to oppose the Wine Train.

A city planner by profession, Donna got paid to write letters on their behalf criticizing the Wine Train's environmental impact, all the while thinking, "You're out of your minds." The Wine Train had not been dead on arrival, and she had seen that coming. To the contrary, the linked green-and-maroon railway cars were soon noisily hauling tourists the length of the valley and serving them food and wine while they watched a big-screen alternative to *Nature* beyond the window and consumed what had been compared to upscale versions of TV dinners.

Phillips told Donna she was a natural advocate for wineries, and Jack agreed. " 'They're just like little industrial parks,' he said," and that gave Donna a new way of looking at it. This turned into her profession, and though the two men were now gone, that early fight revealed to her just how democratic the valley was. Phillips and Davies, representative of the powers that be, made things happen. They may have failed in the Wine Train fight, but their type still ran the county, and that type was no longer freighted with the same concern for probity.

St. Helena isn't the county, she likes to say, but "a textbook case of saying *No* to everything. No good deed goes unpunished. Hugh Davies was encouraged to buy the Chevy dealership for a winery. At the first hearing only one person stood up and spoke against it." At the second hearing many did, and some criticized the family. The sight of Hugh's wife, Monique, in tears struck Donna as a remarkable milestone: The Davies, who had long been an example to other vintners of environmental concern, were now not green enough.

Schramsberg hired Donna because, in effect, "they had to go through the whole application process again, they hadn't properly thought through their application," asking for too much and now having to deal with the consequences of too much success. Their example would reach beyond the town, she feared, "making the county, too, more cautious in the future."

She recommended to Hugh that $75,000's worth of mitigation studies be done. They were, and revealed that less water would be used by the winery than had been used by the car dealership. This was a big plus. Also that the proposed number of visitors was comparable to those at Merryvale Vineyards just up Highway 29. And a traffic study suggested that vehicles going to and from the winery, including those driven by wine tasters, were of no particular danger to passing students. "I'm a lot more afraid of teenage drivers than of someone coming out of a tasting room" is Donna's standard line.

Schramsberg held a public meeting and brought along fourteen employees to answer questions. Hugh explained that he had talked to the school's principal and that the principal had no problem with the winery.

He started a program in which high school students could learn how to make wine, pick grapes at nearby Salvestrin Vineyards & Winery, and ferment them in Schramsberg's new facility, getting academic credit in the process.

He offered to reduce the number of visitors to less than the number that was already allowed at Sattui and HALL wineries not far south of the Davies Vineyards site. But no one was impressed. The opposition had hardened.

2.

Geoff Ellsworth assumed he could defeat the Davies winery with a referendum, then learned that, no, it had now become a legal issue and so had to be appealed through the courts. At the last minute he pulled it off the city council's dissent calendar; he and his allies were learning on the fly.

Then he called Andy Beckstoffer, and a couple of other prominent families, and asked for financial help. Citizens' Voice needed money and it needed it now if it was going to appeal the city's decision. Beckstoffer said he would think about it, but the idea that he might even consider being involved was empowering. Then Hugh Davies called Geoff up. They had been friends, though not as close as Geoff had been to John Davies, but now the voice at the other end sounded to Geoff both cold and unyielding. In close to an hour of talking Geoff was unable to get in more than a few words and he hung up convinced that Hugh was uninterested in his arguments.

Geoff had become a fan of the British fictional character Inspector Morse, because he, too, did crosswords. Meanwhile Geoff spread his communications net wider, and increasingly the phrases "alcohol tourism" and "binge tourism" punctuated the arguments. His contacts included several groups in Mendocino, Marin, San Francisco, and beyond. Sometimes he couldn't recall exactly where some ideas had come from, things were happening so fast.

He began to see similar struggles everywhere in the state and the country. Like fracking. In the American West and upper Midwest this had come about through the early advances made by agents of Big Oil who used zoning boards in little towns to change what was allowed, the people living in those towns unaware until it was too late. The same thing had happened in St. Helena. The city council was allowing Schramsberg to go forward despite the fact that the neighborhood was zoned for local service, not tourism. Schramsberg claimed it would create jobs, which wasn't really the case, but as soon as that argument was heard, other businesses applied for similar zoning variances.

Then Robin Daniel Lail, daughter of John Daniel Jr., inheritor of Inglenook, wrote a letter to the *St. Helena Star* under the headline DAVIES PROJECT THREATENS OUR CHARACTER AND CULTURE. The piece continued in that vein. "This is an interesting facility which morphed from a production facility into a major entertainment center . . . [T]hink about the impact of 66,000 visitors going into and coming from the winery in cars, limos and buses. . . . The proposed entertainment component of the winery is stunning." That letter, Geoff told people, definitely bumped the argument up a notch.

Hugh Davies, rereading Robin's letter in the *Star*, reminded himself: "Don't take things personally. People have differences of opinion. Reason with them, talk on the merits, be polite. Also steadfast. But get it done."

That's how his father would have handled it.

The irony inherent in this particular criticism was that it emanated from a bona fide Napa Valley grand dame whose father had been the embodiment of unfettered free enterprise. Like others in his day who inherited great wealth, John Daniel Jr. hadn't accepted even the possibility of being deprived of anything by the upwardly mobile then moving into the valley. A kind but private man, John had been no friend of the so-called exciting wave of the 1960s, dreamers and would-be vintners like Ric Forman, Warren Winiarski, and Jack and Jamie Davies.

Hugh remembered the story of his father's call on Daniel in his beautiful white Victorian under the spreading oaks that now belonged to Coppola. Jack Davies had dropped in on Daniel hoping to get advice and maybe the blessing of the proprietor of the grandest and what then seemed the most durable Napa Valley family estate. But Daniel had received him coolly and made plain he didn't approve of outsiders coming to the valley and upsetting the established order. Jack had driven back to Schramsberg with the knowledge that he and John Daniel would never be friends.

More telling had been Daniel's opposition to the creation of the agricultural preserve in 1968. The supervisors, all Republican, had seen the wisdom of requiring a large minimum acreage for building a structure on agricultural land, thus preventing the whole from being converted to another bedroom community as had happened to the beautiful Santa Clara Valley. The fiercest critic of the ag preserve had been John Daniel, who accepted no restraints on land owners. He teamed up with other wealthy men in opposition and descended upon the county supervisors in a fury, abetted by his unlikely friend Louis Stralla, the only mayor in St. Helena's history with reputed links to organized crime. They and their allies waylaid supervisors outside the meeting, grasping lapels like those belonging to Don McFarland and issuing threats. Stralla shoved one supervisor up against the wall. But in the end the supervisors defied them, voting in the preserve that would soon be hailed as the valley's savior and the first toll of the death knell for the old order.

Daniel's disappointment at the altering political landscape added to the burdens of a difficult later life and may have contributed to his tragic death. Had Daniel still been alive, Hugh wondered, how would he have come down in this fight over the makeover of the Epps Chevy dealership? History suggested that John Daniel would have defended Davies Vineyards as an example of a successful business hampered by local tampering.

Daniel's daughter Robin Lail was yet another St. Helenan who owned a boutique wine of her own and was using the same arguments evinced long ago in defense of legally preserved ag lands outside of town. Now she seemed in favor of limitations on the aristocracy her father had represented and of which she was still a part.

Harder to take for Hugh was criticism emanating from Andy Beckstoffer, who had also written to the *St. Helena Star* to say his concern wasn't the winery project, but its location. Beckstoffer's name elicited powerful reactions across a broad political and commercial spectrum. It, too, was tied up with the ownership change of Inglenook and the rise of the corporate class, yet Beckstoffer had maintained his independence from both the clamorous gaggle of rich vintners and the intertwined, often warring factions of the environmental and grower communities.

It was Beckstoffer money, Hugh learned, that pushed Citizens' Voice beyond the limitations of piecemeal contributions and might well enable it to fund an appeal of Schramsberg's permit that would end up in court. With this in mind, Hugh telephoned Beckstoffer at his farming compound down in Rutherford.

Few in the valley wouldn't take a call from Hugh Davies. Beckstoffer came promptly on the line but as soon as Hugh began to explain the proposed mitigations and compromises for his new winery, Andy cut him off. "I don't care about the particulars," he told Hugh. "It's the wrong place for a winery."

Hugh hung up thinking Andy would oppose any new winery near Highway 29, from Calistoga to the outskirts of the city of Napa. It was a remarkable position for a man who depended on wineries to buy his very expensive grapes, and an indication that something had moved Beckstoffer in late middle age off the neutral ground and into the ranks of the rising objector class.

What Hugh didn't know was that Beckstoffer considered the whole Davies family elitist and the late Jack Davies one more example of bad corporate mentality. From the beginning Jack had brought grapes into the valley from other counties, thereby putting his narrow interests above those of the community, in Andy's view. This tended to undermine local agricultural interests and in its way discredit the Napa Valley Appellation. This conclusion would have stunned any Davies who heard it, since the family had founded and continued to maintain the Jack L. Davies Agricultural Fund and support the agricultural preserve as a sacred covenant.

Another source of money for Citizens' Voice, Hugh learned, was Leslie Rudd, a partner in St. Helena's Dean & DeLuca and the owner of a winery and vineyards in the valley. Rudd had donated a million dollars to the high school to build an auditorium. The late discovery that his new edifice was to have what Geoff Ellsworth was calling "an alcohol entertainment center" almost directly across the street didn't please Rudd, nor did the fact that school officials told Rudd, in effect, thank you for this auditorium but we'll make our own decision about Schramsberg. And that decision was not to oppose.

Hugh Davies and Geoff Ellsworth both longed for a statement in support of their positions from one of the two most respected wineries within town limits, Spottswoode on the west side, and Salvestrin to the south. The former provides a view of immaculate vineyards for those contending personalities on streets named for grapes, an exemplary neighbor; the latter is a modern-day contender for the Jeffersonian ideal, a modest wine estate employing mostly family that fit unobtrusively into the community. These two viticultural captives of surrounding growth were allowed only a fraction of the visitors the new Davies Vineyards would enjoy. Both were staunch environmentalists and an expressed opinion from either could have made a difference in Schramsberg's urban imbroglio.

3.

The dirt driveway, within St. Helena town limits, passes through an old gate bearing the name Salvestrin. Trees partially obscure a white-frame farmhouse built in 1879 by Dr. George Belden Crane, whose original vineyard nearby was planted in 1879. Here past and present run together like the tendrils of historic vines feeding an enterprise practically timeless.

You can easily miss it, and most visitors do, although Crane represents a latter-day superhero in the valley since he was the first to plant *Vitis vinifera*, not George Yount down in Yountville, as is commonly believed. The Crane house is little changed, lived in today by three generations of Salvestrins, including the one in charge of a small winery and a twenty-six-acre vineyard.

Rich Salvestrin is blue-eyed, burly, burnished by the sun; he wears boots and jeans and a blue work shirt with rolled sleeves. "My grandparents bought the place in 1932," he will tell a visitor on the little patio adjacent to dusty grape leaves. "My grandfather came to the United States through Ellis Island, straight from northern Italy. He went west, worked in mines and on the railroad, married, and then heard about Italian families living in Napa. They came here, and they thought, 'This is just like home.' "

Some of the original Crane furniture came with the house and what was then twenty-three acres. "My grandfather helped neighbors with their vines, and bartered his labor for the use of a horse. My father took over, and in 1950 bought a tractor." That same year St. Helena High School next door had to expand. It took some of the family land but left enough vines to provide a living. "I've been tied to this land for as long as I can remember. I loved playing in the dirt, I learned pruning from Granddad and Dad."

He worked in the vineyard all through school and afterward. Salvestrin is a useful case study of the opportunities and difficulties of small vineyards in Napa Valley today. If put in today, it would cost at least $30,000 an acre, and maintaining it, too, is expensive. So the financial stakes for anyone starting out are great.

Rich began to make wine in 1994. "When I got my hands around all aspects of it, we went into the wine business." The Salvestrins built a winery "because it added value to the crop," but there construction stopped. No nascent event center. The acres support his family, including three daughters and his parents, who still live in the house. A top bottle of Salvestrin cabernet costs seventy dollars, very reasonable for a wine made from fruit of such provenance. "Now the fourth generation will get its hands on the place."

As for current tensions between development and agriculture in the county, Salvestrin has the sunny agrarian's view: "The valley will go the way of reasonableness. We're at the tipping point again, not the hillsides now, but the number of wineries. This place should be about the wine. We shouldn't be selling T-shirts or wine that's not from grapes grown here. People will just have to come to their senses."

*   *   *

The hearing for the Citizens' Voice appeal of the winery permit was heard by a judge from neighboring Solano County in late spring 2014. He had little experience of wineries but plenty having to do with commercial zoning, and he listened to all the now familiar arguments, from many of the same people. He then announced that he would take the documents with him, think about the case, and make a ruling within ninety days.

After the hearing Hugh and Monique returned to Schramsberg. They had finally moved into the big house, all five of them living on the second floor while the attic served as a miniature landscape of childish delight strewn with toys of every description. Many of the paintings that had once hung in the hall and living room downstairs had been taken by Hugh's brothers. The rug now in the dining room had been found rolled up in the barn.

The kitchen bore no resemblance to the one in which Hugh and Monique had shared a glass of bubbly with Jamie toward the end. The old photographs of family and friends gazing down from lacquered pine paneling were all gone, too, as was the bed of calla lilies outside the window. But the view of the pond was the same.

They ate together as a family most evenings at the new center island, in what seemed like a shiny new world. The oldest boy, Emrys, was playing soccer and occasionally getting roughed up. Nelson, the middle son, looked preppy in his Bermudas, and little Huey was already reading *The Great Brain*. No one looking at the boys that evening could have missed their resemblance to the generation before, nor the suggestion of great— and greatly varied—possibilities lurking within these harbingers of the future.

Hugh had discovered, in venturing beyond the isolation of Schramsberg, that some people didn't like his family. This had come as a surprise, one he was still trying to adjust to. But many others did like them, and had written and called over the months to say so, and this meant a lot to him and Monique.

Hugh decided then and there that he wasn't going to get involved in such a venture again, no matter how tempting. And he was pulling back from all commitments other than those to business, family, and the Jack L. Davies Agricultural Fund. Schramsberg's defense against the appeal had cost $300,000, in addition to all the other costs, and if the judge ruled for Schramsberg and Citizens' Voice then appealed that decision, it would cost the winery that much all over again. The fight was not over.

Meanwhile Hugh, youngest son, now the steward of old Jacob Schram's and his parents' dreams, had to make money. He had to get it done.

IV.

ON HOWELL
MOUNTAIN

*A rugged individual makes wine in the path of a
raging natural force, then acts to thwart a
wealthy interloper determined to have his way.*

INTERLUDE:

The Sanctity of Stuff

It could, except for the gasoline-powered four-wheeler, be a mining operation in the Sierra foothills a century and a half ago. Or, more aptly, a timber camp. In reality it's a nascent vineyard very much in the present, which means scraped earth reaching for the sky from an encircling wreath of redwoods and Douglas firs. Dust and rock and implements for dealing with them provide the ambience, while the proprietor—heavy black beard, glinting green eyes, filthy straw cowboy hat, lumbering boots and a black Lab best friend unaccustomed to other humans—provides the action.

His name's Ketan Mody and if you haven't heard of him, you well may. Gesturing past his one-room rough-hewn cabin toward the spot where it used to stand, he says, "A storm came through one night and a friend down in the valley got flooded out and called for help. I drove down"—way down—"and when I got back up here next morning the house was flattened." The big Douglas fir fell across his bed, leaving long wooden splines in the pillow where his face would have been.

The stump's still obstinately there, but the rest went into the new house, for this is a work in progress in every sense of the word. Like the forty-niners once bent on a very different sort of success, he will utilize every object and advantage until he has what he's seeking.

"The problem in Napa Valley is that most people just can't do *stuff*," such as put in vineyards themselves and the thousand other tasks that go with self-sufficiency. "And no one wants to work. How many white guys do you know who actually do something in the vineyard? I see too many of them in their Audis with $2,000 bikes on the back. But if you're not willing to put all your effort into this, you shouldn't be here.

"The only way I could afford it is to do it myself. I wanted a place to work and make wine to last my lifetime, but it's so hard to get into Napa. Costs are so high, the projects so large there's been no place for the small operator."

But he found one, much to the consternation of a neighbor who opposed him for a time. "You have to put your head down and work twenty-four-seven. You might lose perspective, but you're committed."

First he worked in finance "and hated my life," then in a winery in New Zealand. "I was interested in singularity, and place, and realized there's no difference between wine and oysters," each of which speaks to origins. "I came to work a harvest here, and didn't want to like it, but the beauty was shown to me. And the understanding that to know one thing very well I would have to do it for the rest of my life."

With help from his father and others he bought this remote forty acres at close to two thousand feet in altitude. It took him four and a half years to get a vineyard permit. He did a voluntary environmental impact report, on principle, and even now, eight years later, there's still no place to sit out of the sun atop this mass of rock, the sound of the earthmover is constant, the view of heavy Douglas fir stacked and waiting, and a lot of terraced raw dirt to be dry-farmed. The cabernet sauvignon rootstock is in, tightly spaced—"the magic stuff's in the clone selection"—and small yields.

"This is my day job: I'm the plumber, janitor, check signer, cheerleader. I love it, putting in a vineyard with a light hand—no deep-ripping, no soil-smearing. Come at it from a love of place. It's totally fulfilling."

Many vintners in Napa Valley are caught up in what amounts to a parody of viticulture, elaborate dramas of money and celebrity far removed from the dust from which hope springs eternal. "I believe in Napa Valley. There's a sense of community not found in other wine regions. I see more reasonableness now, as well as more insanity. More little site-driven wines, more good information about them finally getting out."

He points due east, toward Howell Mountain across the valley. "Randy Dunn is the model for young guys like me," he says, primarily because Dunn does *stuff*. "If you're willing to do more than cut checks, Napa is one of the best places in the world to be, with people who share the unifying experiences in a semi-mystical glass of wine."

CHAPTER TEN:

Waiting for Fire

1.

Smoke hangs in the branches of Douglas firs massed atop Howell Mountain. Years of drought have weakened them, and now a forest fire has reached the south end of Lake County and is moving into Napa County. Most days Randy and Lori Dunn, who live just below the ridgeline, can see the ragged palisade clearly, but today the trees are indistinct and recede farther as the day progresses. By 7:00 P.M. it's dark, and although the fire is still a dozen miles away, the smell of smoke is inescapable.

The Dunns close the windows, turn on the air conditioner, and go to bed. At 2:30 A.M., they wake up to flashing lights in the driveway: The sheriff has arrived to tell them that a fifty-mile-an-hour wind is blowing the fire their way, and White Cottage Road is being evacuated. Since Lori has recently undergone shoulder surgery, this news means putting on a sling before she can place framed photographs of children, parents, grandparents, and friends into a cardboard box with one hand.

That she has to choose which faces to save and which to discard does not seem fair at such a lonely hour. Randy taps his iPad to track what is being called the Valley Fire—not for Napa Valley, but the valley to the north, in Lake County, where forty thousand acres have burned already. It is safe to say the fire is out of control despite a score of fire engines, two dozen dozers, and a thousand people laboring to contain it.

If the fire comes farther south, it might well climb Howell Mountain's northern flank, race along the ridge, and come down through the firs and ponderosa pines that extend into the very midst of their lives. Then it could consume things as precious to the Dunns as their photographs: house, outbuildings, a couple of million dollars' worth of bottled cabernet sauvignon, and the new 2015 vintage still on the vines; also a vegetable garden, the huge fig tree dropping more fruit than they and the birds could eat, and nearby Wildlake, three thousand acres of wilderness high on the eastern perimeter of Napa Valley. The Dunns have saved it once before.

Lori takes off her sling in frustration and carries the box of photographs out the kitchen door, past a sign that reads GRANDMA AND GRANDPA'S HOUSE: MEMORIES MADE HERE, and down the outdoor stairs to the little cave where some Dunn wine is stored. She leaves the box there and goes back upstairs for her sewing machine and quilt collection. Then she hugs Randy and, still in her pajamas, gets into their white SUV to drive to the relative safety of St. Helena, a vertical half-mile below.

Randy—in Levi's, boots, and a T-shirt bearing the silhouette of his turboprop Commander parked a mile away at the Angwin Airport—now has to decide what job to do first and the order of all those that follow.

On the phone the next morning he is laconic, even on such a day, for that is Randy. Yes, he says, the fire's close, likely to get closer and, sure, he could use another pair of hands. I'm at the bottom of Napa Valley and I put on hiking boots and drive the twenty-odd miles north with a water bottle and a hat, not knowing quite what to expect.

Cars are coming down Howell Mountain, but a few are going up, too, and I join them, topping out on a country road overlain with low, scudding clouds pierced by intermittent sun. The way into the Dunns' property turns from tarmac to dirt, and at the end of the road an ancient Caterpillar D4 snorts at its labors, flaking yellow paint with rust showing through. The machine seems too simple to be effective, yet Randy has built a firebreak, trenching the edge of the sunflower field and pushing up windrows of dirt, rock, and dry pine needles blown from the big trees.

The dozer was army surplus, rebuilt in Okinawa after World War II and later put up for sale. Randy bought it in the town of Tulelake decades ago and drove it home on a borrowed flatbed truck, anticipating his future as a successful and, as it turned out, highly individual maker of fine wine in the modern heart of American viticulture.

It's 9:30 A.M., and Randy's Levi's and T-shirt are already filthy, a fitting match for the dilapidated straw hat sitting crookedly on his head, his white mustache a gleaming brushstroke in the brim's shadow. Behind him is a dusty horse paddock, a stand of apple trees, and a sprawling woodshed and machine shop, its bat-winged corrugated iron roof held down with heavy stones. Mounted on the gable is a neon sign shaped like a bottle, made by a friend from vintage bits of salvaged tubing. It will announce, the next time it's switched on, WINE!

A pickup comes barreling in from White Cottage Road, loaded with all-terrain bicycles. The beefy driver brakes and leans out the window. It's Mike, Randy's stepson and Dunn Vineyards' official winemaker now, involved in all aspects of the growing and rendering of cabernet sauvignon. Unshaven, smiling crookedly, he seems the picture of affability. But the conversation is pointed: The fire's said to be moving in on the Aetna Springs Golf Course, in nearby Pope Valley. Then Mike asks, "Did the horses get into the vineyard?"

They did not, but if they have to be let out of the paddock, they know their way around the property and will have a good chance of surviving. "They're hungry," Mike adds. "I think I'll go get them a bale." And he's gone.

The landscape has been exhausted by years of drought, and the understory of the tall oaks and conifers is bleached. In the distance, tree trunks stand out as dark slashes in brittle blond stubble, the madrone branches and pine needles as dry as dust. What has always been comforting to the eye is now vaguely threatening.

Waiting for fire inspires an almost easeful fear, as if the threat can be banished at any moment—a lessening of the wind, a bit of rain—but it's an edgy gamble. Whether the fire will appear suddenly and ruin their lives, possibly even claim them, or turn and consume the next ridge over, is impossible to foretell. Information about a fire's progress is not often available—the official Cal Fire website is busy and difficult to navigate—and fire is a constantly mutating menace that only those in the middle of it can truly know.

By 10:30, the smell of smoke is stronger. Though the barely detectable breeze is southerly, a big fire can create its own dynamic. Low clouds presumably have kept the bombers from flying in with their loads of liquid fire retardant. No one knows for sure what's going on, only that Angwin Airport is closed and people are fleeing. Randy went there earlier to move some fuel away from his plane in its hangar. Now he starts up the D4 again and mounts it, headed for a last line of windrow between the flats and the hill.

A quarter-mile up a steeper dirt road and just over the crest is the Dunns' estate vineyard. In thirty-odd years, it has earned a reputation for wines of longevity, tannic density, and beautiful bottle bouquet after a decade or more of age. Lean, intense fruit is part of that reputation, in direct contradistinction to the upfront jammy embrace and riveting alcoholic follow-through of many popular high-end Napa Valley cabernets.

Vineyards are good at thwarting flames, providing little fuel, but this one would make a very expensive firebreak indeed. Wine from its fruit paid for the Commander and its lesser predecessors, including a secondhand 1946 drag-tail Aeronca Champ, in which Randy once courted Lori. It also paid for the Diemme grape press, the tunnels in the mountainside, and countless French oak barrels. This was before Randy, in the final rigors of earning his PhD in entomology at UC Davis, took an elective course in enology. He started making the stuff in a plastic barrel in the back of his used Ford Econoline van, sloshing nascent wine onto the floor as he circumnavigated Lake Berryessa between Davis and Napa Valley, where he worked for Caymus Vineyards.

2.

Her face drawn, Lori returns from church in St. Helena midmorning. "The fire will get to Wildlake before it gets to us," she says, her voice breaking. "There're mountain lions up there. And deer, bobcats, bears." She hurries up to the house to collect more valuables.

Their daughter, Kristina, and her daughter Taylor live just down the road, but they spent the night with relatives in St. Helena and will stay there tonight, too. The nagging ambiguity of the day is shared by the hundreds who have fled Lake County and flocked to the Napa Valley Fairgrounds in Calistoga, having lost their homes. Many are bunking with friends, family, or employers on the Napa Valley floor: pourers, waiters, barkeeps, forklift drivers, flower arrangers, pruners, punchers-down of the floating caps of grape skins in stainless steel fermenting tanks, and caterers who often have to cross a mountain range on two-lane roads twice a day to get to and from work.

Randy walks up the sloping drive to the house, past his Ford F-250 loaded with a ladder, wrenches, gas cans, rope, and an all-terrain vehicle that could get him back up here if he has to evacuate but finds the road to Howell Mountain blocked. Houses lost to fire often don't have to be. A person on the scene can preserve them, but it's risky. On Randy's backseat is a lemon-yellow flame-resistant fire suit, a helmet, and a gas mask.

Next on the to-do list is cleaning the house's gutters, which are full of fir needles lofted there by wind the day before. The roof is metal, but an ember in a gutter can destroy even a concrete house if conditions are right—and the Dunns' house is made of wood. He drives the forklift up to the back door as a tethering point and fetches a climbing rope for belaying.

His son-in-law, Brian, has shown up to help, and Randy presses both of us into service: Brian is the gutter man, and I'm the belayer. Wearing aviator shades and shorts, Brian clambers up the ladder, dons the safety harness, and applies the furious leaf blower, walking crabwise with one hand on the rope down to the far edge of the roof. He's a professional firefighter in Sonoma County, and he will have to go back there before day's end.

We then clean the gutters at the winery office, a house built in the nineteenth century by Italians who used the cellar for winemaking. A full century later, Randy Dunn would use it, too, climbing over casks on a dirt floor, employing a tool called a wine thief to draw long vials of cabernet from bungholes into antique glasses, raising them speculatively to his nose. The house had belonged then to Charlie Wagner, owner of Caymus Vineyards down the mountain. Warren Winiarski, winner of the Paris Wine Tasting of 1976, had also lived here with his wife, Barbara, and their small children, in what was then deemed a backwater unsuitable for grapes, being too far removed from the vaunted valley floor. Now this land is as sought after by potential growers as any terroir in Napa. The old viticulturists' redwood stakes are still sometimes found in the woods.

Randy made Charlie Wagner's wine for him in the 1970s and 1980s. In those days, Randy looked a lot like Robert Redford—same beard, same abundant strawberry-blond hair. Charlie allowed Randy to press his own grapes at Caymus and bring the juice back up to White Cottage Road, where it was transformed into the first versions of what would become the distinctive, surprisingly successful Dunn cabernet sauvignon. The praise it received then was the beginning of Dunn cabernet's steep critical climb, and he and Lori soon bought the house.

In Randy's early days of ownership, the house had swaybacked floors, streaked walls, and Victorian sash windows with wavy glass. After he and Lori built their own rancher next door, this place stood empty. One night a mountain lion saw the moon's reflection in a window and leaped through. The next morning, Randy found shattered glass, the curtains in shreds, and a single drop of blood on the floor, shed before the big cat leaped through another window and was gone.

Brian comes down the ladder and drops the leaf blower and harness. He has scoped out the fire from bits of news he has picked up, but even professionals like him have trouble getting good information. "It's probably going to jump to the next canyon," he says. "If it does, it'll come straight through Wildlake." After that, it's anyone's guess, but the fire will move quickly through the chaparral. "The real problem's going to be blowing embers."

Everyone congregates in the kitchen to eat Lori's chicken salad sandwiches and drink cold grape juice made from a mix of Ruby Red grapes and unfermented Dunn cabernet. Brian says, "If it happens, a brush unit will come through to save what they can and move on."

The brush units put out spot burns, essentially pushing the fire around a house. But not if the owner hasn't made any preparations, or if there's no water and it looks hopeless. Wildfire triage.

Son Mike comes in briefly in his Aussie boots, shorts, and a sweat-stained T-shirt over his barrel chest. He's headed home. He, Kara, and their kids live on the north end of the ridge and are vulnerable, too, though their metal-roofed house is covered in stucco. "I guess I'll go back," he says, almost casually, "and get up there and see what I can see."

As he leaves, Brian tells Randy, "If I were you, I'd make a sign and put it up on the road. I'd spray-paint the address and the words 'Defensible, 10,000 gals. Pond and pool.' That's what I'd do."

The Dunns' machine shop and shed is not readily comprehensible to a visitor. Surely any mechanical problem in small-scale viticulture can be solved here, but first you must know where to look: rebar, metal and plastic pipe, boards, enigmatic tools, machines for fixing other machines, a wall of dusty chainsaws, a forest of wrenches both new and grimy, a wall of fittings great and small for every imaginable coupling, and various other mysteries from the deep industrial past.

Take the drill press that once lived in the hold of a ship—its battered Darth Vader visage towering over a new bit that could drill through a foot of steel. Randy bought that, too, in the 1970s, from thirdhand UC Davis surplus. It weighs half a ton, and he brought it home on the same flatbed that had moved the D4. Ask why and he'll say, "It was too beautiful to pass up."

What the shed and shop don't have, however, is workable spray paint cans. Randy and I have penciled Brian's words on a piece of plywood, but the first can he tries is clogged; the second fizzles. The only working one contains orange paint that's too pale to be seen at a distance, so the letters must be traced again with a succession of parched black Magic Markers.

The words go on, but there's no room for "pond and pool," so another board is propped up and assaulted with orange paint.

Randy tosses a hand drill and some sheetrock screws into the back of a golf cart that is now a wheezing farm runabout. We take off, passing the roan gelding on his back in the paddock, rolling in dust.

White Cottage Road is deserted. We prop the first sign against the mailboxes, and Randy screws the second one high against a runty oak. A sheriff's cruiser speeds past, and the deputy's head whips sideways to take in Randy's handiwork. The next day, Dunn Vineyards is to be visited by the influential wine critic Antonio Galloni, who has come from New York to taste Napa Valley's best, including a succession of Dunn vintages. Most vintners in such an enviable position wouldn't want to greet their estimable guest with odd, hand-painted messages in lurid colors, but the signs could give the vineyard a chance.

Overhanging boughs of live oak, Douglas fir, and madrone might deter a passing fire truck in the heat of battle, so we drive back to the shed to get the forklift, one of the white plastic bins used for hauling grapes, and a chainsaw. Soon the offending, powder-dry branches are exploding against the tarmac, where Randy shoves them aside to make way for possible saviors.

3.

The breeze has shifted to the west. Tiny bits of ash alight on car hoods and the lenses of my sunglasses. The odd, unsettling sense of isolation seems inevitable. But meanwhile, trenching is in order—around the main house, the garage, and the two well houses. The implement used for this, the McLeod, is a heavy hand tool with two working edges: a broad, hoe-like blade and a fanged rake. Randy quickly moves earth and needles into rows, creating more firebreaks, while I sweep leaves from low roofs. Soil, systematically exposed in neat circumferential alleys, must be hosed down.

But most of the hoses are in the big cave next to the "winery," a collection of eight stainless steel fermenters under arching metal girders, open to the sky. A great rolled sailcloth can be stretched overhead if the sun becomes intolerable, but before the harvest, the sail stays furled. The grape press is parked to one side of the crush pad, and that's it but for heavy oak doors under a concrete archway that lead to the cave, a world unto itself.

Fifty-odd gallons of Dunn petite sirah, a hobby pressing that comes before the main event each year and is intended for family and friends only, bubbles in a smallish stainless steel tank on the crush pad. A square of cloth has been duct-taped over the top to keep the wasps out. Randy interrupts his labors and says, as he stands on an empty beer keg, "Let's make some wine."

Using a special steel implement with a canted blade, he punches down the clot of purple skins floating on top, a practical step in winemaking that is thousands of years old and increases a wine's color and intensity. Petite sirah is considered a lesser variety in Napa today, though it once was a power because of luscious fruit and inkiness that could deepen the color of even endemic wines. These vines were propagated from old stock. After the grapes are picked and crushed they're de-stemmed and inoculated with yeast to start fermentation. The punching down intensifies color and flavor. After about ten days the wine will be drawn off and the skins put into a small wooden press to recover any remaining wine. The pressed skins and seeds, known as pomace, will be spread in the garden as compost. Says Randy, "The chilis love it."

The wine will go into an oak barrel and stay there for two years before it's hand-bottled, all this the very basis of winemaking throughout history and around the world when wine was primarily for pleasure, conviviality, and conversation, not points.

At that moment a sheriff's cruiser pulls up, having passed both the paddock and the house without slackening speed. A deputy gets out in a drift of dust, his belt weighted with a capable-looking automatic pistol and handcuffs. Randy gets down to talk to him, providing, when asked, his name and those of the surrounding neighbors, all of which the deputy dutifully enters into a spiral notebook. When they're done, the deputy says, "White Cottage Road's being evacuated," the second time in fourteen hours.

Randy says, "Okay."

"Are you leaving?"

"Maybe."

"That a yes, or a no?"

There's a pause. "No," says Randy, and the deputy and his partner pull away, leaving a skein of new dust. They're too busy to bother with a recalcitrant property owner, though they're unlikely to forget him.

Randy pulls open the doors to the cave. The dim space is punctuated by winking lamps tunneling toward the heart of Howell Mountain, the corridor lined by French oak barrels like opposing sentinels forming a blond, symmetrical honor guard. He makes his way toward the farthest barrel, collecting a hose here, a hose there. Draped with heavy rubber coils, he ascends to the buildings above and attaches nozzles that can be directed toward embers or creeping ground fire during that short interval when a fire is possibly controllable.

More water will be needed for an inferno, however—more than is readily imaginable. Thirty feet from where that mountain lion once jumped through the window stands a faded red International fire engine built in 1946 by Van Pelt of Oakdale, California. It's an elegant conglomeration of red domed lights, old cloth hoses folded and stacked like hundred-foot pythons, rubber hoses on hand-rolled wheels, spiderweb-covered railings, and various other accoutrements out of a Buster Keaton film. Most important, though, the antique fire engine has an eight-hundred-gallon water tank, which Randy now fills using a big plastic pipe from his big well's concrete collecting tank.

Randy bought the engine as is from Mike Robbins, the owner of Spring Mountain Vineyard—also known as Falcon Crest on the 1980s television show—when Robbins, despite the success of the soap opera, was in bankruptcy. The fire engine's transmission was jammed, and Robbins agreed to take just $1,500 for this classic, even on the off chance Randy could get it running. So Randy borrowed a crowbar, fixed the transmission in a few minutes, and hauled the fire engine up Howell Mountain on a trailer. He parked it in the field south of the house, where it has sat ever since.

When Randy presses the ignition switch, a blast of black smoke erupts before the motor turns over with authority, filling the afternoon with the resonance of old-time vehicles.

We pull the flat cloth hose onto the grass, up the stairs, and across the office porch, where Antonio Galloni will have to step over it the next morning—if there is still a winery here and cabernet to taste. The hose expands as the engine pumps water through it. For one frightening moment, the nozzle—sculpted brass, a work of art in its own right—blasts a barely manageable torrent as thick as a man's arm before the motor is shut off.

Fortunately, the smaller rubber hoses emit streams of water less likely to break windows. Their pump runs off the main engine, and Randy gets it running, too. The rubber coils throb as they come off the roller. Squeeze the trigger on a fancy nozzle and a shaft of water shoots half the height of a Douglas fir. The fire engine's water tank is full, the hoses are ready, and Randy shuts everything off.

It's late afternoon and there's no sound now from the one house visible to the north, no sign of human life in the encircling view. The breeze is undetectable in the trees, but high overhead, curdled clouds move glacially out of the south. Randy walks around the paddock and down to the pond, where a child's plastic paddleboat sits among the weeds.

He pushes the two-person boat into the water, then climbs in alone and tests the paddles. The boat lists to one side, so the paddles make it go round in a circle. Randy climbs out and wades in deeper. Here we could stand and possibly survive, although it would be a very long night. We would watch the firs crown in paroxysms of flame, the Dunns' house following. We would listen to bottles exploding in the cellar, hot embers raining all around as we felt the pressure of lung-collapsing heat. If we had fire suits and gas masks, though, we could contemplate the smoke through a thin sheet of scuffed plastic. But Randy says ruefully: "I've only got one gas mask."

At dusk we go into the kitchen, where Randy makes margaritas with a single-field tequila called Ocho, for which he trades Dunn Howell Mountain cabernet. This sort of bartering—cab for a case of tequila, cab for a flat of apricots, cab for a reworked airplane part—is as old as agriculture. Meanwhile, I cook hamburgers doused in Worcestershire sauce, and then we devour them, Randy drinking a bottle of Sierra Nevada Pale Ale and I a glass of a previous year's Dunn petite sirah from one of the open bottles next to the sink.

All outside lights are off now, and darkness settles in like a sentence. The thought of dying from smoke inhalation at two in the morning recurs, but Randy has been through this before; he's no fool. And if I stay, I can have another glass of petite sirah.

A friend calls from St. Helena: Rumor has it the National Guard is coming to evacuate any stragglers. Randy hangs up. "If we see anybody on the road," he says, "we'll just turn off the kitchen light."

After dinner, he turns off the light anyway and goes back outside, where he puts on his headlamp. Exhausted, I head for the guest bedroom under the office, where there's a shower with double glass doors to stop any mountain lion. It occurs to me as I pick my way through the darkness that, in this age of calamity, falling embers are a metaphor for a host of real and possible disasters. We're all waiting for fire now.

The last time I see Randy that night he's back up at the well house. If the National Guard comes, they will see a bobbing circle of yellow light and hear the sound of someone wielding a McLeod, working.

CHAPTER ELEVEN:

Wildlake

1.

The wind died that night and the fire north of Howell Mountain was finally brought under control. Antonio Galloni did indeed visit the next day, step over the hoses, and taste several Dunn wines, to his apparent satisfaction.

Also unscathed were the three thousand meandering acres known as Wildlake that once belonged to a hunting club, all just minutes away by pickup from the Dunns' and the object of much of Lori's concern. The property was once called Wild Lake Ranch, but its origins reach further back into Napa's history. Native American grindstones are discernible there along Bell Creek, and remote ruins of a nineteenth-century homestead. Unknown to most people living two thousand five hundred feet below, some of the purest surface water on the west slope of the Howells range begins its descent here and flows down through Dutch Henry and Bell Canyons, the latter feeding into the reservoir from which St. Helenans happily drink.

Years before, Randy wanted to explore there but didn't belong to the club. He did know one of the members who, when asked about the possibility of Randy joining the club for access to the land, happily said, "You don't need to," and gave him a key to the gate.

Randy used it, canvassing the property on horseback with his daughter Jenny, in the last years of the American century. They rode Rattlesnake Ridge between the two drainages, and highlands that run all the way up to the boundary of Robert Louis Stevenson State Park. Nimrods only came up from the valley to shoot deer, so out of season the place felt empty of people. The old cattle pond near the property line where calf-and-cow operators in times past dammed runoff wasn't really a lake, though there were grasses along the edge, and fish in the emerald depths. Sometimes the whole Dunn family came, sometimes just Randy and Jenny, a bright, optimistic girl who loved what they had all come to call, simply, Wildlake.

Jenny and Randy would sometimes hold hands as they rode through country seemingly without end, full of possibility. When she was twenty and a junior in college she came home sick, and within hours she was in intensive care, having contracted a rare, rapacious virus before which the doctors seemed powerless. Despite everything they tried her condition worsened. She lost consciousness, and finally died, a sudden, terrifying cataclysm that stunned not just Lori, Randy, and the family but all who knew them.

The pall was so dark, extensive, and weighty that some thought it would never lift. Most affected seemed to be Randy himself who, unlike Lori, could not talk about what had happened. Mention of Jenny, of their time together at Wildlake, of daughters and anything tangential brought instant, total grief, without apology from Randy.

Their son, Mike, picked up more duties around the winery. Slowly, miserably, everyone there undertook familiar tasks that had been robbed of relevance and joy. Randy still went to Wildlake, not on a horse now but on a mountain bike, or on foot. He drove himself to exhaustion in the far reaches of the three thousand acres, and a day or two later went back and did it again.

*   *   *

In the years that followed the pall slowly began to lift, though not entirely. He and Lori bought a discrete stretch of woods above the town of Angwin, known as Sentinel Hill, and placed an easement on it so it could never be developed. Helping him was the head of the Land Trust of Napa County, the ginger-bearded, loquacious John Hoffnagle. When Randy passed up the opportunity to extract the maximum tax deduction, Hoffnagle thought, "This is different, he really wants to save the land."

Occasionally Randy mused about the possibility of preserving Wildlake the same way, but it was too special, he thought, for the owners to ever relinquish it. And if it ever did come up for sale, it would be too expensive for the Dunns anyway. They wouldn't even get close. Still, he yearned for access, the lock to the gate having been changed. He no longer had a regular ramble in the most—the only—extensive pristine stretch of Napa County.

He learned that one of the fifteen memberships was being vacated, and tried to purchase it. But Marc Mondavi, a hunting club member, got there first. Marc was the son of Peter and the nephew of Bob, and so belonged to the fraternal line going back to the split between the brothers half a century before, when they had fought in the vineyard and Robert had been kicked off the family's Charles Krug property. Marc considered himself a mover, and Randy suspected he had eyes on all of Wildlake.

Then Randy discovered that another club member had simply disappeared. If he could be found, Randy reasoned, he might be able to buy the man's share.

Randy's wide network of friends with practical skills beyond the ken of most vintners and inheritors included an affable neighbor, Bob Lamborn, the maker of a good zinfandel from old vines as well as a crackerjack private investigator. Randy asked Bob to see if he could find the guy, and Bob did—up in Alaska—but Marc Mondavi picked up that share, too.

Randy told Lori, "I'm pissed."

She was glad because being pissed was good for him. Then their daughter Krissy, attending school down in San Luis Obispo, called to say she had just talked to the son of one of the hunting club members and been told that Wildlake was going on the block. So rapid had been the rate of development, particularly of coveted vineyards lending legitimacy to other activities, and so enormous the fortunes pouring into the valley from elsewhere, that no pristine parcel was safe.

Randy learned that many members had lost interest in the place over the years. He later examined hunting club documents and a list of the number of bucks killed there. The tally went from forty deer one year to thirty the next, and so on down to less than twenty. Members said they didn't much want to hunt there anymore because mountain lions were eating all the deer, when in fact it was they who were eating them.

He still didn't know the price. That was because there wasn't one. So he arranged to meet with a couple of club members—not including Marc—and talk about it. Randy asked them, "Can we say it'll be somewhere between five and fifty million dollars?"

They said yes. They did not give him a formal first option on the property, but it seemed that an option was what he had. The property was not listed as for sale, and the price finally arrived at was near $20 million. He had six months to put it together. Everybody but Randy thought—but didn't say—it was impossible for a small-production guy like him, so far outside the local pool of Napa's astonishing real wealth, to succeed. As Randy told a friend, "There are people in this valley who can write a check for twenty million with no more thought than taking somebody to lunch. Any one of them could buy and hold on to the land while they figured out how to fuck it up." But he wasn't going to allow that.

2.

There were twenty-five separate tax parcels within Wildlake. That meant twenty-five mansions and all the infrastructure for each, or a hundred or so top-dollar houses for people who wanted a piece of the valley, and that meant roads, electricity, water lines, helipads, and, of course, vanity vineyards. As much as three hundred acres were readily adaptable to produce premium Howell Mountain cabernet sauvignon. They were close to the well-known Dancing Bear Ranch and worth at least $100,000 an acre.

He consulted with his accountant and banker and discovered that he could borrow $5 million using Dunn Vineyards as collateral. He and

Lori had never been in debt, paying out of pocket for almost everything. If they ran up a line of credit, they paid it off at the end of every year. This would be digging, for them, the deepest of holes. But bankers like to have you in debt, the deeper the better, so why not take advantage of this?

Randy thought of it as creative financing. Give a note for $5 million to some nonprofit that agreed to buy and preserve Wildlake. He could write off, over five years, up to 50 percent of his gross adjustable income. It was manageable, but since he already owed money on Sentinel Hill in Angwin, it was a big risk, too. Dunn Vineyards Howell Mountain cabernet could carry the debt if the then looming Bush recession didn't turn into a depression. Mike and Krissy would be paying it off long after Randy and Lori were gone. But they would be part of something bigger than all of them, and they could handle it.

He went straight back to the Land Trust, not because he feared he couldn't put together enough donors himself to buy the property, but because he was afraid someone would get wind of the sale and stab him in the back.

John Hoffnagle picked up the phone, and Randy said, "Wildlake's available for twenty million. Want to see it?"

Hoffnagle was known for his rasping monotone and genuine enthusiasm for what his profession called "conservation values." He could talk and talk about the redemptive value of undeveloped land of almost any kind: cleared, wooded, rocky, dry, swampy, beautiful, scruffy, road-worthy, inaccessible. But highest on the list of preservation prospects was agricultural land and wilderness.

He had come to Napa in the late 1980s by way of the Yale School of Forestry and the Nature Conservancy, and was by now a thoroughgoing professional with an exemplary record. By the time Randy had met him, Hoffnagle had deep connections with those wishing to see the land forever free of concrete, condos, and, in some cases, vineyards.

The Land Trust had secured protection for some fifty-three thousand acres, about 10 percent of the land in the county and a full percentage point above the number of acres in vineyards. The donors all had sufficient capital to assure that this happened and that someone would look after their donated property after they were gone, but that did not include Randy Dunn. Not to the tune of twenty mil it didn't.

The process of granting easements was rarely simple, or easy. Hoffnagle had to explain to everyone at least once that just turning land over to the Trust wasn't enough, that in most cases some real money had to be put forward by the donors for continued management. He had brought about the acquisition of thousands of acres in the county in more than a hundred transactions of varying complexity, but he had never dealt with anything this large or, as he suspected, this impressive.

The successful maneuvering that would be necessary for acquisition, if it was possible, would heavily depend on the selflessness of other donors moved by the beauty, strategic positioning, and existing wildlife. The Trust had never purchased a piece of property outright, and not everyone belonging to the Trust would be in favor. Some cared not at all about such things, and Hoffnagle had to continually juggle them with those who really believed in preservation—between 10 and 25 percent of the members, he reckoned—and those who wanted only big tax deductions. One donor habitually claimed deductions to which he wasn't even entitled, and told Hoffnagle, "If I'm not audited by the feds every year, I know I'm not claiming enough."

These people included Andy Beckstoffer, owner of more vineyards in Napa, Lake, and Mendocino counties than any single individual. All the easements Beckstoffer had granted—and received tax deductions for—would never have been developed anyway, but such was the law. Here was a chance for Beckstoffer to really step up.

The hunting club's longtime member Paul Woodworth had been granted sole negotiating rights, and he agreed to let representatives of the Land Trust into Wildlake. They traveled in separate cars—John Hoffnagle, Randy, Denis Sutro, heir to the wealth of Adolph Heinrich Sutro, mayor of San Francisco at the end of the nineteenth century, and another member. During Randy's tour Hoffnagle sat on the edge of his seat, unable to stop saying, "Oh my God, look at this. Oh my God . . . Oh my *God* . . ."

Wildlake, if preserved, would create a contiguous wilderness corridor that could eventually link up an expanded Robert Louis Stevenson State Park and comprise thirteen thousand acres. It contained some of the most diverse plant and wildlife in the United States, a bona fide Mediterranean-type floristic province with its eastern-most population of redwoods and a crucial area of study for those tracking the effects of global warming. If preserved, so also would be the striking view from the valley floor for people who mostly had no idea what they were looking up at, but loved and were inspired by it nonetheless.

But somebody had to lead on this, providing not just an argument but also an example, to inspire others to give. The Land Trust would contribute, and manage the transaction, but it had other financial obligations already. And Hoffnagle wasn't at all sure the Land Trust could bring it off in just six months. If so, it would be a record.

They got out of the cars deep in Wildlake and stood around an ancient fire pit, near the ruins of the homestead. Sutro asked Randy, "If the Land Trust is going to take this step, what'll you do to help?"

Randy said, "I'm in for five. I'll take out a loan and hand it over to you."

"Come on, Randy." Sutro was annoyed. "Five what?"

"Million."

And John Hoffnagle muttered, "Holy shit."

It was insane, he thought. Floored by both the generosity and offhand way Randy had said it, he got back in the car with Sutro. He could tell that he, too, was moved, and they rode back to the entrance in stunned silence. Hoffnagle wasn't given to superlatives, but Randy Dunn had just become, with one deft move, his hero: the perfect donor.

Randy locked the gate behind them and came over and tapped on Hoffnagle's window. He lowered it.

"John," Randy said, "if I give you five million dollars, do I get a key?"

3.

Marc Mondavi had been out of town and when he finally heard about the pending sale he "hit the ceiling," according to a participant in the many conversations that followed. He also threatened to sue individual club members for "messing with his rights." The real clash, though, was yet to come.

A dinner was scheduled at Tre Vigne, the still-fashionable restaurant in St. Helena owned by Bill Harlan, to bring club members together with representatives of the Land Trust board. When John Hoffnagle arrived he noticed that both Marc Mondavi and Paul Woodworth had been drinking wine and that a dispute over Wildlake had already begun between them. It turned into a full-blown "dustup," got even worse—and louder—and Hoffnagle decided it was time to go home. The goodwill breaking of bread among members of the hunting club and the Land Trust never took place.

Randy started approaching people he knew who could afford to donate, and some he didn't. They surprised him with their generosity. An outspoken denizen of Howell Mountain, Betty O'Shaughnessy, resisted at first. She owned a house and vineyard on the road that led to Wildlake—her name had been cut into the steel gate with a laser cutter—and Randy and his friend and tennis opponent, Mike Hackett, another pilot, "two-timed" Betty, first one calling her and then the other, until finally she told Randy, "Okay, two-fifty."

"Two hundred and fifty dollars?"

Betty laughed. "Two hundred and fifty thousand."

Koerner Rombauer, a pilot and the son of Irma Rombauer of cookbook fame and fortune, owned a winery down on the Silverado Trail and was a member in good standing of the GONADs, the acronym for the exclusive eating club otherwise known as the Gastronomic Order of the Nonsensical and Dissipatory. His oaky chardonnay had made a lot of money, but what he and Randy really had in common was flying. Rombauer agreed to let Randy show him around Wildlake in an all-terrainer, and without ever leaving the vehicle said, "I'm in."

"Don't you want to walk around?"

"Naw, I get it." And he did—to the tune of a million dollars.

Yet another pilot and close friend of Randy's, Gordon Burns, owner of a wine analysis lab down in St. Helena, gave half a million. Then Larry Turley of zinfandel fame, brother of cult winemaker Helen Turley, vinous consultant to people with very expensive wines like Jayson Pahlmeyer and Bill Harlan, took Randy's call. He listened to Randy's pitch, which went on until at last Turley said, "Okay, Randy, I'm going to sit down right now and write a check."

Soon John Hoffnagle was receiving a fax from Turley at the Land Trust office. The paper had dark blotches on it that Hoffnagle realized was spilled wine, and it affirmed the fact that Larry Turley, too, was donating a million dollars.

Hoffnagle was doing the same thing among his contacts, and writing grant proposals to organizations that might chip in. He got a pledge of five million each from the Gordon and Betty Moore Foundation and the David and Lucile Packard Foundation, and two million dollars from the California State Coastal Conservancy. Some days brought as many as thirty checks, mostly small ones. The total rose, but the fund was still in touch-and-go land.

Then Paul Woodworth telephoned Hoffnagle with bad news: He had only six votes among hunting club members, and he needed eight for a majority if the sale was to succeed. Holdout members wanted more, but there wasn't more to offer. So Hoffnagle offered to raise the price a symbolic $100,000, and throw in an additional five years of hunting rights after the sale went through. That did it.

People had said they couldn't put together a $20 million campaign in six months, and they had. Sterling Vineyards created a special Wildlake label—merlot—in celebration, and offered to donate profits from its sale to the fund. Sterling also staged a gala, in midsummer 2006, and most of the donors came.

From the deck of Sterling's monastic white winery you could see Wildlake on the far side of the valley, high above, a vision half terrestrial, half celestial. "What the Land Trust has been able to do is go above and beyond the call in preserving all this land," said Napa County supervisor Diane Dillon. It was to be called the Dunn-Wildlake Preserve. Then she and another supervisor, Brad Wagenknecht, declared this a "Land Trust of Napa County Day."

Lori and Randy looked on from their seats at the head table. John Hoffnagle rose to praise them both, and to recognize Randy as the force behind the creation of the largest contiguous protected landscape in Napa County. Others stood to thank the Dunns for the single most generous conservation act in the valley's history, and the setting aside of the largest single wilderness parcel.

Some response was called for, but since Randy couldn't do it without crying, Lori stood up. She told of her husband's riding in Wildlake with Jenny, and of how much the memories and the place meant to them both. Randy just sat there with his hands folded on the white tablecloth, sun-braised cheeks slick with tears, grinning.

One morning, in the grass beside the horse paddock, Randy found a young bird. It was either a crow or raven, he couldn't tell which, and had fallen from a nest. He put on work gloves and picked it up. The noise the bird made seemed certain to bring angry parents, but didn't. So he took it back to the house and called a wildlife expert he knew, who told him to mix oatmeal, pablum, and egg yolks. The bird gulped it from the spoon.

Randy called it Raycrow and very soon it was flying to their bedroom window every morning to wake them up, and then around to the back door for breakfast. Later, Randy led Raycrow out into the field and showed it how to dig for worms and insects. Most days Raycrow perched high in a Douglas fir beside the house, and when Randy appeared would swoop down at tremendous speed, flare at the last moment, and land on Randy's shoulder. Raycrow loved to fly, as Randy did, and he admired Raycrow's agility.

Once Raycrow joined a flock of crows at the bottom of the property. When all the birds took off, Randy whistled and Raycrow peeled off and returned and landed on his shoulder. Late that same afternoon Randy saw the bird standing placidly on the back of the big quarter horse, Velvet, in the middle of the paddock. Randy went in to dinner and to bed, and the next morning Raycrow was gone.

Randy walked in the woods, whistling, to no avail. He put notices in neighbors' mailboxes asking if they had seen the bird, but no one had. Whenever crows passed over, Randy looked up and whistled, to no avail. He never saw Raycrow again.

Velvet was a horse the girls had often ridden double behind Randy. Sometimes he thought about that.

CHAPTER TWELVE:

The Death of Shame

*The pastoral idea of America had . . . provided a clear sanction
for the conquest of the wilderness . . . But no one, not
even Jefferson, had been able to identify the point of arrest.*
—Leo Marx, *The Machine in the Garden*

1.

Since the United States Geological Survey never formally recognized the Howell Mountains, they should have fallen off maps of Napa Valley long ago. Other names—the Vacas, a lesser chain bordering the Suisun Valley in what's now Solano County, and in Spanish times the interchangeable Sierra de Suscol and Sierra de Napa—were also in common use. But the Howells hung on, maybe through the force of personality of their namesake, John Howell, a shadowy figure who started the valley's first blacksmith shop in St. Helena in 1856.

The Howells hook up at the top of the valley and form a vortex with the southwest-trending Mayacamas, a lusher range that still outshines its droughty eastern cousin in social cachet, if not in terroir, lofting the eye and the imagination toward Sonoma and the Pacific Ocean.

The Howells are the last wall between the valley proper and the vastness of the rest of the United States. Its soils are mostly silica found in rhyolite tuffs and breccias—broken rock segments cemented together by heat or pressure—and there's also basalt lava, serpentine, sedimentary rock, and volcanic gravels washed down in the stream beds. But few nutrients, which means it isn't suitable for many crops other than vines. It stresses them, and their fruit is said to evince more character and depth of flavor than grapes grown down in the loamy valley. This has led to the outsized popularity of Howell Mountain cabernet sauvignon at the end of the twentieth century, and of vineyards on the steep slopes even though the viticulture's arduous.

The confusion of terrains is greatest at the northern end, just shy of Mount St. Helena, where plunging canyons, obsidian cliffs, hillsides too steep for any ATV, and impenetrable, protracted stands of mixed chaparral and manzanita overhang gin-clear seeps. Creeks flow in the dense shadows of rock, oak, Douglas fir, and redwoods, often inaccessible except on foot and occasionally horseback, when the rider is pitched forward in the saddle and keenly aware of exposed geology and the proximity of the mostly unseen: the bears, deer, coyotes, and mountain lions Lori Dunn worried about during the fire.

The northern boundary of Wildlake remained inviolate for years. Some vineyard development occurred on the road in, removed from the wilderness boundary and in another watershed. But at the same time, with the number of Napa wineries now approaching five hundred and the valley floor planted out, new vineyards were going in anywhere legal, and sometimes not—on mountaintops and strips of land deemed plantable by vineyard managers and their consultants. These all worked for aspiring wine squires who might once have considered this too backcountry but now couldn't seem to live without it, particularly when their right to do with land whatever they pleased was challenged by neighbors and, increasingly rarely, by the county itself.

Ironically, Howell Mountain was significant in part because of the hardscrabble success Randy Dunn had wrought as far back as the 1980s. Then vineyards were few and distant enough from each other to fit into a harmonious whole, viticulture being just one adjunct of rural life. But now it dominated. The monied desire for coveted grapes at any cost clashed openly with communities interested in preserving a semblance of traditional landscapes and community values, and manifestations of this clash were also being felt far from Howell Mountain.

Some days, driving to the gate, Randy could see a haze of dust in the air from new construction or vineyard work south of White Cottage Road, similar enough in appearance to smoke from a nascent fire to make him pause. But it was far enough away from Wildlake so that it wouldn't disturb the enduring wholeness of a former hunting camp still functioning more or less as it had before Europeans arrived two centuries before.

That, however, was about to change.

Mike Davis grew up in San Mateo where, as he liked to tell people, "I had the genetics to succeed as a discus thrower." This he did at Indiana University Bloomington before he got into industrial marketing—sweepers, forklifts—a natural big-rig guy with pale, sleepy Jackie Gleason eyes under a big white cowboy hat.

He "liked people and still finds them fascinating"—helpful if you're selling something, including digital equipment. This led him to found Applied Computer Solutions and then "bet the farm on distributive processing when floppies and desktops had to talk to each other and Cisco and Sun Microsystems were just coming along."

Davis made a fortune from turn-of-the-century interfacing without having to know everything about everything he sold: "A great chef doesn't make the tomatoes or the steak. He just puts it all together. I'm not smart enough to write code," but smart enough to carry Sun's and others' products, "and when the Internet came along, we were ready."

He and his wife, Sandy, sometimes came up to Napa Valley "and were always asking 'what if?' " In time they bought 114 acres on the Silverado Trail and then the question became "What now?"

The answer was hiring Davie Piña to install a vineyard down on the valley floor, have the historic barn on the property moved, put up a windmill for sentimental reasons, and pay architect Howard Backen to create yet another quotidian California space. Davis had wanted a wine label of his own, too, and a life far from the grubbier aspects of the computer phenomenon, but he ended up with something that looked a lot like one of the manufacturing complexes he had left behind.

Joining the fortunate in the happy garden of aspiring vintners, Davis also named his winery eponymously and started putting together a list of far-flung Napa vineyards from which he might buy grapes with a good reputation. He also started looking for good ground of his own at high elevations. At that point he didn't know a piece existed in a more or less straight line up Howell Mountain, miles from where his new winery stood and deep within de facto wilderness.

Davis's winery site on the valley floor had for months been beset with diesel equipment designed to utterly dominate the physical world and remove those parts of it a man just doesn't *need*—trees, rocks, dirt, whatever—and shape the landscape in precise, heretofore unachievable ways. A steamroller and an earth spreader greeted would-be customers arriving before the winery was officially open trying to determine which of the three entrances off the Silverado Trail was the right one, and which of the three sprawling structures and a couple of middling ones was the winery.

What they couldn't know yet, because it hadn't been officially opened to the public, was that Davis's part of the base of Howell Mountain was being tunneled and that he had brought down from Canada a special, very expensive machine known as a "mucker." It would go into a tunnel under the drilling behemoth and remove great amounts of loose rock and earth, a wonder to behold for equipment guys. Three decades of digging into wineries' backsides had left myriad channels that, if linked, would extend all the way to Vallejo. The tunnel-planning, tunnel-building elite thrived on the nuanced ways to do a highly profitable, specialized, sometimes dangerous task, and all these tunnelers agreed that Mike Davis's mucker was the biggest goddamn mucker yet.

In the middle of the winery staging area stood the industrial-strength windmill atop a congeries of heavy timber, its long stabilizer more appropriate on a 747 and its purpose unclear. Some speculated that the windmill was a statement that, in essence, said the new winery's owner—though he had already spent an estimated $28 million—was cognizant of the need to conserve energy. Even, by implication—though this was stretching it—that he believed carbon emissions caused by power plants contributed to, well, if not global warming then to excessive amounts of stuff in the air.

On weekends Mike Davis came to the winery in Levi's, plaid shirt, and the cowboy hat to see what still needed doing. He described himself as "a nitpicker in a blue serge suit factory." He had the ability to spot people on the periphery of his vision and figure out what they were coming to see him about before they got there. He liked to have ongoing staff meetings about every aspect of the new winery that one participant said "could have been figured out in ten minutes by two guys with a pad and pencil."

Of all the things dominating his stretch of the Silverado, Davis most liked his old Sevier barn, a towering testament to agriculture that had been "walked" some distance from where it originally stood by removing the walls one at a time with huge cranes. It was then bolted to a new concrete foundation, elaborately retrofitted for earthquakes, and given a freestanding iron fireplace made in a blacksmith's shop that was interesting but had nothing in common with what the old barn once contained. It was burnished with implements made by the installer that had no purpose, but looked old and authentic and made visitors speculate about what they might have been used for.

By the fall of 2015 Mike Davis had six months to go until his winery was complete and his vineyard regimen set. His winemaker now drew mostly from the other vineyards with which Davis had contracts, and from a couple of his own. One of his many consultants, hired to find and help develop new sites, had found a new vineyard prospect way up on Howell Mountain: about forty acres total, with only thirteen or so acres suitable for vines. Big trees would have to be cut, the ground ripped to remove boulders, and soil moved around to create a viable site.

There was no connection to Pacific Gas and Electric out there in the middle of nowhere, but Mike Davis bought it on the consultant's advice, as he was wont to do. All the effort would be worth it, the consultant told him, and that was good enough for him. The site could be hyped by a publicist as primo Howell Mountain terroir for cabernet sauvignon. The wine would go into barrels branded with the Mike Davis name, as were so many flat surfaces at his new winery down on the Trail, and he would be set, reputation-wise.

Mike would later claim to have never heard of Wildlake, Napa Valley's premier stretch of wilderness right next to the acres he wanted to develop with all the mechanical resources at hand to clear, rip, densely fill with rootstock, and surround with high fencing in hopes of keeping out not just deer but also bears. If his consultant had heard of Wildlake, or the story behind its creation, this either went unmentioned to his client or, if it was mentioned, the fluctuating team of advisors involved in every decision at Davis Vineyards dismissed it as irrelevant.

The economics associated with the prospective vineyard are instructive, in light of what eventually happened. The value of the land with trees in place was about $600,000 but would rise to an estimated $2.8 million with a vineyard installed. A dozen acres of vineyard would cost about $1.2 million to install, and after some maturity the grapes produced could be expected to fetch about $30,000 if sold to someone else. Converted to wine, their value would jump to about $1.5 million, minus additional costs.

The stakes were utterly different here than for Rich Salvestrin down on the valley floor. His vineyard and small winery were a true family operation, instead of a common marketing device. The Salvestrins' lives and livelihood depended on Salvestrin grapes and wine, not on a fortune in electronics or some other distant endeavor. For Davis, profit to be made on thirteen acres wrenched into vineyard in questionable, fragile terrain was a barely existent point of light out there somewhere. But profit wasn't the point, brand was. Howell Mountain cabernet would symbolically enhance Davis wine, whatever it actually tasted like. And the remoteness of Wildlake's environs would add to the wine's cachet, the vineyard a jewel in a new diadem that was antithetical to wilderness; it might, with luck, help distinguish the label among the collective bling of new brands.

But before he could do any of this, he needed a timber harvest permit from the California Department of Forestry and Fire Protection, aka Cal Fire, famous—or notorious, depending on your point of view—for allowing the cutting of timber, salable or not.

2.

Karin Troedsson's problem was unique, or so it seemed to her that bright morning turning into the dirt driveway high in Chiles Valley, tributary to the Napa Valley. This nineteenth-century farmstead had belonged to a German immigrant who had a built a house befitting the sea captain that he was—square-framed, broad front porch, a fine but not spectacular view of vegetable garden and vines and the steep, undisturbed hillside across the road, dense with oaks, Douglas firs, and digger pines.

This had been the home of Napa's long-standing environmental advocate Volker Eisele. He was the late author of the celebrated—and despised—Measure J, a law that required any proposal by the county to change land-use regulations, or to grant exceptions to individuals, be subjected to a referendum vote by the people. Volker had died of a stroke earlier in the year, leaving a lacuna at the top of the county's environmental ranks, and his widow, Liesel, had offered the use of her front porch for a forum she thought Volker would have approved of.

The group had already begun to gather in the shade of the old vine heavy with ripening blue-black table grapes. Karin was the attorney for the Land Trust of Napa County and today must perform simultaneous, seemingly irreconcilable duties: preserve the Land Trust's reputation as an unbiased arbiter in matters of vineyard development and protect its largest single holding now threatened with full-scale disruption on its eastern border. The block of sequestered wilderness was Wildlake, and the prospective developer Mike Davis.

This was no mom-and-pop, do-it-yourself operation, but the full-court industrial press: felling trees, dynamiting and ripping earth, extracting boulders, shifting soil from one side to the other, burying water lines, installing a wind machine, and stringing steel trellising with miles of wire.

Costs were all prospective, and all high. One vineyard developer working at altitude in the same range to the south had charged a client between $40,000 and $250,000 an acre "depending on the rock," of which there's much. "We used a lot of dynamite, rock crushers, and big iron. The tree part isn't too expensive, but because you can't just burn everything, the chipping or hauling of stumps is expensive, too."

So are fences, gates, ongoing roadwork, and road use taking months with the toing and froing of dozens of workers, vineyard managers, assistants. Digging successful wells at that altitude for irrigation could cost as much as $100,000 apiece. The dust would be more or less continuous and, as with vineyard runoff in perpetuity, would end up in Bell Canyon or some other reservoir far below. By then the trees would be mostly gone and the land unrecognizable to those who once thought they knew it.

The Land Trust's membership, like many institutions, was neatly split between distinct factions. One wanted to preserve land for its own sake, as a refuge for wildlife and human beings in the future, a dedication that required no further explanation in the land of John Muir. The other faction cared for little other than tax deductions that came to those who gave up development rights on their land in perpetuity. The tension between them was, if muted, real.

Some members took deductions for land that would never have been developed anyway, because of its rare ability to produce extremely valuable grapes, or because it was by nature undevelopable. In some cases this was, if not an outright scam, a close approximation. At best it was hypocritical to the Muir faction, which had included Volker Eisele before his death. He and Liesel had put the entire hillside visible from the porch on the other side of Chiles Valley Road into a conservation easement. Though they had taken the deduction, no single house and tiered garden would ever be carved into that fragile terrain, even though allowed. Volker had insisted he was placing the easement on the land for the right reasons, as a preserver of it, not a tax evader.

Tall and slim, Karin wore jeans—it was the weekend—and her straight reddish hair touched her shoulders as she took a chair and opened her briefcase. She took out a sheet of paper on which she had jotted down the reasons the Land Trust was concerned about the creation of Mike Davis's thirteen-acre vineyard on Howell Mountain. Also at the table were Randy Dunn and next to him Mike Hackett, a retired airline pilot and a once-ranked tennis player as well as the director of Save Rural Angwin, a grassroots organization with a range of conservation objectives. He and Randy had been tennis partners until Randy damaged his hips and had to swap his racket for a bicycle, but they remained friends.

Next came a representative of the Sierra Club in round glasses reminiscent of the fiery suffragette from Prohibition days, then a slim, well-dressed, dark-haired woman named Christina from California Fisheries and Water Unlimited, an anti-logging group. And just taking chairs were Leonore and Jim Wilson, she a poet and he a former quality assurance manager at the Budweiser brewery in Fairfield. Both were foes of the gargantuan development project to the south, known as Walt Ranch, proposed for bucolic little Capell Creek where they lived.

Alan Galbraith, recently elected mayor of St. Helena, arrived in a dress shirt without a tie and suit trousers left over from his former life as a Washington lawyer, his thinning white hair combed back. Then came Geoff Ellsworth in his fly-fishing vest. In the past the group might also have included Hugh Davies, president of Schramsberg Vineyards directly across the valley from the Davis Estates, but Hugh's fight with Citizens' Voice over the Davies Vineyards expansion in St. Helena had vastly complicated environmental politics.

Hugh had been close to Volker and one of the last people to see him alive, driving up to Chiles Valley following Volker's stroke and finding him seated in the living room with a blanket spread on his lap, surrounded by books in German—Goethe, Mann, Rilke. Hugh had held his hand while Volker tried to speak, but he wasn't able to, leaving Hugh and others wondering what final wisdom this veteran organizer had so valiantly tried to voice.

Also expected on the Eisele front porch—ardently hoped for, actually—was a Sonoma County activist named Rick Coates, of Forest Unlimited, the take-no-prisoners advocate of trees. Coates's political legerdemain was said to border upon wizardry. He regularly went after Cal Fire, which despite its firefighting capabilities was the bête noire of environmental and conservation groups trying to save trees everywhere, from the Pacific to the High Sierra and from the Mexican border to Oregon.

Rick was said to have all the moves, and his reputation as an enigmatic, effective force preceded him wherever he went. He had been informed of Napa's problem by phone, but his appearance today was more hoped for than assured, the drive from Sonoma long and arduous and, this being a Saturday, traffic-plagued. "He said he'd come," said Christina brightly, "for the cost of a tank of gas."

On the table sat a hard cheese, rarely seen before at the Eiseles' because Volker had detested cheese of any kind. As a child he had been fed it while in foster care in Nazi Germany, and he never got over the experience. There were crackers, too, and grapes from the overhead vine, plus stemmed glasses next to a bottle of the Eisele Estate's syrah rosé.

Hackett, spreading his hands to include everyone, said, "We're here because Mike Davis spent twenty-eight million dollars on a winery on the Silverado Trail, with a modern windmill, caves, and what he hopes will be grapes from Howell Mountain. He plans to clear-cut a thirty-odd-acre parcel on the edge of Wildlake. The cumulative effects would be very damaging to the Bell Canyon Reservoir, and to the wilderness. We want to stop it."

The discussion that followed was typical of struggles in the organizational phase: statements of allegiance, bona fides, accomplishments, interests in this battle about to start, suggestions. These included bringing peer pressure to bear on Davis, and possible legal steps by the Land Trust to block the vineyard. Karin pointed out that the Trust had never before opposed—or supported—a land development project, "but Napa Valley is one of the biodiversity hot spots in the United States," and Wildlake was a prime part of the mix. "It would be amazing if the Land Trust said that, even though we have someone trying to develop there, we wouldn't object. We don't have any choice."

Uneasy about it all, she added, "We've been Switzerland"—meaning neutral in Napa's long-standing land-use hostilities—"for so long. And we still have to be sensitive about our image, so we can crawl back into our role as protector of land when this is finally over."

Mike Hackett went through a litany of possible ways to put off the decision by Cal Fire in order to allow more information, and opposition, to surface: extend deadlines for hearings on timber harvest and the environmental impact study, stress the deleterious impact on St. Helena's drinking water, which already had a significant algal problem as temperatures rose each year, and build opposition through media by publicizing the impact on birds, primarily nesting.

Someone offered to come up with a list of migratories, and another for special plants and animals. The western pond turtle was a star among threatened species, present in Wildlake. And make clear that crucial wildlife corridors, planned for decades between Howell Mountain and Mount

St. Helena, would be disrupted. Randy added laconically, "There'll be a lot of bears in that vineyard," and the reality of what would happen to them was abhorrent.

"Shaming" was discussed as a possible way to force a person to reconsider a choice that would clearly be destructive of both nature and community. And no better way to shame than to bring influential people like Land Trust board members forward who might speak to Davis.

"Noise and poor air quality are huge issues," Randy said. "We're talking fifty to a hundred guys coming in every day, twenty cars back and forth on a gravel road. They'll spread invasive plants." He had called Mike Davis, he added. "I wanted to tell him I thought he could put the property in easement and still come out ahead." Davis got back in touch, thanked Randy, and said he was going to see the project through.

"Maybe if he sees the light," said Karin, "he'll get us out of this nightmare."

A small, well-used sedan came up the Eiseles' driveway, passed the massive oak, and parked under the linden trees. A rail-like figure in running shoes got out. He had a white beard and white hair held in a ponytail by a rubber band, and he carried a manila envelope: Rick Coates.

After introductions he took the last chair, sipped some water, and ate a grape. Karin told him, "We've asked Mike Davis for meetings but gotten no response."

Coates asked how far along the whole project was, and Hackett said, "About thirty million dollars' worth," upping the estimate a bit.

"This guy's not worried about making a profit," added Randy.

"No, he just wants to win." Coates's smile was rueful. "Winning stimulates this type like nothing else."

One recourse was to challenge the timber-cutting permit, he suggested. "Always remember that the California Department of Forestry is not your friend. Ask for permission to cut trees, and they'll say 'May we sharpen your saws for you?' " It was a familiar joke. "I only know of one harvest plan that's ever failed to get approved. The best thing to do is try to blunt the official comments with denials, buy more time, and eventually get into court."

He opened the envelope and took out a sheaf of paper. "These are copies of a step-by-step outline for opponents of Cal Fire's review system. Environmental comments are unlikely to stop this, but submitting different drafts can slow the process. You can win lawsuits on procedure, so delay as much as possible" so the agency will make a misstep and open itself to legal challenge. "They hate losing in court."

After the meeting broke up Randy offered to take Rick Coates to see Wildlake, and he agreed. They drove over Howell Mountain from Pope Valley, and Randy took him deep into wilderness that had the same effect on Coates that it had had on John Hoffnagle. As they shook hands afterward, Randy felt that he and the others had an ally with the knowledge and experience to get this thing stopped.

3.

The next day Randy was to telephone individual members of the Land Trust board and remind them of an extraordinary meeting being held by the board about whether or not to challenge Mike Davis in court. If they did challenge him it would cost money, and possibly split the membership.

Karin wouldn't give Randy individual Land Trust members' cell numbers because she hadn't been authorized to do so. Such were the intricate steps in the long, close-up dance of environmental opposition, particularly in the crucial early stages when large egos and large fortunes are at play. Randy understood that she was taking no chances, waiting to see if the field broke open and some light beckoned. Karin repeated, "I'm worried about the Land Trust's reputation. We've never taken a position before on land development," and hung up.

"This time," Randy thought, "you'll have to."

He found some members' numbers by calling the tasting rooms of wineries the members owned, and having to deal with women no older than his daughter Krissy. Most had never heard of this old-timer telling them "I'm looking for . . . ," as if just anybody could get the phone number of the proprietor in the exalted firmament of vintners, and provided little help. He continued calling while making salsa from the proliferation of bright red tomatoes piled next to the sink—lumpy heirlooms and other varieties, all awaiting the knife. Already cut up were onions and peppers—Anaheims, jalapeños—and these, too, were periodically fed into the blender, puree all over, and Lori driven from the house by the mess.

Cradling the old landline receiver with a shoulder, Randy wrote down one hard-earned number and then punched it in. "I want you to be aware of . . . ," he said to the man who answered, and launched into a description of the mayhem Mike Davis might wreak on Wildlake. "There's no way really to measure how much physical effort and energy would go into this development," Randy said, "but it's huge."

The pot on the stove burped and spat, and he turned down the heat while he talked. Two-thirds of the volume of the potential sauce must boil away, carefully watched all the while so the bottom doesn't burn and spoil the flavor. The member's voice finally emerged from the speaker: He couldn't make the meeting, he said. He was sorry. "Since you're not going to be there," Randy said quickly, "maybe you could tell some other members."

At last he punched in what he and Karin thought was the most important number of all, that of a former board member who possibly owned the largest acreage under vines of any individual in three counties, Andy Beckstoffer. Despite being a Republican who put business before most other things, Beckstoffer had been on the right side of environmental skirmishes for decades and a significant contributor to the Land Trust. His attentions were desired in this fight.

Randy had known Andy for decades, during which they had found themselves thrown together at Land Trust and other events. Now Randy told him that he and the Trust's attorney were hoping Andy would call Mike Davis directly and let him know the depth and social complexity of the project into which Davis was about to step. It was a yellow jackets' nest, and disapproval would follow, possibly ruining his reputation before he ever got established in the valley.

Andy knew vineyards and could speak to the drawbacks of what some considered to be Davis's potential frost pocket on Howell Mountain. Also one that would disastrously impact a hard-won wilderness that had its own broad, enthusiastic band of defenders. Beckstoffer knew the complex loyalties among growers, vintners, and a broad cadre of professions dependent on them; he could authoritatively point out various reasons Davis might want to reconsider. Back off from Wildlake was the message, choose a Howell Mountain vineyard site somewhere else, like the one Randy had suggested on good land near the college in Angwin. Let Wildlake be.

Beckstoffer agreed to make the call. "But I want somebody on the Trust board to call and ask me." More protocol. "And I can't do it today." Beckstoffer was on his way up to his vineyards in Lake County and, because fire had closed the roads, was swinging far to the west so he could drive up the coast.

If Beckstoffer made the call, it didn't have the desired effect. But by then the Land Trust had decided to take a stand; the fight had gone public.

Since Alan Galbraith had recently been elected mayor of St. Helena he was still finding his way around the small-town bureaucracy. Many of his constituents knew he had been an attorney in Washington, DC, before retiring and moving west with his wife in 2008. Few knew just how large and influential his firm, Williams & Connolly, had been, or that he belonged to a socially prominent New England family well known in academia and politics.

Visitors to the Galbraiths' shady residence in St. Helena saw the array of carved wooden elephants lining the mantelpiece and were likely to assume that Galbraith was a dedicated Republican. A few knew that Alan's father had been the distinguished liberal economist and author John Kenneth Galbraith, as well as a close friend of William F. Buckley, and President Kennedy's ambassador to India, where the carvings had originated.

A member of the California bar, Alan Galbraith had come west often on business and married into the Coombs family, with its long-standing involvement in county affairs, including the founding of the city of Napa.

Alan put time in on the St. Helena planning commission and backed responsible growth, which meant restraints on projects that might significantly alter the town's character, like short-term rentals that could be destructive of neighborhoods. So elephants on the mantel weren't necessarily a key to unlocking Alan Galbraith's politics.

He had left the meeting on the front porch of the Eiseles' house in Chiles Valley concerned. The following Monday he asked the city engineer what he thought about the proposed timber cutting high on Howell Mountain. The city engineer didn't like the sound of it. The downstream Bell Canyon Reservoir that supplied the city didn't need more sediment from on high. St. Helenans still remembered when the Viader Vineyards, under the same sort of development proposed by Mike Davis, had dumped sediment into the reservoir after a heavy rain a dozen years before. The fallout from that calamity had been considerable, and both officials were afraid it could happen again.

The city engineer wrote a letter to Cal Fire asking for a delay in granting the permit, and so did Mayor Galbraith. The city had just enough income to cover services, but nothing was set aside for a disaster like the loss of good freshwater for the town.

After wrestling with the specter of discord within the Land Trust—and a possibly damaged reputation beyond it—Karin Troedsson had decided to defend its largest, most arduously acquired, incomparable holding, Wildlake. She contacted the seasoned warhorse of environmental campaigns, the drolly named Shute, Mihaly & Weinberger in San Francisco, the favorite law firm of the late Volker Eisele and other activists who had been involved in the winery definition fight, Measure J, and other significant battles. She wanted a good letter of protest from a seasoned litigator, and hoped that would be enough, for there was a large difference between sending such a cautionary letter and the actual filing of a lawsuit. This was something Karin had no intention of doing, if Mike Davis refused to back off, but Randy Dunn, she felt sure, would.

With remarkable alacrity, Karin thought, the firm sent to Cal Fire's chief forester in Sacramento, and to the head of Cal Fire's Northern Region in Santa Rosa, a thirty-three-page tour de force that bristled with acronyms and dismantled the agency's argument that the trees could be legally cut:

> The most fundamental flaw in these documents is their failure to comply with these laws' mandates to provide an accurate account of the environmental setting . . . the Property lies within a regionally significant, 12,000-acre wildland complex that includes lands managed by California State Parks, the California State Lands Commission, the Bureau of Land Management, the Land Trust, and the Biological Field Studies Association. Despite this fact, the DEIR [Draft Environmental Impact Report], TCP [Timber Conversion Plan], and the THP [Timber Harvest Plan] all give the incorrect impression that the Project sits in a predominately agricultural area, and improperly attempt to minimize the conservation value of the surrounding lands.

The arguments, though long and complex, seemed irrefutable. But what California's greens like Rick Coates knew—and many latecomers to this fight would soon learn—was that Cal Fire could be indifferent to moral, aesthetic, social, environmental, and even legal arguments opposing timber cutting that did not seem certain to prevail in court. Particularly when, for other reasons—like crushing expense—the arguments were unlikely to ever get there.

Karin also wrote to the agency. "For the first time in our 40-year history, The Land Trust of Napa County is submitting the enclosed comment letter regarding a pending application for vineyard development . . . as a concerned neighbor that abuts this proposed project . . . [the] Timber Conversion Plan improperly indicated that The Land Trust does not object to their application, and we feel an obligation to publicly correct that misrepresentation."

Within days Davis sent out a letter of his own urging a select fifty of the Napa Valley Vintners members to copy, sign, and pass it along to Cal Fire on the last day of public comment. "I have reviewed all 900 pages of documentation and found nothing that should stop your approving this project," Davis wrote, revealing either a lack of awareness of the valley's past land-use struggles or a calculated decision to ignore them. He hadn't mentioned Wildlake, or the overlay of historical, social, and environmental issues involved, and had wrapped the project in what sounded to many like Tea Party rhetoric: "In the United States we have a distinction between public and private lands just so projects like Davis Estates' can move forward."

Davis concluded: "Here are just a few of the now famous Napa hillside wines: Mayacamas, Stony Hill, Harlan Estate, Bond, Dana, Ovid, Continuum, Ladera, Joseph Phelps, Outpost, Cade, Diamond Creek, Pride and Dunn. Who's to say that Davis Estates Friesen Vineyard"—the proposed name—"won't be the next new worldwide 'cult' wine that brings attention and revenue to the Napa Valley wine industry?"

Reading that, Karin Troedsson concluded that peer pressure was no longer a viable means of bringing people into line with the common good. Others who read it went further, suggesting that shame was dead. For Rick Coates, it was notable that Mike Davis had been a discus thrower, and he concluded that for Davis the real pleasure lay not in the feel of the discus itself, or in the throwing, but in the distance thrown and winning. That's what this was all about.

Rick Coates, after explaining the inconsistencies, obfuscations, and outright dishonesty of Cal Fire, sometimes felt like an ancient oral historian. Others thought of him as a character in a Sophoclean tragedy, declaiming on the action of a cruel and arbitrary god. What he had to say to largely powerless citizens like Mike Hackett and Randy Dunn sounded, if read aloud, like tortured verse rising from the cinders of bureaucracy's cremation site:

> Only after the recommendation for approval is made does
> Cal Fire read and respond to public comment.

> This is an exercise only to satisfy the legal requirement to
> respond.

Employees assigned to read the comments have a list of standard responses.

The responses attempt to justify the department's decision.

The "science" quoted is either junk, cherry-picked, or discredited.

Legitimate research is distorted, misrepresented . . .

The entire process is fraudulent.

Coates could have compared these points to Thomas Jefferson's about the arbitrary and unjust actions regarding the American colonies by King George III, written early in Jefferson's political career and underlying much of the reasoning behind the later Declaration of Independence. Coates knew the science was "junk" because he had taken the time to read the articles quoted and, having done research himself, knew the difference between good and bad.

If Cal Fire employees encountered a comment suggesting they had made a legal error, they would halt the process, attempt to correct the error, and then reopen the Timber Harvest Plan to public comment for ten days. Every time they had to do this they got more annoyed and prone to making mistakes.

Coates also knew that the Cal Fire recommendation would eventually end up on the deputy director's desk, and that he would sign it on behalf of the director, a pro forma arrangement unless there was a serious political price to pay. Which was why these citizens had to figure out a way to get Wildlake before the public, and soon. Time was running out.

V.

CAPELL CREEK

A landscape is to be transformed against the wishes of those living in it, and corporate and environmental advocates clash with an intensity not seen before.

INTERLUDE:

Arise!

The board of supervisors is meeting in a new venue off Corporate Drive south of the city of Napa, instead of downtown where a recent earthquake damaged the county administration building and left the historic courthouse in plastic-shrouded rehab and side streets full of rubble. The hearing in progress concerns the controversial project involving vineyards and maybe houses on steep hillsides where water is scarce and roads narrow.

Signs on sticks are in mostly middle-aged hands—SAVE OUR WATER, SAVE 28,616 TREES, FORESTS = HEALTHY AIR, and my favorite, WATER OVER WINE, a succinct summation with biblical resonance. If that's really the choice then the answer's obvious but, as with everything having to do with the environment, it's also devilishly complicated and ways to ameliorate or bypass restrictions almost infinite.

People come to the podium one at a time to voice displeasure and regret for loss of oaks, productive wells, habitat, and community. A grape grower, channeling Jefferson, says, "Agriculture's the highest and best use of the land. Let's keep it that way." He points out that recent legislative changes have allowed event centers at wineries, part of every new business plan now. They mean more traffic, more arable land taken out of production, more demand for water and waste disposal, and more pollution. Vintners who praised preservation of agricultural land when applying for permits, and agreed to abide by current law, now can't live without an event center.

"We have a diminishing quality of life," says another speaker in a down vest. "We've lost our way, people are talking of leaving." The familiar activist Chris Malan stands to say, "I'm lucky to live here, but do we want to continue to strip our land? It's a moral question," and gets applause.

The project under consideration is the Walt Ranch high on the eastern side of the valley, 2,300 acres, of which about five hundred will be "disturbed," meaning cleared, and three hundred of those are to be put under vines. The fear is that houses will soon follow, vineyards having become stalking horses for serial McMansions and more ambitious development.

The Walt property belongs to Craig Hall, a former owner of the Dallas Cowboys but primarily a developer and a significant player with extensive connections in Texas. He's also a "vintner," the symbolic term evoking wine and history that once softened commerce's sharp elbows, but no more. Though relatively few vintners actually make wine, winery owning is assigned roughly the same cachet as collecting art, and the Halls do that, too, much of the latter reportedly from Eastern Europe where during the second Clinton administration Kathryn Hall was ambassador to Austria.

She's a Democrat and friend of Bill, but her husband's political beliefs, like most things about him, are ambiguous. They are among the wealthiest couples in a valley known for them, and Kathryn—an attractive woman in tasteful white knit—drove to this meeting in her familiar blue Porsche roadster with the khaki-colored top. I approach and ask her if she'll discuss the Walt project with me after the meeting.

She goes off to consult with her lawyer and her winemaker, since in recent years winemakers have come to perform increasingly ambitious lateral arabesques for their employers. Not only do winemakers tweak wines for the market, but they also serve as courtiers and confidants of vintners navigating Napa's political thickets. The former ambassadress comes back and says, "We're not going to talk about that."

Local activist Geoff Ellsworth leans against a wall, having progressed from St. Helena's issues to the county's. This morning he wears a tie and a seersucker suit, to all appearances a businessman jotting memos on a clipboard. Others in the room are, like Geoff, part of the perennial bloom of citizen activists who flare, flame out in various struggles, and flare again. They're clearly fed up with deforestation and vineyard development in the hills that demand much water, but they burn with a new intensity, and I'm struck by how many more there are than in times past. And by how much older they seem.

Geoff says softly, "Projects like these are ruining the quality of life here. One woman was just weeping. People like her are the ones most sympathetic to keeping the agricultural preserve whole, but the preserve's very existence has lulled us into thinking we're protected when we're not."

Less than two centuries ago trees grew so densely on the western ridge that a raindrop could take a week to reach the earth. It's difficult to imagine this valley as one of the southernmost reaches of the temperate rain forest that starts in Alaska, but it is. As recently as the nineteenth century grizzlies romped here, scooping salmon and steelhead from the Napa River, and its tributaries ran year-round in a paradisiacal setting brimming with groundwater and wildlife.

"We don't have defenses here against raw capitalism. It encroaches on the common welfare, adversely affecting water, air, noise, and traffic. And elected officials do nothing."

CHAPTER THIRTEEN:
The Riddled Rabbit

1.

HALL Wines sits at the south end of St. Helena, its welcoming gesture a thirty-five-foot, six thousand six hundred-pound, blindingly stainless steel rabbit leaping from among vines next to Highway 29. The sculpture is full of holes, as if its creator anticipated the chorus of public derision that fell like karmic buckshot on his creation as soon as it was unveiled. According to a book produced by the Halls its name is Bunny Foo Foo, after a character in a children's poem. Grazers in Napa vineyards are in fact hares, not rabbits, but personal choice is as sacred in California as redwoods and surfboards, and more malleable.

Earlier, the architect Frank Gehry had come up with a design for an undulant shell, a photograph of which appeared in the *New York Times* showing the famous architect and the Halls next to a maquette. It resembled a doll's mansion topped with crumpled burlap, but the Halls canceled that project without explanation. The winery that was eventually built looks more like an office building with environmentally correct accoutrements.

It is LEED certified, and in the foyer hangs a twelve-foot bespangled black satin medallion made of found material that could be titled *Elvis Dreams of Microorganisms*. Upstairs, red glass globules dangle, apparently signifying wine but looking more like plasma. The winery also boasts a tunnel lined with fancy bricks from the Habsburg Empire that the Halls brought back with them from Austria, after Kathryn's diplomatic mission for President Clinton was over.

And that's about all visitors to HALL Wines are presented with, other than a costly tasting of another overripe cabernet sauvignon reaching for cult status, and the Halls have indeed received one 100-point Parker score. The Halls cleared a trailer court from this site before they built the winery, eliminating a significant portion of St. Helena's rare affordable housing. The curious may buy their book, *A Perfect Score: The Art, Soul, and Business of a 21st-Century Winery*, from a press that also publishes Newt Gingrich and Rand Paul.

The book informs readers that "despite homegrown political complications"—citizens' complaints—"we love it here." Weekends begin when they get into their convertible with their two Cavalier King Charles Spaniels, and head toward their favorite trailhead on the outskirts of Calistoga. They hike up the hill. "The valley stretches out in front of us like a sprawling vine . . . What a fantastic way to start the day!" It's far from a property they own in the eastern sector of the county where twenty-eight thousand trees await felling.

Craig skims the surface of past financial problems in the book, mostly those related to the 2008 recession and to wine, with this aside: "Kathryn always says that *Leverage* is my middle name." Anyone wishing to know more about him, and the origins of his wealth, is left with mostly fawning stories from the Texas press and public documents. Peer into that cellar hole of corporate remainder, at the bottom of an exceedingly twisty staircase, because it's worth the effort when considering the impact Hall has had on his chosen valley, one that far exceeds the spectacle of Bunny Foo Foo.

An epileptic child, Craig Hall grew up in Ann Arbor, Michigan, "a hub for left-wing activism" according to *D* magazine, a quasi-promotional glossy out of Dallas. Craig had to take phenobarbital, a depressant, for his epilepsy and tended to get injured in sports—breaking an ankle in tryouts for high school football, breaking his nose in tryouts for baseball. While he speaks of times when he wandered alone in the woods, dreaming of being a poet or perhaps a social worker, there was an altogether different side to him: an eight-year-old who turned a half-dollar investment in soda-making syrup into a thirty-seven-dollar profit, and who later took on multiple paper routes and lied about his age to sell knives door-to-door. Craig told *D* that by the time he was a high school senior he had saved up $4,000.

He bought a scruffy rooming house and let rooms to University of Michigan students caught in an inflated rental market, then pooled two hundred dollars from fifteen acquaintances, and repeated the move.

His poetic aspirations and his early belief that business was boring and ignoble had apparently been reassessed.

Craig's parents took him to a psychiatrist because of his obsession with money. "I messed with the guy," Craig claims, telling the psychiatrist that all the images he showed Craig, in an attempt to elicit meaningful responses, reminded him of dollar bills. Craig added, "It was fun."

What's the reader to make of a boy so sure of himself that he toys with a grown medical professional? Was the kid who had wandered in the woods still there, but in the new, protective clothing of budding entrepreneur? How did the psychiatrist interpret Craig's bizarre reaction to a simple psychological test, and were his parents reassured, or distraught? Did their son care? Most striking is the distance between the savvy protagonist of this self-serving tale and the rest of foolish humanity.

Is it possible that Craig wasn't "messing" with the psychiatrist at all, but telling the truth, that everything Craig looked at *did* remind him of money?

Intent on being a millionaire, he dropped out of college. University degrees matter in Ann Arbor, but he eventually moved to Texas, where the opposite is true. By that time he had raised millions for apartment complexes near Detroit, and diversified quixotically into for-profit health care and even racquetball. But real estate was the real deal for Craig, and Dallas the place to be.

He teamed up in 1984 to buy the Dallas Cowboys from oilman Clint Murchison Jr. By then Craig and silent partners owned thousands of apartments and millions of feet of office space. They had close to five thousand employees, if *D* magazine is to be believed. They also carried huge debt. The tax shelters that had made all this possible in the first place were sensibly withdrawn by Congress in 1986, and investors wanted their money back. Craig sold his share of the Cowboys and other personal assets, but it wasn't enough.

The *New York Times* defined Craig's predicament: "The fragility of Texas' real estate market was underscored last spring when . . . Hall, once the nation's largest real estate syndicator, filed for protection under the federal bankruptcy code." Real estate syndication is the gathering of passive investors willing to risk money in buying, operating, and selling property for a lot more money, and it remains Craig Hall's real profession.

His 1992 filing for Chapter 11 protection prevented the government from seizing the rest of his assets. The Resolution Trust Corporation offered to sell him some of the mortgages his partnerships had placed with banks, but at deep discounts, so he had to raise $102.5 million in three months to bring it off. "There was a lot of blood on the table," Craig would later say, and it wasn't his. A former investor told *D*, "There was a time I'd just as soon not be behind the wheel when Craig Hall was crossing the street," implying that he would have run him down.

A reporter for the *Dallas Morning News* later wrote, "Mention the name Kathryn Hall to many in Dallas, and the universal response is a glowing smile and a kind word. But mention the name Craig Hall, and some people wince, voicing adjectives such as 'sleazy' or 'slimy.' "

Craig met Kathryn Walt Cain, a lawyer and once candidate for mayor of Dallas, and they lunched at an Indian restaurant, exotic in Dallas. Craig married her. By then he was collecting investors to buy more Dallas real estate, installing in it art that now belonged to both of them, and branching out again into unrelated ventures—oil and gas, computer software, even a blood laboratory. The Hall Office Park near Dallas was now his as well. "No one could understand why Hall was developing on farmland . . . ," said *D* magazine. "But his instincts about the path of growth were dead on." And easily transferable to Northern California.

In Napa, the former poetic, untutored dreamer would find self-realization in the amorphous role of "vintner" and a process was by now numbingly familiar: husband and wife desire a small vineyard and a few cases of wine to further enhance their lives—and set out to achieve this at any cost. With the Halls, this blossomed into something larger than most. First they bought the old Sacrashe Vineyard in the hills of east Rutherford, tunneled into the mountain, and built a showy house designed by David Schwarz just up the road from the Auberge du Soleil, where luncheon could be had overlooking a landscape suggestive of Burgundy.

Suddenly Craig Hall cared about terroir, that other kind of real estate. He bought the site of the old wine co-op south of St. Helena on the visitor feeding tube of Highway 29, which came with a grandfathered right to bottle a lot of wine, where HALL Wines would rise. And he began talking like other vintners, rhetorically asking himself if, in two hundred years, his distant Dallas real estate empire would still be there.

He answered himself: "I don't know. But Thomas Jefferson used to drink Lafite Rothschild, and I've gone over to the estate in France where they still make that wine. The idea that you can build a business that will endure over time and make a difference to people and their experiences—that's what it's all about."

Making a difference "to people and their experiences" is what real estate development and tourism are all about, not agriculture. That is hardly a premier cru sentiment, and certainly not Jeffersonian, although it is good public relations and represents the new imperative in Napa Valley: Show reverence for the past and for the future, and ruthlessly exploit the present.

2.

The assessor's records indicate that HALL Wines' LLC owns the thirty-three-acre winery site on Highway 29 valued at a measly $5,205,231, and the vineyard at an even more measly $468,364. But the structure was valued at $56,331,205, so the total, with all the fixtures thrown in, was about $80 million. Kathryn Hall wasn't new to her vintner role when the winery opened, having—with her brother—obtained an Alcohol Beverage Control Board license to manage vineyards and make wine near Ukiah, in Mendocino County. HALL Wines shares an ABC license with the Halls' smaller winery in the hills above Rutherford, bought after flipping two office towers in downtown Dallas. According to *D* magazine, Craig sold these fully leased for millions in profit.

The Halls' first winery and the house in Rutherford are owned by 199 Rutherford Associates LP, registered in Dallas. The limited partner was Mike Reynolds, variously presented over the years as HALL Wines' winemaker, general manager, president, exalted multipurposer, and finally "developer." In 2007, on the eve of recession, another entity was formed for the Rutherford property and deeded over to a new LLC, Hall 60 Auberge, also registered in Texas.

That money was rumored to have been provided by First Republic Bank, which had financed the failed Lake Luciana and Aetna Springs projects up in Pope Valley years before. Hall had already acquired the long-defunct cattle operation above Capell Creek and rechristened it Walt Ranch, but Walt Ranch was owned by neither the Walts nor the Halls, but by a company called Hall Brambletree Associates LLC, a real estate syndicate whose members typically did not have to be identified or enumerated.

Hall's intention, he said, was to plant vineyards, not to build so-called ranchettes like those going onto another of his vineyard development sites up in Alexander Valley. Mike Reynolds was in charge there, too, as well as at Walt Ranch over the mountains in eastern Napa County, long the sniffing ground of Texans.

Reynolds has an MBA from UC Berkeley and a degree in winemaking and viticulture from UC Davis, thus two-upping his boss, who has neither. Earlier, Reynolds had worked for the notoriously difficult Jess Jackson. But before that Reynolds worked in an entirely different environment—Schramsberg—as winemaker and then general manager. Within old Jacob Schram's redoubt Reynolds was known as bright and business-eager, but that he would come to sit on the board of the California Wine Institute and belong to the Young Presidents' Organization would have surprised his colleagues at that time. And likely no one at Schramsberg could have dreamed that Mike would one day end up as the partner in the wine business of a Dallas real estate developer.

Winemaking is a profession once associated with art, even nobility. But a path to wealth beginning at wine's back door had opened up. Developers might still be making themselves respectable with wine, but now winemakers could—and eagerly did—move in the opposite direction. Such an endeavor would once have been considered déclassé, but viticulture had become a gloss for almost any profitable transaction, even if in direct conflict with the vision that had inspired Jefferson and created the agricultural preserve in the first place.

The Hall Financial Group, the umbrella over Hall's various operations, registered in Texas, includes HALL Wines and WALT Wines. It apparently also provided financing to two downtown Napa boutique hotels and the Senza Hotel on the northwest side of the city of Napa, with parks, fountains, Japanese iris, boxwood, wisteria-draped arbors, and cherry trees.

An early study of Walt Ranch showed freshwater wells, eight miles of seasonal roads, and almost ten miles of hardened roads much like those Hall put in at his Alexander Valley development in Sonoma County as preparation for the ranchettes. There vineyards provided both justification for the development and selling points for highly profitable residential real estate. Again the name listed as the developer was Mike Reynolds. Preliminary studies by the Hall Financial Group suggested that this Sonoma model was now being followed in Napa County.

Craig Hall suffered a severe economic setback—his second—said to be due to over-leveraged real estate, wrong-way hedges, and a cratered oil and gas venture. He had recovered by 2010, perhaps assisted by the bank bailouts at the end of the Bush era, but this, too, is something of a mystery. His eighteen-story, 500,000-square-foot building, the first in downtown Dallas after Hall's One Arts Plaza, was to house Hall Financial Group, as well as other financial clients. Additional phases were to take the project's value up to about $750 million.

Meanwhile, a lot of money was flowing in, and a lot of money was flowing out. Craig Hall had also told *D* magazine: "I have a bad habit of putting things on steroids. You could drop me on Mars, and I'd be starting businesses."

And people in Napa County were indeed wondering if something otherworldly hadn't landed in their midst.

CHAPTER FOURTEEN

The Grandmother Tree

Someone's mind is on fire to possess, uproot, subdue,
While another riding a bulldozer, hums a little tune to himself . . .
The days are becoming shorter, not simply because it's winter.
Oh poor trapped earth, the sun grips the map of your death.
—Leonore Wilson, "Western Solstice"

1.

He's the athletic-looking fiftysomething with salt-and-pepper curls that dangle, Nero-style, over a broad forehead. He wears the same sneakers and running pants he had on when he and his wife, Leonore, traversed the steep valleys of east Napa County to sit on the Eiseles' front porch to discuss protecting Wildlake. But a powerful impulse to preserve land had been born earlier in Jim Wilson, just across the road from his house on little Capell Creek that he had built with his own hands.

His glasses—squarish lenses—sit on the end of his nose, his soft, reasonable smile that of a man schooled in two poles of human endeavor: fermentation science and German literature. The sweatshirt's left over from biking days when he rode thirty-six miles round-trip daily from their high valley to the Anheuser-Busch brewery in Solano County. He led Anheuser's resource conservation team in trying to figure out how to save water and energy, and was so successful that his "best practices" were adopted elsewhere. He even got the company to put up a wind turbine.

He and Leonore had been college sweethearts who married young and moved into the trailer next door to her mother's house on the family's Capell Creek property. It sat at the end of a near-impossibly steep, winding driveway Jim poured himself, one that climbed past two valley oaks so thick of trunk and broad of branch that the Wilsons called them the Grandmother and Grandfather trees. He started building a house next to the trailer, and almost immediately Leonore had twin boys. Less than a year later she had another son, so while Jim framed and floored and fashioned a fireplace from stones he hauled up from the creek, she tended to three little boys in diapers.

The family spent most of the time outdoors in the sunny, beautiful, untrammeled country all Californians hear about but relatively few experience, a remnant of the Napa County of the century before and the one before that. When not tending to home and family Leonore wrote poetry. After the main house was finished Jim built a second cunning little redwood "birdhouse" for doves, pheasants, and ducks. Not for eating but for playing with.

He rode the thirty-six miles round-trip to work for many years, and when he was gone Leonore took the boys next door to her mother's. She later taught English and creative writing at Napa Valley College, and published a book of poetry. Their sons grew up and moved away but still return regularly, often from great distances, and since the Grandfather tree died always take time to walk out into the meadow and stand in the shade of the Grandmother tree.

Jim's interest in mushrooms rivaled his interest in cycling. He knew well that the madrone trees on the property across the road were indicators of prime terrain for fungi. There he was shown by an old Tuscan also living on Capell Creek how to recognize boletes, Caesar's, and chanterelles, and how to tell these and other types from those that can kill you, called death caps.

Jim dried the ones easy to recognize on the woodstove and stored them for year-round eating. He paid an expert $200 to drive the tortuous road into the valley and inspect with him mushrooms Jim had staked out beforehand, wanting to feel comfortable in the knowledge that he could eat even the ones most experts avoided. But all he really wanted to do, after he retired from Anheuser-Busch, was ride his bicycle.

Leonore's boys represented her family's fourth generation on the same rudimentary ranch on Monticello Road, a mile-and-a-half stretch of county running straight up the mountain at their backs. She had been brought here at age three, her grandfather having acquired the property and small house in 1919 in a bet on a prizefight in San Francisco. Her mother still lives in the frame replacement of the original house that burned, and first learned of plans to develop the sprawling property across Monticello Road like most everyone in the neighborhood—from the pages of the *Napa Valley Register*.

For years the steep 2,300 acres had been known as Munson Ranch, even after it was bought by a Texan preceding the current one who had talked about building a resort and maybe a casino in partnership with descendants of Wappo Indians but had sold to the Halls instead. By then Texans were synonymous in some minds with an invasive pest, anthropomorphic glassy-winged sharpshooters popping up when least expected in Pope Valley and along ridgelines and little creeks like Capell, pushing development schemes and then drifting blessedly away, leaving behind plans for resorts, golf courses, vineyards, wine "estates," and prospective McWineries.

Vineyard development higher up was something else again. It would demand not just a lot of water but also increase traffic on a challenging country road, even more so if houses were built. Such projects had languished after the successful lawsuit against Pahlmeyer in late 1999, but now an analysis was being done for yet another Texan who already owned two wineries down in Napa Valley proper.

People living on Monticello Road were concerned, and the more they heard about it the more concerned they got. Hall had paid $8 million for the property in 2005 and had test water wells dug, supposedly for vineyards with Bordeaux varieties to be planted. "There are no plans to put houses up there," HALL Wines' ubiquitous general manager, Mike

Reynolds, told the *Register*. Readers may well have thought he was speaking for another family vineyard and not suspected that possibly hundreds of investors in Hall's latest real estate syndicate owned a small piece of Munson/Walt Ranch, where surveyors and geologists and soils, water, and plant experts started showing up. One of them told Jim Wilson he didn't think the county could possibly approve such a massive project on these steep, unstable slopes.

The erosion control plan alarmed water quality managers down in the city of Napa whose drinking water would be affected, and the neighbors feared not just for their own wells but also sheet erosion runoff that would further destabilize fragile soils, darken Capell Creek, and play havoc with aquatic life. The extended five-year drought to grip the state wouldn't officially begin for another six years, but anyone paying attention to the weather and scientific predictions knew that something different, unpleasant, and lasting was in the offing.

In Napa and the little offshoot valleys, people who had nothing to do with the making or selling of wine and wanted their families protected from fire, desertification, and wholesale development began to complain. Whether or not the Halls would get what they wanted depended on the integrity of a regulatory system put in place years before. Hall had paid for an Environmental Impact Report, and about the time it was finally released in 2014, Leonore's mother walked out to her mailbox and discovered a large envelope inside. Across the road were slopes dense with live oaks and madrones, chaparral, meadows, and pocket wetlands where in season water collected and provided habitat vital to Capell Valley's wildlife, a natural setting that had for almost half a century borne silent witness to her daily routine.

She tore open the envelope and found a letter from Craig Hall inside. "Dear Walt Ranch neighbors," it began, though she still considered herself a neighbor of the old Munson ranch. The letter went on to state that the Halls intended to put in "premier" vineyards and were considering "what additional development rights to maintain while putting whatever was left over into a conservation easement." That phrase—*additional development rights to maintain*—struck her as odd, a possible reference to expensive residences nestled among vineyards and sold at high prices to satisfy investors living far from Napa. If getting such houses built hadn't actually been planned, the wording suggested, the right to do so was being assiduously "maintained."

The letter failed to mention that much of the land going into a conservation easement was too steep or unstable to be built on, by then a familiar ploy used by wealthy property owners to claim land already in de facto preservation and still avoid paying taxes. "By way of perspective," the letter reminded recipients, "the Agricultural Preserve rights for this property"—it was not in the agricultural preserve, which was the floor of Napa Valley proper, but in the steep watershed—"include the right to build 35 wineries, 35 recreational vehicle parks, 35 campgrounds, 35 hunting lodges and other developments," an apparent warning of what might be attempted if the Walt Ranch vineyard scheme was opposed.

Leonore's mother showed the letter to Jim Wilson and said, "I don't like being threatened."

Neither did her son-in-law, who drove down to county headquarters in Napa, climbed the stairs to the planning department, and asked two different people behind the counter, "What's going on up on Capell Creek?"

They looked oblivious. It was then that Jim Wilson realized his bicycle riding was over for the foreseeable future.

2.

A small community already occupied a discrete portion of those same hills, hard up against the Walt Ranch property. It was called Circle Oaks, long established and mostly invisible from the road. Many living there were retirees who had built their own homes and watched the seasons come and go, far from the action in Napa Valley proper. They had their own water company to dispense and protect their most precious resource, and they had learned with dismay, back in 2005, that a new test well was being drilled just across the line from theirs. That meant the prospective Walt Ranch development could legally draw down on its neighbors' water supply, if it so chose, for vineyards and houses.

Circle Oaks neighbors began to ask each other, "Who would do such a thing?" One of them, Cindy Heitzman, the elegant, white-haired executive director of the California Preservation Foundation, had for years risen early each morning for the ninety-minute drive to San Francisco—sometimes it was twice that—where she tried with like-minded people to protect the state's historic treasures. These are mostly built structures, but she was also concerned with landscape, for without some integrity of the whole the past becomes attenuated and eventually lost.

Unlike some historic preservationists, California's are aware of the value of the environmental community as the other side of the preservationism coin. Now environmental degradation was to be in her face in an unexpected and distressing way. Cindy Heitzman never dreamed she could wake up one day in Circle Oaks and discover that, next door, some thirty thousand oak trees were being cut. There had long been talk of resorts, even a casino, in these hills, pipe dreams of outside speculators who had been showing up since the twilight of General Vallejo. But thirty thousand stumps?

If this tragedy were actually to occur, the very best she could hope for was to spend every day working in the city and avoiding the sights and sounds of destruction where she lived. Not so her husband, David. A luthier (guitar maker) by trade who worked at home and found solace and inspiration in the absence of all things developmental, David had been an admirer of early Napa Valley architecture when he and Cindy met, and of artifacts the early proprietors left behind. Bald and lean, with an ascetic air that dissolves when he smiles, David once made guitars out of redwood planks from a decommissioned Charles Krug storage tank that for a century had held an incalculable amount of zinfandel, petite sirah, carignan, cabernet sauvignon, and other varieties.

When the winery had to retrofit for earthquakes and get rid of some old equipment, a client of David's took a bottle of Schramsberg over to Krug, hoping to persuade Peter Mondavi Jr., or his brother Marc, to sell him an entire eight-by-twenty-foot monster tank. "But all my client got was a bottom," says David, who made the guitars from it and called them "BOBs" (bottom of the barrel). He also made a hybrid called a guitello, played like a cello, that "still smells great."

David had long had reservations about the Halls, whom he did not know. "There was something twisted about them giving money to good causes down in St. Helena while at the same time kicking people out of the trailer park and removing their homes."

His opinion didn't improve when he learned that Hall and Mike Reynolds might use the road through Circle Oaks for access to their vast property, and that twenty miles of new roads were to be built, with as many in fences that would adversely affect wildlife. It sounded like infrastructure for a housing development to him, and he tried tracking the ownership of Walt Ranch. What he discovered, he told Cindy, were more than sixty corporate entities associated with the name, "but no one you could call and talk to, and no listed assets. We even tried to buy a Dunn & Bradstreet report. D&B said there was nothing there."

When the Walt Ranch Environmental Impact Report (EIR) was first released, Cindy realized "we couldn't stop this with a meeting of the Homes Association. We got organized and asked for an extension in order to comment, and got a month to respond to sixteen hundred pages. Where the hell do you begin?"

One day they saw a neighbor carrying a clipboard, gathering signatures for a petition opposing the development, and the Heitzmans joined her, something people still did in communities without locked gates. They held a meeting of the Circle Oaks Homes Association where "everybody vented. David pointed out that we had to look organized and credible to raise money," and they did, forming a nonprofit 501(3)(c), producing a business plan with bullet points, a bumper sticker, and a map, and canvassing the 189 houses in Circle Oaks.

Cindy had seen all this happen before in her efforts for the California Preservation Foundation. "You can't wait to mobilize. And we went from a bunch of ragtag, hand-wringing neighbors to a full-frontal assault."

They called themselves Defenders of East Napa Watersheds, with Cindy coaching members in running meetings and setting an agenda. When they needed a lawyer, Cindy found a good, sympathetic one who worked for a very good price. The Defenders created an education committee because the issues had to be explained to people, and they were complex, as all environmental issues are. They then assembled a thousand

signed letters of protest and delivered them to the county board of supervisors and the planning commission simultaneously. "We even went to
public meetings down in Napa, carrying signs, which was Jim Wilson's
idea."

They decided not to be litigants in what promised to be a bruising
legal battle over water rights. "Walt Ranch will turn on those," Cindy
predicted, but the Circle Oaks County Water District was better situated
to sue on its own. One neighbor happened to be president of Napa Sierra,
the county arm of the Sierra Club's regional Redwood Chapter, and married to a member of the Circle Oaks water board. Both were Yale gradu-
ates. "There are lots of people up here like them, and they know how to
do research," the same cohort Craig Hall had left in distant Ann Arbor.
"Hall and his people assumed we were just a bunch of hicks."

They found various experts to help them: noise experts, frog experts, a
geologist, two hydrologists, others. Most had to be brought in from outside the county because locals feared testifying against the Halls would
rob them of a livelihood. "We had gone from 'Oh my God' to being
ready: raising money, doing mailings, getting strategies and attorneys for
a challenge like the county had never seen."

After the comment period was over, Circle Oaks decided to join with
other like-minded groups rising spontaneously all over the valley. They
were driven by local concern about the future of their particular communities, part of a larger genesis similar to little Citizens' Voice in St. Helena
opposing unsuitable or patently illegal wineries on Diamond Mountain
and in Soda Canyon. Yet another, fighting a helicopter pad near the Napa
city limit, joined the lengthening list.

The Defenders decided to invite them all to a meeting right after New
Year's 2015 at the Oxbow Public Market, down in Napa, to discuss an
alliance. The meeting was led by what Cindy called "the dream team,"
including her husband as president, Jim Wilson as vice president, Dan
Mufson, a retired pharmacologist, as secretary, and Rich Cannon, a retired
shop teacher, as treasurer. The very name of the organization announced
the remoteness of the terrain and called to mind historic coalitions that
had slipped into oblivion but were being revived now by the threat of
greater development.

Another big vineyard project had been approved because their neighbors rose to oppose it too late. And right next door to Walt Ranch was yet another that came to be known as "Little Walt." Over the ridge to the north were more active or looming threats. New or resurgent organizations were essentially battling the same phenomenon as in the past but in different guises now, all over the county. They took on names like Soda Canyon Road, Watersheds Alliance for Atlas Peak, Protect Rural Napa, Calistoga Citizens for Green Community, Save Yountville Hill, Mt. Veeder Stewardship Council, and Save Rural Angwin. But as yet they had no umbrella organization.

The twenty organizations each sent one person to a meeting, and among them they came up with a name: Napa Vision 2050, "a countywide coalition formed to advocate for responsible planning to insure the sustainability of the finite resources of Napa County." They had tacit allies among growers and vintners who for the most part remained out of sight because the subtleties were many and the retribution real if you valued consultancy fees and grape contracts.

Concern within the wine industry for the desires of those outside it had declined precipitously in recent years. In the summer of 2015 a spokesman for the Winegrowers of Napa County would stand up at a national convocation on tourism held in Napa and falsely state that ten percent of the valley's residents were "basically against everything." He dismissed their concerns as unimportant, even laughable, without addressing what those concerns were.

3.

The board of supervisors early on had been asked to hold a preliminary hearing on the Walt Ranch application and had refused. The Halls did offer to meet with critics on their own, at the Meritage Resort and Spa south of Napa, where Geoff Ellsworth arrived in time to see Craig Hall in his Tesla changing from a business suit into an everyman's plaid shirt before going inside. But that public relations gesture satisfied no one.

Finally the planning director, Dave Morrison, put together the public venting about the Walt Ranch EIR held on Napa's Corporate Way, the meeting that had brought together county supervisors, planning commissioners, sign carriers, and other objectors and exposed Craig and Kathryn Hall to the collective ire of the community. "Six hundred people out of a population of thirteen thousand showed up on a weekday morning," recalls Cindy Heitzman. "It was pretty outrageous."

Since the meeting had been Morrison's call, he had put his job at risk, existing as it did at the pleasure of a pro-development board. It might well turn on him at any moment to deflect attention from its own failings. A similar board under the influence of the Winegrower's newly elected candidate back in 1989 had fired the best planning director Napa ever had, towering Jim Hickey, who had the temerity to ask the question the county's ruling body had danced around since 1968: *What is a winery?* Answering it had launched the long-delayed soul-searching that was still playing out in dozens of far-flung fastnesses on both sides of the valley.

Out of that old fight had come the "75 percent solution"—the requirement that three-fourths of the grapes going into wines designated as being from Napa had to actually be from Napa. That compromise struck most outsiders as a dubious accomplishment: "Shouldn't there be one hundred percent Napa grapes in Napa wine?" But to get to even that partial victory reformers like Eisele and Beckstoffer had to agree to "grandfathering," or legalizing what for recently built wineries would be illegal behavior like operating clothing boutiques and de facto restaurants.

Even the Farm Bureau, usually a proponent of good land use, had of late felt the undue influence of developers within its ranks who lobbied tirelessly for more vineyards and tree felling in steep, fragile terrain, defending it as "farming" when in fact it was a real estate play. But at least the Farm Bureau didn't speak out against the position of the Defenders of East Napa Watersheds. This, as Cindy Heitzman pointed out, "said volumes."

By 2014, Walt Ranch had produced no revenue since being acquired in 2005 and was burning up considerable capital. Criticism of the Halls in Napa Valley was no longer relegated just to the riddled rabbit or the Gehry flirtation, but focused on the possibility of a phantom development above Capell Creek.

"Napa County is special, unique," wrote one lifelong resident to the

Napa Valley Register, "and I don't feel that preservation is a top priority for the Halls. In fact it takes a backseat to developing properties with park-like settings for the urban crowd, with fabulous views of other people's vineyards. Hall knows this makes for increased property values for the next sale. It's a pity they don't seem to understand Napa County and what it's about."

When the Halls arrived in Napa in the 1990s they had quickly become benefactors of charities, the arts, and political causes, but were not de facto members of the social elite, such as it was. Garen and Shari Staglin, also wealthy Democrats, were friends, and so were some among the Republican mélange who regarded the Halls as merely agreeable Texans. In general Craig came across as inoffensive, personable, unknowable.

He described himself in the pages of the *Dallas Morning News* as chairman and chief executive officer of Hall Financial Group. Many who knew him in Napa didn't think much about his complicated financial affairs and believed him when he said he had no intention of building houses on Walt Ranch. But then the Walt Ranch project began to cause public ill will, not just toward the Halls but also toward the valley's wine industry.

A friend told Craig bluntly in late 2015, "If you bring criticism down on the vintners, they'll throw you under the bus."

As the Halls tell the Walt Ranch story in *A Perfect Score*, they were simply trying to plant vineyards on property zoned for agriculture. But because part of it was above 5 percent grade they had to do an erosion control plan as well as the Environmental Impact Report. Their water "experts," according to Craig, told the Halls that they had one of the best "water areas," that their erosion control plan was "similarly positive," and would actually improve the quality of Napa's water, something the city's quality control manager denied.

Few people seemed to believe the Halls' assertions. After the draft Environmental Impact Report was released in 2014—1,500 pages—a public meeting was held at which a man told Kathryn Hall she was the devil, and overnight a dead rabbit was left in the winery entrance.

Craig and Mike Reynolds wrote to the county protesting the "ever-increasing burden" applicants face. "Changes to the process as have been experienced in this application will only serve to discourage future applicants for agricultural uses and may lead to challenges on the viability of the Agricultural Preserve."

People reading that took it as another threat. Some, looking further out, thought that if Hall didn't get his way he was willing to bring down half a century's worth of invaluable land protections, changing more or less single-handedly the very nature of the valley and sullying the vaunted Napa Valley brand. Rather than risk being thrown under the bus by Napa Valley vintners, Craig Hall seemed on the verge of throwing *them* under the bus.

Unlike most, he had the resources to simply pull up stakes as he had elsewhere and move with his recently procured assets to some other beautiful place. Valley residents were reminded of the planet's new class of refugee fleeing neither religious hatred nor wars but the ordinary restraints of civics. Drifting one percenters increasingly seemed unburdened of scruple, accountability, and any sense of the past. Politically invested, adept at converting others to a singular purpose with money, out of the reach of irate citizens, befuddled officials, and often the law, they perceived the very Earth through the bars of a dollar sign.

Sometime after the hearing took place on Corporate Way, the planning department announced that the absolutely last, decisive hearing on Walt Ranch would be held in early April 2016. Final comments on the revised Environmental Impact Report would be received at that time and a decision made by Dave Morrison as to whether or not the Halls/Walt Ranch/Hall Brambletree/hidden investors would get a permit. Until then, there was nothing for the principals to do but jockey behind the scenes until the real fight began in court, where everyone knew by now it would eventually land and where the testimony of "experts"—a highly varied concept—would be very important.

4.

He walks into a café where he is guaranteed anonymity and orders tea. He stipulated earlier by phone that his name cannot be associated in print with what he's about to say, a carefully considered decision to speak out about what's happening in Napa and surrounding counties by a seasoned professional, despite risk to his livelihood.

"Deep Root" isn't his choice of pseudonyms, but it will suffice. He is one of hundreds of "experts" in planned development that include geologists, hydrologists, soils and climate adepts, even landscape designers and assessors of prospective vineyard sites in rough terrain, and also an accredited preparer of Environmental Impact Reports who knows more about such things than most of his competitors. Deep Root has a long history of assessing the effects of development in the wilds of the North Coast counties, "and really knows," as a friend puts it, "how the mountains move in Napa."

Deep Root has less interest in wine than in land's ability to recover from what people do to it. Also an abiding belief in the ethics of the various professions, and a passion for natural balance that soon burns through his caution, leaving in its wake an altered view of reality in anyone who might be listening to him parse the damage done to remaining pristine meadows and woodlands, all in the hope of providing those parcels at least a chance of survival.

"If you leave a landscape alone for forty years," he says, "it will actually get back to being one." He redesigns them on paper to accommodate the unrealistic desires of owners and developers, and is daily stressed by the collision of ignorance, greed, and enormous sums of money.

"If a guy shows up in a $130,000 Tesla and asks me for help, I say, 'I'll take a fifty-thousand-dollar retainer and talk to you tomorrow.' There's a lot of that type out there, and it's scary. They know almost nothing, and a lot of them see vineyards as a way out of their financial problems because vineyards are all about real estate, not wine."

He's well acquainted with big developmental projects in the Howell and Vaca ranges, the classic middleman in an increasingly uncomfortable position. "The rich need a fall guy, so that if the project blows up, they can 'disburse.' The money isn't real to them. They recruit local people as shepherds and fall guys, and after the deal's done they either buy them out or eat them up by contributing to their difficulties and then taking them over."

He's talking about vineyard developers and land evaluators who readily lend themselves to distortions and inventions of the geomorphology to make their clients' projects look benign on paper. "Water is allocated that doesn't exist. Some investors buy a water right just to shoot up the value of the property then sell. It's all about making a lot of money off the land, not about the land itself, or wine, which have become part of the smokescreen.

"More than ever, it's about what's passed on to later generations. Or isn't passed on because it no longer exists."

The only solution to rampant development, he believes, is to make pristine land as valuable as so-called improved land, taking the incentive away from those who care about nothing but making more money at the expense of all else. Local government agencies that should protect the land, he adds, mediate on a constantly shifting front, too many elected and appointed officials failing to live up to expectations of the people and often subverting the spirit of the law, if not the law itself.

"The planning commission's objective is to wear people out so they will eventually go away and the agencies can take the easiest way forward to give developers' clients what they want. The supervisors tell the planning commissioners what to do, the planning commissioners tell the head of the planning department what to do, and he tells the professionals beneath him what to do. The latter all drink beer and hate vineyards not because of all the work but because vineyards introduce an alien culture, not agriculture, but 'lifestyle.'

"Planners see wineries as speculative ventures to be flipped, forcing the planners into the role of abetting speculation. It goes against the mandate inherent in their jobs, which is to preserve agriculture. This works well for owners and developers because most people don't care, but the trouble in Napa County, from the speculators and developers' point of view, is that people do care. They're pissed, and many have turned into hawks."

An initial permit is inestimably valuable and, for the most part, the beginning of the end of that piece of land. "No one ever goes back to monitor—ever—what's been agreed to, and that's when the real damage is done. Vineyard managers clear-cut trees they shouldn't, then sit back and wait to see if anyone objects. The force of law should be felt by the property owners who pay for this, but it isn't. Then in ten years they flip the property—lately to the Chinese, the new class of the rich and inexhaustible.

"Napa Valley's an eighteen-billion-dollar economy based on tourism, and they're at the point of running out of resource. So it's all about adding value and leverage to existing real estate," that is, event centers, new wineries amid converted vineyards, de facto restaurants, new transient occupancy tax–reaping hotels, houses, and ranchettes.

Most property owners in Deep Root's experience need a lot of money to support extravagant lives. "Most own property elsewhere, too, and are maxed out. They have no cash. The Halls are different—they have real money. For them, it's the ranchette game. As soon as he gets a permit for Walt Ranch vineyards he'll create thirty-five limited liability corporate entities, each with its own name, roads, and leech fields already put in, then add more roads to accommodate houses. Twenty years from now the payback will be enormous.

"When the possibility of a Walt Ranch development first came up, some professionals wouldn't touch it. There were very real problems, including 'ice cream terrain' "—too unstable to be built on—"and the presence of huge ancient live oaks whose complex root systems essentially hold the landscape together."

In the beginning "an engineering company went in and built access roads, took water, and messed with the wetlands. It cost some engineers their jobs if they objected to cutting into the ground so close to wetlands that the water drained away." The initial Environmental Impact Report "contained inaccuracies and false claims," he says, "that could eventually be blamed on the engineering company if need be.

"Cutting thirty thousand mature oaks, some with diameters of close to two meters, is unconscionable. Some oaks were three, four hundred years old because, by chance, no catastrophic event had occurred there during all that time, including no big fires. The roots held it all in place during earthquakes, so even cutting one big tree could destabilize a sizable piece of land.

"No one wants to think in terms of land forms now. It's too much trouble to discern them, so instead they use one law to fit everything, which is fundamentally the problem. The rich take as much advantage of the rules as they can, that's just what rich people do. What's criminal is that the state agencies in charge don't challenge them. Instead, they cave.

"There's just too much power here—Nancy Pelosi, Mike Thompson, so much influential wealth invested in Napa. Starting in 2009 during the recession, horrible decisions were made by the county because no one was paying attention. To update the Environmental Impact Report the county employed third-party corporations that were also working on vineyard projects. And many of those companies were eventually swallowed up."

During that time the county provided money to update the General Plan, the same process that altered the definition of agriculture to favor tourism. "That changed everything. The former planning director wanted to balloon to 12,500 acres of new vineyards, the big question being who was behind it. Real estate developers, that's who. They said they had done analysis, but it was often based on faulty science. And the laws had changed because of greenhouse gases. But the real problem was that they didn't involve the public in these decisions. As soon as the EIR on Walt Ranch was done, and the county cranked up to handle the new thirst for vineyards, residents started waking up. Opposition to the wineries in general grew out of that."

Deep Root watched prospective developers use regional instead of specific analysis, which is more restrictive. "They targeted blue oaks first because that's the species that indicates the best vineyard land." That was stopped. "So now they're protecting blue oaks and killing the rest. It's all about massaging the resource. When the state fails to provide the best science to stakeholders, local government, and environmentalists, there's no way to locally enforce regulations. Since the state doesn't engage with the public, or effectively communicate with other government representatives, we have chaos, lawlessness, and continued degradation of the land."

To Deep Root, long committed to environmental protection, Walt Ranch represents the biggest, most lucrative real estate pivot the county has seen since the change in the definition of agriculture, and of great symbolic value. "Hall said he subdivided land for vineyards, but I think it's really a real estate scheme, even if it takes twenty years to bring off. The fall guy was the planning director who had had a conversation with the board of supervisors, done what they wanted, and stepped down."

After Morrison arrived, according to Deep Root, questions arose about the amount of wetlands on the property. "The Halls cleaned up their EIR, and the director of the board of supervisors ordered Morrison to release it."

Deep Root believes Morrison "saved the asses of the board of supervisors by taking on the project. If he hadn't, opponents would have gone to the state and showed them the EIR that generated thousands of letters because it was so bad." But the objections took more than a year to read and respond to. "Then the county cleaned up the EIR and announced that there's to be a review in April 2016," only months away. "What's needed to kill it is lawyers working with red meat from people like me, who know the land and are no longer under confidentiality agreements because the process has taken so long. If the county doesn't kill it now, they're done. The people won't stand for it, and the paper trail's too long to cover up. A court of law would eventually force out the truth."

For wineries, he adds, other large problems loom. "They still aren't acknowledging the methane that comes from all aspects of making wine, which is huge. So is the biomass left over. For years it was hauled to Oakland, with more huge emissions. Insane. Napa Valley wineries have ten times the carbon footprint of comparable European ones and they have done everything so as not to have to calculate the real footprints. But now that agencies can focus on individual wineries with satellites and other tracking methods, behavior's going to be affected. Public data will change everything."

His tea has grown cold and the morning regulars have all gone home.

"Don't entirely blame the rich, just pity them their vanity. It's a Disneyland, and it's all business. Better to look at your own life, do due diligence on yourself, and take their money."

CHAPTER FIFTEEN

Enocracy

1.

Twenty sixteen had promised to be the hottest on record as early as February, with buds appearing a full ten days early. El Niño refilled the reservoirs after five years of drought, but the rains stopped temporarily in January and the sun climbed the southern sky with a determination more summery than springlike.

Other forebodings hung in the air. It was a year of presidential election, candidates calling for revolution, but quite different kinds, and global warming still the unmentionable specter for many. Strands of pale blue smoke rose against the deep green of the Mayacamas, through air utterly still, as the vines were pruned and discarded shoots burned throughout the lengthening days, their smoke visible all over the valley.

Those seeing them tended to fall into three distinct groups. The first, composed of workers, property owners, and the downstream beneficiaries of the life wine had wrought, saw the smoke as a sign of a necessary natural process. The second, visitors and the romantically inclined, perceived physical beauty and a reminder of an ancient practice that transcended time. Third, those concerned with the future of the valley and the world into which it was so fortuitously set saw the release of life's most basic element—carbon—into an atmosphere that grew more dangerous by the day.

The second—or was it the third?—public airing of the Walt Ranch project was presided over by the planning director, Dave Morrison, and so many people packed into the board of supervisors' room that they spilled out into the hall and threatened to block the elevators. More than a hundred people rose to speak, most of them in condemnation, but one of the most interesting—and unexpected—statements came from a lifelong Napa resident who did not speak but who had provided each of the planning commissioners, the night before, with packets containing the most riveting documents in the fight so far.

Her name was Lois Battuello and she included maps in the packet that once superimposed on the vineyard plan seemed to clearly point to potential house sites. She added that any effort the supervisors could lend to opposing Walt Ranch "would be appreciated by those who have not been given a voice otherwise allowed by the normal process for development schemes."

At the end of the hearing Dave Morrison announced that his decision was being postponed—again. New material had come to light, he said, and the planning department had to deal with it. Craig Hall and Mike Reynolds cried foul, claiming that all relevant facts about the proposed development had been amply aired. But Morrison stuck to his decision: He would wait until the new material had been absorbed, and announce his final judgment on June 13, 2016.

Morrison had grown up in Fresno, one of the Central Valley's sprawling metropolises built around farming. It had turned into another struggling mass of urban problems caused by the failures of corporate agriculture, with decreasing profits for the small farmer. His father had been a truck driver and his best friend's father a crop duster, but Dave majored in anthropology and economics at Fresno State, with a minor in studio art. As a planner, the Walt Ranch proposal was the biggest thing he had dealt with: three volumes of regulations and five thousand pages of comments that had to be read and answered. And new comments and information kept coming in.

In some ways, Dave Morrison felt, Napa was following the example set by the founding fathers who established the tradition of deliberative debate. But some applicants were unfamiliar with that tradition. They tended to condemn the idea of global warming, whereas others espoused it furiously. Out of curiosity Dave did some research and discovered that only about 20 percent of the countries of the world had done anything at all about global warming, including America. More surprising, only about 20 percent of California had done anything about it. So Napa County was a minority within a minority.

The state under Governor Jerry Brown set strict standards for measuring greenhouse gases, which have to be below 40 percent of 1990 levels by 2030. Loss of carbon sequestration occurs when trees are cut, but Napa County has upwards of 130,000 acres of oaks. Pointing this out didn't placate opponents of cutting even one. The county was working on all emissions, including what would be required of the almost five hundred brick-and-mortar wineries, and as many as two hundred more operating out of other facilities. Relatively few were aware of what those emissions amounted to and what would eventually have to be done about it.

Dave once asked a group of Napa vintners how many of them would accept an offer of two, even three million dollars an acre for their land. Only one hand had gone up, even though they could have built a winery somewhere else, put thirty million in the bank, and still gotten a 98 Parker score with the cult wine formula. They all wanted to be in Napa, where many wineries operated not for business but for vanity. So the economics had broken down because irrationality had been introduced.

2.

A week before Dave Morrison's announcement on Walt Ranch was due, the county held its local election. The sitting supervisor in District 4, the bellwether, was Alfredo Pedroza, the establishment candidate. Already acting chairman of the board, Pedroza represented the extraordinary elevation of a twenty-nine-year-old novice by an unapologetic wine and tourism industry. According to one voter who talked to but didn't vote for Pedroza, he was "clueless but seemingly pliable."

The Winegrowers of Napa County openly endorsed him, and although the Napa Valley Vintners' policy didn't allow endorsements, Pedroza was their favored candidate as well. Two decades before, the Vintners had stood on principle as much as expediency, but since then the differences between that organization and the secretive Winegrowers had blended in a haze of entitlement. Political decisions concerning the material well-being of the collective memberships trumped all else. This alienated some among the Vintners' more than five hundred members who objected to what one called "power plays," but they hung on to their memberships because they needed a trade organization to push their wines.

The notoriety of the Vintners' annual wine auction had burnished the Napa brand outside the valley, but it excluded county residents by virtue of cost and association. Once envisioned by Robert Mondavi and other founders as a countywide celebration of Napa's arrival in the world of fine wine, the auction had become a spectacle under glass for fawned-over billionaires manqué whom vintners were eager to have buy their lavishly presented wares. Bidding was manipulated by individual vintners while a carefully culled journalistic cohort was kept at bay, relegated to peripheral seats and denied access to bidders who didn't want the outside world, including their own employees, to know the price of their frivolity.

Locally, the auction was perceived as proof that the valley was divided into two distinct classes: vintners and their fellows from the corporate world, and everybody else. One resident referred to this event, mimicking Oscar Wilde's denunciation of fox hunting, as "the unspeakable in pursuit of the undrinkable." Millions were spent on bottles, travel, and dinners with vinous stars. The money went mostly toward medical care in the valley, and though no one denied the good this did, the spectacle was something else: a safe zone for vintners avoiding the most pressing long-term problem, climate change, which was bound to radically alter not just quality of life but also the valley's most famous product.

Pedroza was known for his ready smile and often irrelevant answers to questions, having never before run for county office. He had been appointed to the board by Governor Brown to fill a vacancy left by the departing supervisor Bill Dodd, who was running for the California Senate. Dodd raised money from the same people who backed Pedroza, and now had more of it than any other senatorial candidate in the state.

A Republican backed by the Winegrowers before he flipped to the Democrats, Dodd, too, had been largely ignorant of agriculture when first elected and voted for almost every developmental project that came before the board. Changing parties had been a breathtaking display of ambition in a state where Democrats reigned, but his backers didn't care which party he belonged to. They knew their man, just as they knew his replacement, Pedroza, perceived as Dodd's doppelgänger.

The fact that Pedroza was Latino had greatly improved his likelihood of being appointed, but it disappointed progressives and environmentalists who saw Mexican workers as the unsung but crucial element in Napa's long-running success. They would have preferred someone interested in land preservation, but many Latinos whose fathers and grandfathers had labored in the fields went speedily over to the interests of the *ricos* when they got the chance. This was viewed as the natural acculturation of a minority gaining access at last to the engine of commerce, but others saw it as a reaction of aspirants more interested in affluence than good land use.

Much of Pedroza's financial support came from developers like Craig Hall, but also from Charlie Wagner of Caymus Vineyards, which had paid a million-dollar fine for overproduction and had lucrative issues pending with the county. So did Palmaz Vineyards, which had been fighting neighbors on Hagen Road for years to get an unlawful helipad and had backed Pedroza, as had Silverado Resort, Pedroza's new neighbor, a California real estate PAC, and the president of Syar Industries, which was seeking to expand its mining operation within the city of Napa. Syar didn't wish to undertake expensive alterations to reduce emissions despite the fact that Napa had a high incidence of cancer among California counties.

Among the Democrats was, for now, the place for aspiring politicians to be, regardless of their beliefs. The state legislature was firmly in Democratic control and Hillary Clinton expected to prevail over the bumptious Donald Trump in the presidential election. When in the valley the Clintons stayed at Craig and Kathryn Hall's, whose neighbor above Rutherford, Nancy Pelosi, was minority leader of the House of Representatives, another friend and social companion. For them, Napa's land-use problems were pennies on the tracks of the presidential express.

On the June night of the local election, it looked early on as if Pedroza would garner more than half the vote and so avoid a runoff. The collective total for the green candidates—Diane Shepp, a founding member of Napa Vision 2050, and environmentalist Chris Malan—reached 43 percent, where it stalled. A concentrated effort by the two women might have built a unified movement and encouraged the dispirited electorate confused by their dual candidacy. Chris, for all her accomplishments, had proven the persistence on the Left of "Nader Syndrome," which it is said had cost Al Gore the presidency years before.

A victory party was held at Ristorante Allegría in Napa, the crowd flowing out onto the patio. The *Register* reported that "a smiling Pedroza stood amid the cool of the night as election results came in. . . . He talked about listening to the people who didn't vote for him. While other candidates could take positions on such controversial issues as the proposed helipad, he couldn't because these matters could come before the Board of Supervisors in coming months."

Diane Shepp's summation of the election was "same-old, same-old," which summed up the view of many. One close observer stated flatly, "The Board of Supervisors is run by the [V]intners," whose director of government relations told the *Register* his "community likes where we are, they like where we're headed," adding, "our agricultural land is the most valuable in the country. Our grape prices are the highest in the country. Our wines are the best . . . And our environment has probably not been cleaner, greener or better in many, many decades." This dubious statement could have come from a ranking executive in a corporate conglomerate, which in a way it had.

The president of Napa Vision 2050, Dan Mufson, said that door-to-door campaigning had exposed a very different valley from the one described by the Vintners' director of government relations, one in which the people worried increasingly about water and traffic, revealing a growing antipathy to an industry that would so skew Pedroza's financial advantage. "We just don't like to see the influence of so much money on our local elections, and we don't think it's fair to the citizens of Napa." It could also be seen as a downstream manifestation of the *Citizens United* decision in the Supreme Court that has allowed unlimited corporate money to find its way into local elections.

A week later, Dave Morrison announced that he was forwarding the Walt Ranch development proposal to the board. He had tried and failed to find "a compelling and provocative reason" not to. Morrison expected the board to accept it, then for the project to be appealed by the forces arrayed against the Halls, and lawsuits by various groups to follow. The crucial decision was in and the verdict clear: development had won, limits on growth had lost.

"We're toast," said a longtime member of the Farm Bureau. "It's the end of a noble experiment."

The board of supervisors would begin hearing the various appeals on the Walt Ranch development above Capell Creek, but meanwhile the Halls entertained the Clintons at their home above Auberge du Soleil. And on weekends demonstrators continued to show up in front of HALL Wines on Highway 29, carrying signs that said HALL-O-CAUST and CHAINSAW WINE. Tourists kept turning up, though not necessarily to visit the winery. The enormous steel rabbit full of holes was just too good a selfie opportunity to pass up.

3.

The call comes in the furnace of an early-summer afternoon, the county election still fresh in every mind and Highway 29 swimming in thermals. The parking lot of the Oakville Grocery's packed with highly reflective out-of-county cars. Inside, the long community table is elbow-to-elbow with devourers of wild mushrooms with melted cheese on whole wheat and other delicacies.

"It's all bullshit," Deep Root's saying, his voice enlivening the ether. "The environmentalists should get together, but they're always fighting. They may be ready to move against the Halls, but they have different objectives and actually *hate* each other. Chris Malan is obsessed with sediment and fish. Jim Wilson cares only about emissions and trees. Meanwhile the citizens are opposing every proposal for a winery put forward, anywhere, and that's not going to stop."

A semi loaded with bottles passes; another tourist comes in from the parking lot in North Face paraphernalia, looking for a mountain to climb. He finds arugula and mozzarella on sourdough instead.

"What the environmentalists don't understand," Deep Root continues, "is that they could end all this simply by suing the county over winery emissions. The governor has mandated that everybody must measure their carbon footprint, and that has to include winery-related releases. No one wants to face this or even have the subject raised because the consequences are *enormous*, as are the emissions themselves.

"The Halls pushed the envelope, and the other vintners are finally angry because the Halls are calling attention to activities and requirements for big wineries. Don't you see? Everybody's afraid of a lawsuit that will force wineries into compliance with state regulations. The Halls have spent eight million dollars to buy their twenty-three hundred acres, five million to officially study them, and two million on the little vineyard that was there when they bought the property. They could still lose that investment, but so what? He's a *billionaire*!

"The planning director will offer to help citizens and the applicant iron out their differences, and when all's said and done Hall won't get all his acres of vineyards, but he'll get enough. Then he and the county will figure out how many ranchettes he gets to build.

"It's hilarious. The enviros could shut it all down tomorrow if only they could agree. But the Sierra Club won't sue to make wineries comply with state mandates because they want leverage in the future by still being able to *threaten* to sue over emissions. Meanwhile all of them would rather fight each other than win. But somebody will eventually sue the county over this, and the battle that follows will be huge. It will be *bloody*."

Sunday afternoon and Angèle's is almost empty, the narrow view through the restaurant's inset windows of the roiled, muddy torrent of the Napa River. For a moment the affairs of the valley have been set aside for reflection and a taste of something other than the valley's universal beverage, for there are times in the affairs of men and women when distillation's quick effects and sharpened perceptions are preferred to the mellowness of wine.

On the bar stands a stemmed glass, quite pretty on the burnished wood, that contains gin, a touch of vermouth, and an olive. Unhurriedly raising the glass is Alex, a prominent player among the Winegrowers of Napa County who isn't utterly inured to environmental values, just to people who put those values between the Winegrowers and their desires. Many of those members are lucky spermers—the offspring of founders—who inherited established fiefdoms and the wherewithal to start new brands, race Porsches, whatever, without undue effort and with little knowledge of or interest in political or environmental issues.

The word *winegrowers* is archaic and basically nonsensical. Jack Cakebread knew that and accepted the moniker anyway. "The Winegrowers interviewed Pedroza after Jerry Brown appointed him to fill Dodd's seat," says Alex, musing. "The board had made him chairman right out of the gate—a twenty-nine-year-old with virtually no experience."

The statement's left hanging.

"The question of tourism comes up, whether or not five hundred event centers would be good for the valley. A member asked, 'Since we have ours, why do we care?' So we discussed it—you know, what our position should be. A show of concern was necessary, we decided, because it's good public relations. We should be seen as supporting existing regulations purely on grounds that doing this helps prevent new regulations."

The river slips by, sucked at by the outgoing tide in San Pablo Bay.

"A member of the Winegrowers said we should be seen as upholding the values of the winery definition. He meant limiting activities at new wineries and observing the seventy-five percent Napa grapes rule. Trouble is, half our members don't know what the winery definition is. Some are beginning to realize, though, that the world isn't infinite, and that a lot of people in the valley don't like them."

After one public hearing on Walt Ranch, a Winegrower exclaimed, "There's a lot of negativity out there!" The statement might have come from the high turret of some impregnable castle. Members tend to see the groundswell of opposition—most things, in fact—as if from a great distance, but Walt Ranch has brought much into focus, much of it unpleasant.

"Everything could have been handled better by the Halls," a tacit admission that other vintners are now feeling the heat. Meanwhile Hall has placed his own people within both the Grapegrowers and the Farm Bureau to bully opposition; the industry's distinct elements of leadership that once led citizens to believe change possible though discussion and compromise were gone now.

As for Randy Dunn, "his vineyards are right on top of Howell Mountain, he's got his," a handy dismissal far off the mark since Dunn's vineyards are relatively small, long-standing, and representative of phenomenally successful viticultural pioneering. But Alex doesn't really know what's transpired on distant Howell Mountain, never having heard of Wildlake.

Since Craig and Kathryn Hall are Winegrowers, now their problems are the Winegrowers', too. A dozen years before, Jayson Pahlmeyer was ostracized after his vineyard developer graded above Atlas Peak Road, a cause célèbre. Could the same thing happen to the Halls? "Pahlmeyer broke the law," says Alex, "and the Halls haven't been charged with anything."

And what would be the reaction among the Winegrowers should the Halls reveal, despite earlier disclaimers, that ranchettes are in fact going to be built on Walt Ranch? Alex, whose olive is now marooned in an empty glass, laughs heartily: "And what would be so terrible about that?"

VI.

WATER INTO WINE

A dedicated few take it upon themselves to protect Napa's most crucial resource, pitting them against an establishment determined to divide, rule, and chasten.

INTERLUDE:

The Drip

Cold lurks on the back edge of night, part of the contradiction of waking up in Northern California: down vests and bare arms, Bermudas and cable knits. I see these on runners at dawn—but never in the vineyards—and standing in line at the Napa Valley Coffee Roasting Company and other high-intensity caffeinating substations the length of the valley.

By 11:00 A.M. the vests are long gone and gazes, like moisture, trending heavenward. This dependable furnace of the sun, in conjunction with chilly nights even in summer, may be what produces wines such as Napa's, in conjunction with well-draining soils, much of it blown or washed down during formation of the Sierras millions of years ago, and pushed up time and again along contending tectonic edges.

The quality of that wine draws to Napa journalists concerned with all things of the palate, and I am invited to join a gaggle of them dining at Cindy's Backstreet Kitchen in St. Helena. The next day we're to take a tour of Newton Vineyard, our host a multinational that owns fashion and fragrance houses and estates in Champagne, Cognac, and other well-established wine regions, including Napa. They're a youthful lot: bloggers, a foodie website founder, and 'ziners. Then there's me—the sole print journalist.

The menu's full of promise—you have to be inept to eat badly in the valley—but first it must be vetted for lactose, soy, gluten. Then the delectable procession of dishes—Hog Island oysters, piquillo peppers stuffed with cumin-braised beef, rabbit tostada with red chile salsa—is carefully appraised, our insides lubricated by constant trickles of chardonnay, merlot, and Newton Vineyard's unfiltered rocket juice that sells for fifty-two dollars a bottle.

Discussion of Hollywood gives way to the millennial use of tweets and sound bites, then wine as an antidote to stress, the difficulty of finding adequate accommodation in Mendoza, and the fact that a winery like Newton, with right-of-way through its neighbors' property, can't allow in as many visitors as the winery might want. Though this limitation is basic to life in Napa Valley, and is the reason the place still looks so well, it confuses those assembled. "Why not?" one asks. "It's private property!"

Sensory journalism has evolved like any other, words electronic synapses with vast, near-effortless reach that have drawn enthusiasts of every persuasion, upended the old swirl-sniff-sip-jot hierarchy, and destabilized notable egos, but there's been a cost.

Among those riding up to Newton the next morning there's no awareness of the agriculture/urban clash fundamental to all that has happened here. Napa's more than three million visitors a year also mostly assume the place has always been as it is, nature bent to human wants and as predictable as vineyard views uncoiling on the far side of tinted coach windows.

In most wineries the old saw "visitation" has undergone another Orwellian transformation—"hospitality," genteelly implying that wineries put themselves out to receive you when in fact they're enhancing their bottom lines by selling all manner of things directly. This euphemism is about tourism, not agriculture, the hospitality industry wanting as many bodies as possible, and wineries increasingly devoted to harvesting events instead of grapes.

I met the late Peter Newton here, back in the 1980s. A sophisticated Brit, he had made a lot of money investing in Sterling Vineyards up Highway 29, the one with the gondola lift. It was bought by Coca-Cola, then sold to Seagram and then to the liquor conglomerate Diageo, and finally to Treasury. I dug my fingers into the dense coat of Newton's Grand Bleu de Gascogne hound while he talked about his little mountain, with its imported exotics for gardens he designed, reminding me of Jefferson's passionate amateur interest in the horticultural.

The juniper topiaries here still look like corkscrews, the roses are still so numerous they take two days to deadhead. The Torah gate leads to the residence, the lotus-shaped front door adding a strange, melancholy splendor to a house safe behind white stones raked in the Buddhist manner. Our tribe is introduced to the Secret Garden with its Thai spirits house; the English garden with its hanging mulberry and curtain of pleached blue spruce; and the Sleeping Beauty Garden with tree roses and a stone fountain brought over from England. The others turn back for the inevitable lunch, but I'm transfixed in the midst of an infinity-edge lawn high above a valley of Lilliputian vineyards stretching north toward the upthrust knob of Mount St. Helena, as if gazing directly into the past.

For a tour of the high, sixty-acre vineyard we board a six-wheeled Swiss all-terrain Pinzgauer of the sort that moved soldiers around Afghanistan. The reverse roller-coaster ride up to the pinnacle passes some of the costliest mountain viticulture on earth. Thin black plastic lifelines dipped into a reservoir far below, to irrigate what would be a semi-desert but for the nearness of the deep, cold Pacific Ocean. Until recently it regularly lofted enough moisture over coastal ranges to fill ponds and assure harvests, before the age of drought.

Talk has been of crush, cuvées, cultured versus wild yeasts, and the subtleties of French oak. Now, gazing directly across the valley at Howell Mountain, we discuss those plastic IVs for vines no less frail than the substance that fills them, water. The average rainfall for Napa has been about twenty-five inches annually but recently—in 2013—it was a quarter of that. Lack of water is on all minds, though climate change is mentioned gingerly everywhere in the valley and the phrase *global warming* can still disrupt a dinner party.

When Newton's prized cabernet was imperiled that year, the vineyard manager tells us, they discussed trucking water up from the valley floor. Some rain did fall at the last moment, but what, he's asked, would the buying and trucking have cost, if it hadn't?

He hesitates before saying, "Just under a million dollars."

CHAPTER SIXTEEN:

The Rutherford Dust Society

1.

The common element in all Napa's conflicts has been neither industrialism nor tourism, but water. Sometimes a minor player, usually a major one, water dogs almost all discussions. It was waste runoff that first drew Andy Beckstoffer into the world of Jean-Charles Boisset, and the use of city water that heightened contention between the new Davies Vineyards and the citizenry of St. Helena. Runoff from a proposed vineyard next to Wildlake on Howell Mountain brought St. Helena into that fray, too, and both state and federal regulatory machinery. And in the Walt Ranch epic, water played the lead in all its guises: purity, destructive potential in flood, utter ruin when absent.

People who would never have worked together but for these various connections came together in the flow of it: Beckstoffer, Geoff Ellsworth, Randy Dunn, Rick Coates, the Land Trust of Napa County, Chris Malan, Vision 2050, and many more. And out of these points of connectivity arose the year's final conflict, one that drew the cloak from the establishment's abject self-interest, damaged the community, and sparked possibly far-reaching changes that are still playing out.

Go back now to the final years of the twentieth century when the most obvious problem associated with this most precious resource was the Napa River itself. For most of its journey the river is a little-noticed presence, burrowing so deeply into its ancient bed as to be pitiful if even noticed by those crossing the bridges up-valley. It would occasionally re-emerge after heavy rains as its old self, reminding people of its destructive alter ego, the flood dumping much of the valley's soil into San Pablo Bay.

Ancillary damage to vineyards was considerable, and largely unaddressed, as if the river was an instrument of God and its rages an excuse to attack it in weak moments, including dumping car bodies, urban runoff, and waste into it. Meanwhile the things living in it were, for all practical purposes, disappearing. Then one day a man whose land bordered the river asked if all this might not be changed. His name was John Williams and his winery bore the unlikely name of Frog's Leap.

His earliest memory was of running a hand across the velour cover of his grandparents' Victorian settee, in upstate New York. The velvety resistance of the nap was softness itself, the dust mysterious and provocative, motes lofting through angled sunlight like memories of a distant past. Years later, he would taste a cabernet sauvignon made in the valley of the Napa River, near the sleepy hamlet of Rutherford, and be reminded of that touch and smell.

John attended Cornell University where he came under the influence of the noted enologist Konstantin Frank. A polymath, Frank was said to speak nine languages and made to be desperate by the refusal of Finger Lakes vintners to embrace the proven enological greats of cool climate European ancestry—pinot noir, chardonnay–choosing inelegant grape hybrids instead. John learned two things from this: Institutions and industries, once committed to a course of action, don't welcome dissent. And wine can drive you mad.

He also learned the importance of money because he ran out of it in the early 1970s and joined a work-study program at the Taylor Wine

Company. Then he left for Northern California, where he met a doctor, Larry Turley, who knew the famous Robert Mondavi, who in turn knew a vinicultural tyro named Warren Winiarski. Like many hopefuls in the days of perilous winemaking, Winiarski had been Mondavi's cellar rat before setting up a small independent operation on the eastern side of an uncrowded valley, in a district known quaintly as Stags Leap. Now Winiarski needed a cellar rat of his own.

John's duties included most everything in and around the winery. In the process of learning he tasted some of the most beautiful, subtle wines of his life, from vineyards with strange names like Fay and Cask 23, and realized that the sort of wine old Frank had championed back East was imminently possible here and might rival those of Pauillac and Margaux. In those days the grapes were picked when not too ripe, alcohol was controlled, fruit and acid maintained, and sufficient tannins imparted through barrel storage to produce elegantly balanced wines. These aged gracefully, were best drunk in concert with food, and left in the drinker the vague impression of dancing with a ravishing partner.

Meanwhile he sold odd bottles of Stag's Leap to tourists who happened by, pulled hoses, and bottled the 1973 vintage when it was ready, no reason to suspect that through his hands was passing a soon-to-be mythical substance that would radically alter the trajectories of the Winiarskis, John Williams, the valley, and much of Northern California by winning the most famous tasting ever, from the valley's point of view.

John made Stag's Leap's 1974 and 1975 vintages, too, but heard nothing in 1976 about the competitive tasting of French and Californian cabernets and chardonnays in Paris until one day he looked up and saw the thin, agitated figure of Warren running down the hill toward the winery. He was waving a copy of *Time* magazine in which there was a story about the Californians winning "the Judgment of Paris," the judges all being French critics, not American. Stag's Leap had come in first in the red wine category, and Chateau Montelena had won in the whites.

After that day strangers began arriving, all wanting a bottle of the 1973 vintage at the astoundingly high price of seven dollars. John was jerked from winemaking duties to selling the stuff until Warren told him to shut the winery door and open it only if an expensive car sat outside.

John returned to New York determined to become the Robert Mondavi of the Finger Lakes. But the reign of the hybrids had endured, along with the reluctance of winemakers to change, despite the fact that John's East Coast experiments were written about admiringly by Frank Prial in the *New York Times*. So he went back to Napa and into the cellar of Spring Mountain, in St. Helena, owned by Mike Robbins, another devotee of French wine.

John hung out with other winemakers enamored of the same style—young, adventurous types like Tony Soter and Cathy Corison. Married now, and a father, John bought a piece of property in Rutherford in partnership with Turley and started working for himself. He called it Frog's Leap, in droll homage to Winiarski's Stag's Leap as well as the aquatic life on John's parcel next to the Napa River, but Warren was neither flattered nor amused.

Years later, after the Smithsonian Institution in Washington, DC, set up an exhibition in the National Museum of American History commemorating the 1976 Paris Tasting, John wondered if viewers would realize that the crabbed notes in the displayed cellar book about the 1973 vintage had been written by him, spiritual heir to Konstantin Frank. But John had not been driven mad by wine, just so deeply into the arms of vino that escape was now impossible.

2.

The barn is old, red, and lovely, topped by a weather vane fashioned into an elongated leaping frog and surrounded by a riot of blooming wild mustard. This and other chest-high nitrogen fixers compose a dense, nutritious jungle overrunning the vineyard and trying to hide the winery's name painted unspectacularly on a fence rail. Despite sheets of black plastic stretched over a large mound of aging manure, winery and ground look more nineteenth than twenty-first century.

White-bearded now, the unassuming proponent of organic agriculture for two decades is talking sustainability: "We got the farming down but then I realize that there are thirty-five cars parked here belonging to workers. You don't want to come off holier than thou when half the things you do still contribute to pollution."

He still hopes for a parking shed with a roof of solar panels to recharge the batteries of the hybrid cars he would make available to employees, and one for a tractor that runs on solar energy. But that's another dream in the broader narrative of organics, an attempt to instill in farmer and consumer alike a greater appreciation of the taste of place. Inherent in that taste, they say, are healthier communities at both ends of the production cycle.

He grabs a spade, parts the mat of vegetation to more fully reveal the rich mix of cover crop, and turns over black soil full of worms and white nodules on the roots of plants where the nitrogen resides. He learned this and other lessons in the late 1980s after visiting Fetzer Vineyards, up in Mendocino County, which had undertaken an organic regimen early on. John hired a Sierra foothills farmer and itinerant agricultural consultant who traveled the state advocating effective holistic practices.

His advice led to Frog's Leap using certified organic grapes in 1989. It was making about sixty thousand cases annually from two hundred acres, plus another fifty owned by other organic growers who share his concerns. At the time some organic growers followed the biodynamic principles of the late Rudolf Steiner, the Austrian founder of anthroposophy and the Waldorf schools, but weren't officially certified.

Steiner's world-famous lectures, delivered in Koberwitz, Silesia, in 1924, were on agricultural theory and still widely discussed. But Steiner's "biodynamism" differed from merely organic farming as orthodoxy differed from freethinking. Though some of the ideas were logical, including the closed system that generates its own fertilizer from animals roaming fields and vineyards and limiting outside influences on crops and land, other Steinerisms elevated eyebrows, like planting and harvesting in accordance with phases of the moon, and putting crushed stone or cow manure in a cow horn and burying it for the winter, transforming it into a mysteriously potent force.

The cow horn and other Steinerisms are just the "sacraments" of biodynamics, in John's view. They do no harm to the farm, unlike fertilizer, which leeches into the ground, and spraying with herbicides and pesticides as most do in Napa, which drift onto neighbors' land and crops. "I believe in cosmic forces," John ventures, "but I can't run a vineyard this size by the calendar alone. Organic farming has evolved into a deeper understanding: If you want healthy soil, you don't want the guy tending it to be so poor he has to live in his car or under a bridge. And you don't want your winery using up too many resources."

He leans his spade against the barn.

"In the end, if you respect the principles, you take better care of everything. That's got to lead to better wine."

In 1997 an epochal flood scoured the banks of the Napa River and left behind ugly, twenty-five-foot mud walls. John had just agreed to purchase fifty acres to expand Frog's Leap, and a portion of those acres had washed down toward San Pablo Bay. The seller agreed to knock $60,000 off the price, and John immediately called a riparian expert. After looking at the damage, he told John that fixing the riverbank would cost $30,000, adding, "In cash."

John said okay.

"Well, that never happened so fast," meaning the decision to spend so much money.

The expert dumped big "toe" boulders at the base of the bank, drove stakes into the bank above, and wove mats with live willow branches. He put sand on the mats and watered it, and the following year willows began to grow in. Meanwhile John went up and down the river, looking at what he called "the levee wars": neighbors trying to deal with undercut banks overgrown with invasive species, including nonnative blackberries, host to malevolent insects like the glassy-winged sharpshooter that spreads the bacterium causing Pierce's disease, which can kill grapevines within a few years.

"It was a never-ending battle. We needed a systematic approach."

What really opened his eyes were the old car bodies he found dumped in the river in the vain hope that soil and debris would accumulate around them and make a difference. Meanwhile siltation in the increasingly narrow channel had decimated salmon and steelhead. The human overlords all needed regulating, and the only way to get that was by having neighbors agree.

"A snowball's chance in hell," John thought.

Judging by the comments he had heard over the years, of all the growers along the river only Andy Beckstoffer seemed likely to favor draconian measures for fixing an old, intractable, now desperate situation. What the rest needed was subtle educating, and the only way to do that was by bringing everybody together socially and very gradually introducing an alien idea.

The first meeting of what would become the Rutherford Dust Society was just the occasional coming-together of growers and winemakers in the neighborhood. This time they were to discuss planning a tasting of wines made from grapes grown on Rutherford's broad plain, made famous by the recently deceased avatar of Napa Valley winemakers, André Tchelistcheff. The tasting would be in faraway New York, to remind Francophilic Manhattanites that some exceptional cabernet sauvignons from Napa tasted much like those from France and were just as good— often better—when made in the old-world style.

At one point in the meandering conversation, John Williams said, "You know, there really is no Rutherford," meaning no political and social designation within which people voted and then acted in concert. "We're talking about promoting a community that doesn't exist. I haven't been to your wineries, and you haven't been to mine. There's no living history here beyond the 4-H Club. We should find out who we all are."

The effect was silence, followed by reluctant grunts. When John later raised the question of the ailing Napa River and problems it caused adjacent growers, one of them said, "I don't give a shit about the Napa River. But I've got a Pierce's problem that just won't quit," and he conceded that controlling invasive plant species that harbored pests was needed.

John started visiting his neighbors. One of them, irascible old Joe Heitz, demigod of Martha's Vineyard cabernet fame, did something highly uncharacteristic: He hosted a lunch for the nascent Rutherford coalition, and John knew he had struck a chord. "I began to see a nexus," he later recalled, "and not just a marketing organ. We were facing fines after the passage of ballot-box propositions for vineyard setbacks from streams and flood control and so I went to Davie Piña."

3.

Piña has an office on Silverado Trail, in Rutherford, and is the vineyard developer who would eventually be chosen to plan Mike Davis's new vineyard up on Howell Mountain. An old-line presence in the development community, Piña had several clients whose vineyards bordered the river. Flooding from broken levees had caused them all problems, and Davie listened with interest the day John brought a stranger to a meeting of Rutherford growers.

His name was Phil Blake and he represented the Resource Conservation District, the county agency dedicated to helping property owners conserve land and protect agriculture. The RCD, as it's called, represented "government," the widespread bête noire already being reviled in political clashes around the country by those who would coalesce into the Tea Party. Extreme property rights proponents were well represented in Napa Valley, and energized in the late 1990s' epic clash between the vintner Jayson Pahlmeyer, environmentalist Chris Malan, and the Sierra Club.

One of the Rutherford group was also a member of the Winegrowers, which opposed government involvement in property management decisions, particularly when related to the environment. Since everything did relate to the environment, the position was increasingly untenable. Yet the vociferous Clarke Swanson—inheritor of the frozen food empire—was unfriendly, as were the owners of the Caymus and Round Hill wineries.

The group drank a few bottles of zinfandel while Blake showed slides he had brought along. He was known for an extraordinary knowledge of land use that cut across disciplines, for his luxuriant mustache, and his penchant for "anywho" as a substitute for "anyhow." Blake offered the services of the RCD to help restore the riverbanks to anyone who might want them.

Other neighbors insisted that "the river's something you don't want to touch." The collective lore about the river's power and mysterious ability to confound the plans of human beings was rich and went beyond dumping in wrecked pickup bodies to teach it a lesson. "Flood control once meant putting a Caterpillar D8 on the riverbed in summer," someone said, "and driving south."

Some at the meeting insisted that the river didn't belong to the county, but to those whose property it flowed past and who could do with it as they pleased. In reality the river belonged to everyone, though it remained a notional no-man's-land in some minds, masking a fear of rules from the county that required effort and lucre. But evidence mounted that such rules and subsequent action could save property owners money, and spare them grief. Davie Piña would later admit, "I had expected people to say, 'What the hell is this? No!' Instead, I saw heads nodding. They knew something had to be done."

Building levees, the usual solution to flooding, was ultimately useless without riverbank restoration because water would forcefully eat into the levees and cause them to fail. Even if the Rutherford group proceeded as suggested, it would take at least three years for the studies and actual work to be done. It would also cost a lot. Some money would come from the county, some from the property owners, but the latter would have to come up with theirs first.

The eventual cost was reckoned at two dollars a running foot, which for Piña Vineyard Management clients was about $7,000 apiece. But this was a lot cheaper than the possible loss of an acre of land valued at $150,000 or more. There were other benefits: a reduction of riverbank growth that harbored the dreaded insects, and levees that could be permitted instead of the current makeshift ones that had to be built without permits.

It was all pretty low-key, John thought, to his surprise. His rebuilt riverbank served as a demo plot, helping convince others to follow his example "even though I was already considered a communist by some because I dry-farm and recommend that Rutherford become a herbicide-free zone."

Most of the property owners eventually agreed to the joint effort, while others undertook the repairs on their own. Someone had to oversee this creature, and it was agreed on that the person to do that should be the one who came up with the bright idea in the first place.

But when people turned to John Williams, he said, "No, not me, Davie."

Piña was soon learning that rivers are a great deal more complicated than he had imagined. Also that he needed help answering clients who called and asked whether or not progress was being made, and whether or not funding would come from the county, and what the exact rules were, and what their effect might be. "I just told them the positive stuff," Piña says, "trying to move the project along."

The technical side he could handle. The scientific and political questions were something else again, but slowly, against steep odds, the snowball in hell grew.

Many years and $21 million later, almost five miles of the Napa River in the center of the valley have been more or less restored. Almost twenty acres of vineyard land were given up to improve the river corridor, an act of generosity by those recognizing the joint roles of science, government, and landowners. Flood damage has been greatly reduced on these stretches, with habitat restored, and work on another three miles, from Oakville to Oak Knoll, is under way.

At the river's south end, after decades of discussion, controversy, and scientific consultation and help in flood control from the U.S. Army Corps of Engineers, new wetlands have appeared. Wilder habitat has brought new wildlife, including otters, but not many salmon, and steelhead are still rarely seen. Other aquatic species continue a desperate struggle going back to the limits of human memory in Napa Valley.

Most of the river channel remains a degraded sluiceway for dirt washing down from on high. Despite mitigation methods that slow this exodus of soil, the dwindling rain still brings with it fine soil, including fertilizer and other chemicals, that cover any eggs that might have been laid, the direct result of vineyard development.

This hasn't prevented the industry, which has collectively done little to help the river, from pointing out that it has gotten healthier. Though demonstrably true, this is practically meaningless ecologically since so much of it remains degraded, and the spotty improvement has been used as an excuse for more development higher in the watershed. Vineyard developers have proposed eradicating trees at the very time the valley—and the earth—require more both for immediate well-being and for mitigating climate change.

The water question was given new urgency in 2016, when out of the *lumpenproletariat*—Napa-style—rose some of the same discordant voices that had split the valley over Walt Ranch. What they called for were some limits on development, neither new nor radical, but no observer would have guessed this from the industry's unhinged reaction.

CHAPTER SEVENTEEN:
Fifty Feet from Forever

1.

Thomas Jefferson's faded agrarian dream had devolved into a celebration of commerce as the ultimate expression of democracy, just as the notion of enlightenment had devolved into tourism. In Napa, a class system based on wine as the generator of wealth encouraged economic inequality and social isolation and skewed once-venerable institutions and ways of life. Claims of just how much was being made in the valley varied and were often unreliable, but it was estimated as an $18 billion economy. The effect of this aura was alternately inspirational, disruptive, and increasingly unreal.

The prospect of hundreds of new event centers in a narrow valley thirty miles long beggared agrarian values and threatened to spoil a local record of accomplishment. Public discussions were held on whether or not wineries and developers should obey the law, a distinctly odd convention by American standards. Public grievances were aired before safe collections of interested parties, the names of the groups utterly anodyne and the participants complicit.

The Agricultural Protection Advisory Committee was one, though a more appropriate name would have been the Vintners' Liability Prevention Committee. In 2015 the committee was presided over by the same stentorian corporate oracle in a voluminous polo shirt who facilitated the takeover of the Robert Mondavi Winery by the colossus Constellation and earned $6 million for his trouble. Now an aspiring St. Helena hotelier, he deftly let the steam out of the kettle of public disgust without requiring vintners to actually do anything. This was proclaimed an accomplishment by corporate peers and senior county staff, whereas the many citizens who took time off to testify were left slack-jawed by the committee's ineptitude.

Brave affirmations of the status quo ante would have been amusing if the lack of so-called code enforcement hadn't remained shockingly weak. Vintners would now be asked to file reports of compliance with the production levels they had been granted, a kind of self-audit, but they would not be required to actually sign these documents because that would put them within reach of the law, had the law been reaching.

The supervisors continued to legalize illegal construction and other amenities after the fact, so winery owners might sell these properties with legal-by-fiat additions, similar to developers illegally bulldozing trees in the hills for projects that were then deemed legal. And individual supervisors, out of indifference, self-interest, or whim, looked kindly upon applications for expansions that by law should have been disallowed. The county's conduct in the new century was in stark contrast to the previous one, when office-holders for the most part acted with respect for history and public institutions and displayed rigor that in retrospect seems quaint. Electing candidates dedicated to maintaining the integrity of the watershed and agriculture at the expense of real estate development remained difficult, and costly. Officials and corporate spokespeople lauded these things in the abstract, and violated them in practice; sums large enough for environmentally minded candidates to compete electorally with the wine, tourism, and real estate engine remained practically unreachable for grassroots organizations to raise, another condemnation of the effects of the *Citizens United* decision by the Supreme Court.

The fractured environmental movement had cluttered its own path

to office with competition from within; self-interested professional organizations paid homage to agriculture and tradition while backing candidates who undermined both. Increasingly citizens believed that another
way had to be found to bring governing bodies into alignment with common desires and the law.

Mike Hackett grew up playing in the woods behind his parents' house,
halfway between Seattle and Portland. He and his friends made forts and
generally lost themselves in early-American fantasies, but home life was
different. His father, a railroad engineer and both alcoholic and worka-
holic, urged his square-built, athletic son into tennis and other sports and
lived vicariously through him. But he also brought grief, casting Mike as
the ameliorating force between him and Mike's mother and three sisters.
This left Mike, in his own view, "pretty good at reading people, particularly when they're being disingenuous," a talent that would one day come
into play in a very different place.

Like a lot of westerners, Mike ended up in a profession tinged with
romance—flying—and while in the navy lofted P-3s out of Moffett Field.
When he got out he went to work for Hughes Airwest, then for Northwest. When that airline was taken over by Delta he retired while still a
relatively young man, and he and his wife, Carolyn, moved to Cupertino,
south of San Francisco Bay.

They visited Napa, were overcome by the physical beauty, and like
so many other couples decided to move there, buying a "view" house
above the valley in 1976. Mike planted three thousand Douglas firs to
sell as Christmas trees and then, at the height of the dot-com boom, sold
out and bought a more modest house outside Angwin, high on Howell
Mountain, which still had the cheapest real estate overlooking the valley. He thought of this as their final resting place, "the High Sierra with
vines," and settled in to play tennis and enjoy the proximity of not-quite-
unspoiled backcountry.

Also in Angwin was Pacific Union College, a small Seventh-day Ad-
ventist outpost possessed of a lot of real estate. Mike watched as the school
"bled red for years," and then an absentee board of directors decided to

sell off some of its land. The easiest way to do that, in strict accordance with American business scripture, was real estate development—in this case using a loophole in the law that allowed some new residences in the restrictive agricultural watershed.

Mike hated politics but wanted to leave a legacy, and the best way to do that, he decided, was "to save Howell Mountain from destruction." He and like-minded neighbors, some distant, formed Save Rural Angwin, adding a new tribe to Napa's broadening grassroots community. With the help of Volker Eisele he told people, "We need to be able to stand up to the developers," particularly "one of the richest men in the world who doesn't need the money" (by now a too-familiar living caricature in Napa), and their elaborate proposals for an urban bubble in the woods.

The county board of supervisors hadn't yet become the recognized graveyard of conservation dreams, and it had put off ruling on clearcutting parts of Howell Mountain, distracted by destruction on the valley floor caused by the 2014 earthquake. Save Rural Angwin joined the larger anti-growth group Vision 2050, with the knowledge that small communities all over were struggling against superior forces. At that early-2015 meeting down at Napa High, Mike saw that people were generally angry about rampant development and the complicit board of supervisors. He thought the departing planning director had "left a legacy of saying yes to development first always," justifying it by citing the recession, and thus contributing mightily to the ongoing disaster.

Claims of lost revenue were used to justify lax law enforcement that continued, and direct-to-consumer sales had become *the* business model even though abhorred by all but wineries and banks. Day and night the county reverberated with powerful machines as wineries rose, expanded, burrowed into the earth, raised up monoliths to their owners, ran giant fans to cool themselves, dipped hoses illegally into nearby streams, and otherwise opened the throttle on the machine in the garden.

Big trees came down all around Angwin, on other ridges, and in steep terrain on both sides of the valley, largely out of sight because they were high up and screened by the very trees destined to come down. Prospective small and gargantuan planned vineyards that rocked the natives north to south, west to east, Walt Ranch being the big one. But lots of competitors waited for more hemorrhaging of the regulatory dam, most hoping for a washout.

2.

Back in 1991, Napa County had passed the hillside ordinance requiring growers to obtain county approval for vineyards planted on steep slopes. A decade later Chris Malan and the Sierra Club's lawsuit victory over Pahlmeyer forced growers and their vineyard "managers" (read: proxy dynamiters and bulldozer operators) wanting to develop new hillside vineyards to subject their plans to the California Environmental Quality Act. This was a much tougher and more expensive standard, justified by abuses in the past, but it enraged vintners and potential growers accustomed to doing as they pleased in the hills. The legal victory of the heirs to John Muir's passion consolidated industry groups that in the past had found less in common.

Clearing and building continued in the hills on both sides of the valley, ill regulated, increasingly alarming. Those cutting trees up in the watershed were already required to spare at least 60 percent of the tree canopy and replace any oaks cut with twice as many planted elsewhere. But this, too, was difficult to monitor and meant an enormous, ongoing diminution of canopy for a generation and more, at a time when action on climate change was being stymied by politics.

Jim Wilson's proselytizing on behalf of living trees was powerful and persuasive enough to convince most within earshot. He convinced Mike Hackett, and they teamed up in early 2016 to put together what became the Water, Forest and Oak Woodland Protection Initiative. Included was a requirement that any landowner wanting to remove oak trees from plots of five acres or larger had to first get county approval and then preserve at least 90 percent of the canopy, as well as plant substitute oaks elsewhere at a ratio of three to one. And buffer zones around all streams would be increased.

Mike, who had previously known little about land use, now knew more than he ever thought possible. Talking to Volker and Randy Dunn had been part of it, but so had reading agricultural reports and propositions and attending meetings all over, which meant long drives in mountainous country. His and Carolyn's style of living changed radically, and though she supported his efforts on behalf of Save Rural Angwin 95 percent of the time, the other five percent she just wanted to pick up and move.

When Randy asked Mike to run the meeting on the Eiseles' front porch, up in Chiles Valley, to organize opposition to Mike Davis's vineyard next to Wildlake, he readily agreed. The preservation of trees and streams became the last thing he thought about when he went to bed at night and the first thing he thought about when he got up in the morning.

A lot of insight also came from Jim Wilson over on Capell Creek. Wilson was obviously an idealist and far removed from the realm of vintners, both geographically and spiritually. Deeply and adamantly opposed to Walt Ranch, he was equally devoted to the basic, a priori notion that human beings should be planting trees nonstop wherever possible as a bulwark against looming climate change, not the opposite. Cutting them down for vanity vineyards and ranchettes was not just shameful but also stupid in the light of global warming, and the refusal of those in titular control of the valley to recognize this was the signal failure of his time.

Oaks were Jim's thing: colossal spreading canopies of great natural beauty and function, miracles of transpiration in an incipient desert, mighty vertical reservoirs and anchors of shifting soils and whole hillsides that without big trees would run straight down and into the waterway—all justification enough for saving them.

But oaks also served as harbors for wildlife, leafy, oxygen-expiring ganglia enduring with difficulty a now century-long invasion of determined realtors in the making and their enablers. The arboreal and the human, one beneficial, the other reductive, were locked in a desperate race for dwindling viable land and a chance to save, or use up, the most essential resource: water.

Mike Hackett, on the other hand, was interested in conifers, specifically the towering Douglas firs that screen Angwin's environs from the otherwise inescapable sun. He and Jim Wilson talked about these different species—the leafy and needley—and came to the decision that tree protection as it existed was insufficient and destructive of headwaters. Trees fed downslope rivulets that joined each other, in season, ever-burgeoning freshets on facing sides of the Howell and Mayacamas ranges and all ending up in the Napa River.

A strengthening of county law limiting tree cutting was desperately needed, particularly for oaks and conifers, and expanded protection for stream banks—so-called setbacks where, if nothing was cut, vernal wetlands and streams would survive and prosper. That meant changing the law. Since that was impossible with the current makeup of the board of supervisors—a local reflection of the dysfunctional U.S. Congress, they would have to get the initiative before the people. That meant hiring lawyers to draft it, collecting signatures, and putting the whole question on the ballot in the November 2016 general election. To fail at this, many thought, would be a crime against nature and humanity.

Looking back, Mike would see mistakes made from the beginning, proof of their own naiveté. They talked to Chris Malan about the initiative and Mike wanted to bring her, with her knowledge, experience, and contacts, into the crafting of a voter initiative. But publicly banding with her meant they would lose a lot of support within the industry, so it was agreed that she would act in an advisory capacity only.

The real problem was Napa's byzantine political power conglomerate: the Napa Valley Vintners, svelte corporate outgrowth of the old coalition made up of Louis Martini, John Daniel Jr., Robert Mondavi, Fernande de Latour, and a few others who in 1944 signed a formal agreement to promote Napa wines; the Winegrowers of Napa County, the gilded husk of Jack Cakebread's old ad hoc breakfast club; the Napa Valley Grapegrowers, Andy Beckstoffer's early cause that had since trended toward development; and the Farm Bureau, the last holdout for family farms, such as they were. In recent years even the Farm Bureau had begun to lean away from environmental safeguards and toward developers. That catch-all category included vineyard creators, the difference being that now the development itself was the prime objective because these properties could be more easily flipped, with huge profits. Farming was the trailing, even ancillary activity. And developers were elbowing their way onto boards and committees all over.

Mike Hackett readily joined Jim Wilson as an emissary, assuming—knowing, he thought—they would find some support in all the groups, with the possible exception of the reactionary Winegrowers. Also that real stewards of the land—there were many, though they avoided the spotlight—no matter which organization they belonged to, would approve of tightening controls on clearing land that resulted in runoff and make their voices heard.

Better regulations would improve the river, Mike thought, conserve water, and help offset climate change, something the governor had mandated statewide. In view of all this, the initiative would seem to admirably meet the needs of the age. So he turned on his cell phone and called the Vintners' government relations director, Rex Stults.

They met at Cindy's Backstreet Kitchen, and Stults—self-assured and, despite his inflated title, respectful—seemed genuinely interested in the idea of the initiative. Mike told him why he and Jim Wilson thought limiting the cutting of trees and increasing buffer zones along streams would better protect the county. Before leaving he asked Stults to run the idea by his executive board and get back to him.

Meanwhile proponents of the initiative had begun raising money. Randy Dunn gave them $5,000 seed money and they hired Shute, Mihaly & Weinberger to draft a resolution, which was submitted to the county for approval. After the initiative had been reviewed, the backers would gather the required number of signatures—roughly three thousand—from registered voters in favor of the initiative so it could go on the general election ballot the following year, November 2016, when a new president was also to be chosen.

But Stults didn't call Mike Hackett back. So Mike called him again and was told, "We've budgeted a quarter of a million dollars to fight this." But Stults seemed to suggest that if changes were made to the requirements of the initiative, the Vintners might support it, or at least remain neutral.

Mike offered to come down to St. Helena and this time he took Jim Wilson with him, not to Cindy's but to the Vintners' industrial-chic headquarters in St. Helena across the street from the public library. They found not just the government relations director waiting but also the Vintners' attorney, Richard Mendelson, one of Napa's many winery advocates, and David Graves, cofounder of Saintsbury Winery and a member of the Vintners' board. Mike and Jim felt ambushed.

Making the best of it, Mike offered adjustments to the setback requirements in the initiative. The presentation went well enough, he thought. In closing, Mike said, "Help me here. I need an answer from the Vintners," adding, "if I were a vintner, I would want this."

He went home with the impression that they might reconsider their position. He and Jim returned once more and told the Vintners' reps—a changeable lot—that in essence they weren't anti-vineyard or anti-winery and just wanted to stop loss of forests and water. But Stults still didn't call. Mike assumed that the Vintners, preeminent powerhouse in the valley, had just wanted to see what the initiative proponents might be willing to give up. Both Mike and Jim figured they had been played.

3.

Next they went to the Grapegrowers, who wanted to meet at the winery belonging to Don Munk, Craig and Kathryn Hall's vineyard manager. The assembled growers seemed to question the need to clean up the river. Mike could usually stop a conversation anywhere by asking if defenders of the river's condition would let their grandchildren play in it. But this time a developer said, "Yes, the river's cleaner than it was thirty years ago," what had become the stock response.

It soon became clear that the Grapegrowers were anti-regulation, period. The executive director, an outspoken young woman named Jennifer Putnam, objected to the use of the term *clear-cutting* because, in strict forestry parlance, leaving any trees at all disqualifies it as a clear-cut. "I have a degree in forestry," she added acidly, as if this was relevant; the initiative proponents were wasting their time.

Mike set up a meeting with Hugh Davies at Schramsberg, confident of finding support there. Climbing the wooden steps next to the magnificent eucalyptus that drops graceful sheaths of bark year-round, he saw a now historic winery lovingly maintained and still breathing of the past.

Hugh received Mike not in his office but in the Tower Room on whose wall were framed letters of appreciation and memorial photos of Jack and Jamie Davies, even Ronald Reagan. Hugh listened to Mike's pitch and said, "If I wanted to expand sometime, this initiative would make it impossible." It had never occurred to Mike that expansion here on the mountainside could be a consideration.

Hugh then asked for proof that the river was in worse condition than it had been a decade before. Mike thought, "Anyone can see by looking at it that the river's still a mess." Demanding new, conclusive numbers was a common stall by those opposing regulation, and Mike was surprised and disappointed that Hugh was using it. Forty years earlier, the Environmental Protection Agency had classified the Napa River as impaired by sediment washing down from development above and including pathogens and chemical fertilizers that deplete oxygen in water. Algal growth exacerbated an ongoing problem, as did polluted runoff during storms and the occasional release of raw sewage. Fish remained seriously affected, native coho salmon having gone extinct in the 1960s, and Chinook salmon were now endangered. Steelhead, the oceangoing trout, had been threatened for years and now numbered fewer than two hundred adults. Reputable biologists believed the steelhead, too, was on a path to extinction if stream and river flows didn't increase.

Ignoring the baleful impact of all these things on the river, after decades of study, seemed cynical to Mike Hackett. Yes, the river was cleaner than it was thirty years ago when raw sewage went into it as a matter of course. Since then, the exemplary efforts of the Rutherford Dust Society had been exploited by some outside that organization claiming the organization's restoration efforts proved the river was "getting better" and no further action was needed.

Mike departed with a very different idea about Schramsberg than he had brought with him up those rough steps, under the spreading branches of the huge old tree.

Mike was given an intern by one of the initiative's support groups, Forests Forever, to help come up with the new figures Hugh had asked for. But before they could be compiled Hugh called Mike and told him he was dropping out of Save Rural Angwin. Now Mike was dumbfounded. This scion of the Schramsberg Davieses, long associated with environmental safeguards, founders of the Jack L. Davies Agricultural Fund, and a former disciple of Volker Eisele, should have been a natural ally. Not so long ago Hugh had openly challenged his fellow vintners to accept unpopular environmental restraints, but no more.

Had the St. Helena fight been so painful as to permanently turn Hugh against the things he once ardently supported? Or did he accept the inevitability of the harvesting of the last resource? Only time would tell.

The Winegrowers of Napa County never invited either Mike or Jim Wilson to come talk about the initiative. Mike went to see Diane Dillon, the up-valley supervisor and a veteran of the land-use wars, and explained the initiative and the difficulties proponents in her constituency were having. He asked if she thought the industry had been essential in her getting reelected, a naive question from her point of view. Without answering she got down a map of Napa County north of the city and spread it out before Mike. "Seventy-five percent of the wineries are in my district," she said. Mike was wasting his breath.

Surely, he thought, the Farm Bureau will support this. After all, the organization's made up of farmers. The oldest of the four organizations wielding the most influence—the Vintners, the Winegrowers, the Grapegrowers, and the Farm Bureau—the Bureau had backed Volker Eisele and Andy Beckstoffer when they launched the Winery Definition Ordinance in the 1980s.

That had imposed the 75 percent rule and limited promotional activities at new wineries, both necessary rules in the minds of most players and observers at that time. But the Bureau had been a battleground ever since. Good land-use stewards in prominent positions over the years had dwindled in number and influence and were now in the minority, and Mike and Jim Wilson were troubled as they drove down to their headquarters in the city of Napa.

The board was waiting. At first they were respectful, but as the discussion progressed Mike noticed that Craig Hall's vineyard manager had brought along more developers and they smirked and made snide remarks. The executive director, Sandy Elles—"a Kumbaya type" in Mike's opinion—asked why Mike hadn't come to the Farm Bureau first, and then sat silently while the vineyard developers expressed opposition. He left with the impression that the Bureau had made up its mind before he and Jim ever got there.

Later, they redrafted the initiative to garner support, reminded that Volker had done the same thing when drafting the resolution for Measure J back in the late 1980s. It had given voters final say in how agricultural lands were to be developed, and Measure P had extended that law for another fifty years. To casual observers those initiatives were often confusing, but both J and P had been stunning achievements and, considering the direction the valley was going, now seemingly miraculous.

The primary problem with the new initiative remained the size of stream setbacks, so-called water quality buffer zones. Mike and Jim went to the California Department of Fish and Wildlife on the Silverado Trail and other agencies to find out if smaller setbacks could still be effective. And Randy Dunn took all the available information about developed parcels in the county to a mapper to see exactly how many would be affected. The answer was that half the designated parcels in the county would be, and 80 percent of all undeveloped land. Class I, II, and III streams were everywhere, it seemed, and suddenly more important than ever.

Scientific studies stated that a minimum of thirteen hundred feet from development is required to protect wetlands, and three hundred feet for all stream classes. Could these be responsibly reduced? they wondered. Looking further into the question as the initiative gathered strength, they began to worry that ordinary voters might not support this, and in the end they reduced the distance of the setbacks from streams down to fifty feet and then to thirty-five, a major concession but a political necessity.

Over the next few weeks, outside supermarkets, libraries, and elsewhere, they and others gathered signatures and e-mail addresses. Other environmental organizations pitched in, the most basic expression of democracy the valley had seen in years. It promised at long last meaningful if modest limits on a process that was denuding sections of ridgelines and high valleys and imperiling streams, facts few of their opponents on the other side even bothered to deny.

The economic argument—"It's too expensive"—had become the only one that mattered to the industry. Mike heard that the Vintners' board had sent a mass e-mail to the entire membership saying that Vision 2050—and Chris Malan, a red flag waving in the face of male vintners— was trying to impose an unnecessary rule on the county. The Vintners would have nothing to do with it, and upped the amount of money it was willing to spend in opposition to half a million.

But the voters seemed enthusiastic. The signatures of more than six thousand had easily been gathered, almost twice the number required, and were proudly presented to the county for verification well before the deadline.

CHAPTER EIGHTEEN

Chinatown

1.

What was a victory procession in the minds of the organizers of the Water, Forest and Oak Woodland Protection Initiative and of the signers of the petition, was a march to the gallows in the collective mind of the opposition. Proponents didn't yet suspect the full extent of the industry's hatred of the measure and of them, or the extent to which the leaders would go to kill it.

Proponents had become upstarts and worse in the industry's mind, daring to challenge the county's collective power structure and bound to feel its wrath. *Audacity* was the word used most often by leaders of the Vintners, the Winegrowers, and the Grapegrowers. Even the plodding Farm Bureau, more annoyed by political neophytes than offended, signed on to a joint steering committee whose objective was preventing the initiative from finally reaching the ballot, though its supporters thought it already had. For, once there, it would probably prevail and so hamper looming projects, the most important—the only—true consideration in leadership's collective mind.

A new politics now prevailed: Increased environmental hardship to come was an accepted reality, but public admission of it was not. Climate change remained as socially and politically untenable as it was scientifically undeniable, and "global warming," with its suggested human complicity, an outright pariah.

Most annoying had been the discovery that voters were eager to sign the petition and align themselves with the inevitable climate change disasters to come. Didn't the signers know the gift they had been given, surrounded as they were by luxurious spin-offs of wine production and their adoring visitors from all over the world, as well as endless vines wherever they looked, including—increasingly—upward, a plethora of good restaurants, neighbors who worked for large corporations, grand spas that made the fusty hot springs and mud baths of old Calistoga anomalies? Didn't they have the opportunity to visit tasting rooms whenever they liked, when other Americans had to travel dozens, hundreds, even thousands of miles for the experience? Where was the gratitude?

It never seemed to occur to opponents of the initiative that many Napans cared deeply about the fact that the county's cancer rates were among the state's highest and that they were surrounded by the residue of Roundup and pesticides applied by the ton, as well as by dust, automotive exhaust, smoke, traffic, strangers, outsized new structures, high prices, ineffective, indifferent, and possibly corrupt public officials, condescending "vintners" who weren't, and a constantly disrupted landscape. The contrast was stark.

The Grapegrowers called a clandestine meeting of the steering committee at their headquarters in Napa. A survivalist impulse had quickly seized the collective leadership, with early discussion of dirty tricks to thwart the initiative, including sabotaging the signature-gathering process before it succeeded. Jennifer Putnam of the Grapegrowers said they had to get the word *water* out of the original name of the initiative "because 'water' is a trigger with voters." Debra Dommen, sturdy puller of the Orwellian plow, according to two attendees, told the assembly that she had called Stu Smith, the bearded, highly vocal private-property-rights advocate, and told him to reactivate his followers. "They'll act so wacko they'll make us look good."

The Farm Bureau's Land Use Committee members were largely silent. Their director was offended because Mike Hackett and Jim Wilson had gone to the Vintners and the Grapegrowers first, and this caused loss of face inside the collective organizations' inner world. Some on the Farm Bureau board thought the organization should preserve what was left of its independence. A second steering committee meeting was called at the Farm Bureau, and unaffiliated experts brought in for advice, including Phil Blake of the Resource Conservation District who said that the initiative, if passed, would have no real effect on agriculture.

But what no one said aloud was that farming had become the easiest and most acceptable cover for all sorts of development. The Napa Valley Vintners had, in a meeting of its Community and Industry Issues Committee, referred not to the Water, Forest and Oak Woodland Protection Initiative, but to the "Anti-Farming Initiative," more Orwellian double-speak without mention of wackos or dirty tricks. When a Farm Bureau representative dared ask aloud, "Do we really want this fight? We're already seen as big ag and big water consumers," the Winegrowers and the Grapegrowers ignored her. They wanted blood.

From their perspective, the industry must be perceived as united and unassailable. It was a defining moment in the modern-day vintner/citizen relationship in America's most famous terroir, which had sprouted a home-grown Darwinism whereby the establishment must prevail at all costs and teach lessons to upstarts in the process. Ironically, the leaders of all four groups were women. By maintaining lockstep with their reactionary male counterparts, they showed they could compete in what was still very much a man's world, but the spectacle left a bad taste in many mouths.

In the ensuing weeks these now bonded organizations would be christened the Four Horsemen of the Apocalypse. Initially a joke, this quickly became a harbinger, a proud one for some: Being compared to the Four Horsemen, they said, could be seen as a powerful expression of righteous wrath.

The county's tax assessor duly announced that the signatures had been verified and that the Water, Forest and Oak Woodland Protection Initiative would indeed be on the ballot in November. The Grapegrowers' director then sent out the collective public letter claiming that the four organizations were "deeply disappointed that this quasi-environmental initiative was proposed," one "loaded with misinformation and hidden costs," code for the diminishment of members' bottom lines. "There is no question that Napa County has already taken a forward-looking approach to environmental protection," and, should the initiative become law, it would "complicate" the system already in place.

For "complicate" readers were obviously supposed to substitute "restrain profit." Vintners, growers, and developers insisted that they must be allowed, at all costs, to proceed with "farming," that now established euphemism for radical landscape alteration. Anyone questioning this was not just treasonous but a de facto enemy.

Two decades before, reaction to criticism within the industry would have been measured. But in the interim two fundamental changes had occurred: the compounding of profits that could be made in wine and related pursuits, and climate change. The latter could no longer be ignored or discredited with a straight face because climate change had begun to cost everybody real money. Rising temperatures and dwindling resources curtailed development and wiped some projects off the drawing boards. As befitted the age of calamity, the new Darwinians now wanted even more of their share of what was available, a particularly pernicious version of the "tragedy of the commons," the fact that someone will always take more than they are entitled to from common resources.

With such self-interest in full view, Napa joined the nationwide clamor for a deregulated America by those large financial interests that profit most from it. Long a shining exception to prevailing land use in California and the nation, Napa was turning on itself in a frantic desire to fully exploit its name and resources now, threatening the valley's very ethos.

The Water, Forest and Oak Woodland Protection Initiative had become an issue in its own right. Resistance—or at best demurral—came from some proponents of open space who were afraid the initiative would interfere with another initiative already on the 2016 ballot authorizing a quarter-cent sales tax dedicated to protecting land. This included the Land Trust, whose director advised Mike Hackett to drop the initiative because it was so controversial. And even Andy Beckstoffer declined to endorse. "I'm going to sit this one out," he told Mike.

Andy had once said of the Grapegrowers he helped found, "You don't go against the brotherhood," and he didn't. He, the Land Trust, and what should have been allies were telling Mike and Jim to back off, postpone, drop out. Mike wanted to say "Fuck you," but all he said was "No . . . no . . . no . . ."

Then, a few days after the tax assessor had approved the initial phase of the Water, Forest and Oak Woodland Protection Initiative in early spring 2016, including the collected signatures, he announced that the initiative was not going to be on the ballot after all. The reaction was one of loud dismay. He tried to explain the unexplainable: County counsel had, after initially reviewing the summary and title of the initiative, as he was required to do, engaged outside counsel to vet it. This was not a matter of course nor something the tax assessor had requested. Rather, county counsel had acted on his own. And in those outside lawyers' opinion, proponents of the initiative failed to meet the "full text" requirement.

This meant, in short, that in the lawyers' view proponents should have attached copies of older regulations from a previous measure known as the Voluntary Oak Woodland Management Plan of 2010. The proponents' lawyers hadn't included that language on grounds that it wasn't customary to list full texts, but the final decision remained with the tax assessor. A veteran of land valuation and a recognized old-school environmentalist with a salt-and-pepper beard and a ranch outside town inherited from his parents, he was also a career public employee with decades of experience in Napa and deep entrenchment in the county's official culture.

Denying the people a vote on what was perceived as a technicality stunned many observers. The clear impression was that the county, at the behest of the wine industry, was quashing the initiative for political reasons. The proponents' lead attorney at Shute, Mihaly & Weinberger said diplomatically, "The county got it wrong. The full text rule is a straightforward one." Expecting plaintiffs to list every law and appendix of every prior law that might be affected by a new initiative was unrealistic, she added, and the county assessor had "gone out on a limb" to reject the measure.

Of the flood of questions that followed, the most often asked was "Why?" The initiative had been prepared by this respected firm, which had much experience and was a lead proponent for initiatives all over the state. The whole process had turned into an aural version of the Japanese classic *Rashomon*, with each hearer interpreting it differently: Some insisted that it was proper, others that it was weak-kneed and ill timed, and yet others that the fix was in. But everyone agreed it was a public relations disaster, one that indicated extraordinary concern behind the scenes and an extraordinary willingness by the county to game the system.

The proponents' attorneys appealed the decision to the local superior court, known to favor the county, and that's just what the court did again. But what had begun as a popular cause for saving trees had become a pressing political problem, as well as an ethical one. As Mike Hackett was asking himself, so were others: "When does bias become corruption?"

2.

The supervisors' offices share a wing of the county administration building in downtown Napa next door to the jail and a block from the river. Tones are muted and a hush hangs over all. The young man rising from his desk with his right hand extended is a bit disconcerting to a visitor because of the supervisor's youth, only twenty-nine and yet a major player in a battle-scarred arena overlain with blemishless paint and taupe upholstery.

Alfredo Pedroza's not only the first Latino to be supervisor, but he's also the youngest board chairman ever. His big smile and ready handshake are well-practiced and his dress borderline preppy: muted plaid shirt, sport jacket, high-topped suede shoes, twined silver belt buckles, and a watch that, though not a Rolex, looks like it weighs as much.

Settling into his chair, Pedroza launches into an affecting origin story: a grandfather who came to Napa from the Michoacán region in western Mexico in the 1960s in the Bracero (manual laborer) Program and spent long years in the vineyards here. The supervisor's father, seventeen at the time, had a sixth-grade education and joined the crews of a vineyard developer. The Pedrozas lived in north Napa city—District 4, the same one that had just elected him—and Alfredo himself spoke no English when he entered kindergarten. He would attend Sonoma State University and eventually work in a credit union before being elected to the Napa City Council, the beginning of a banker's political ascent.

Even when Bill Dodd announced he was stepping down from the board of supervisors to run for the state senate, "The opening on the board wasn't on my political radar. Then a group of folks came and asked if I was interested in being appointed to fill the vacant seat." He won't stipulate precisely who those "folks" were beyond the Chamber of Commerce and other "organizations." Pedroza applied to the governor's office with a heartfelt endorsement from Dodd, who had switched from Republican to Democrat to get the new job, and got the appointment.

Pedroza's possible role in the demise of the initiative has become part of an ongoing debate on a track toward urban legend. He says he met beforehand with Mike Hackett, Jim Wilson, and Chris Malan, and justifies his statement in the newspaper—"We don't need an initiative hanging over our heads"—on grounds that he was referring to "the common good" and not equating himself with the wine industry.

When it's pointed out that some of his own constituents signed the initiative petition, he moves straight into big-picture mode: "We all need to talk about these things . . . We all want clean air and water . . . Regulation increases the cost of doing business for the small farmer." Only reluctantly does he then agree that there aren't really any of those left, and that tree cutting, stream setbacks, and clean water have been talked about for decades, if not a century.

What's clear is that initiatives in general rub the young chairman the wrong way. "We don't need initiatives to force discussion, that's part of our job," though the initiative process has been forcing discussion in California since the Progressive era when Governor Hiram Johnson, circa 1911, saw it as an alternative to voters overwhelmed by the clout of big business.

One of the most persistent stories dogging the Water, Forest and Oak Woodland Protection Initiative imbroglio is that on June 9, 2016, two days after the local election, Pedroza allegedly walked into the office of the county counsel and said, "We've got to figure out a way to kill this initiative."

Both Pedroza and the county counsel deny that this happened. The county counsel will not even say whether or not Pedroza came into his office that day to discuss the initiative because "that would require disclosure of privileged attorney-client communications." Many taxpayers assume county counsel represents them, not the supervisors. And Pedroza will not say when he decided to hire outside counsel, why, or how much it cost taxpayers.

Pedroza says, "I don't recall if I went into the county counsel's office on June 9 . . . When I get off the elevator in the morning I can go to the right, to my office, but I can just as easily go left . . . I don't think I did that day." He checks the calendar on his smartphone but doesn't reveal what he finds there. "I don't think so, that was not my intention."

A funereal hush has settled over the supervisors' inner sanctum. The chairman is perched on the edge of his chair, black eyes impenetrable. "If my constituents don't like the job I'm doing," he adds, "they can fire me in four years."

Proponents of the initiative now had a choice: start over with a longer list of particulars and amass new signatures before the August 12 deadline or go back to court. In the end there was no real choice, and their lawyers filed with the District Court of Appeal in San Francisco, asking for a reversal of the lower court that would certify the Water, Forest and Oak Woodland Protection Initiative.

Shute, Mihaly & Weinberger was the preeminent firm in initiative procedures, authors of Measure J that had also been denied by lower courts and went all the way to the California Supreme Court before achieving victory. Now they argued that upholding the lower court's negative decision in Napa would set a bad precedent for all upcoming initiatives in the state. Signature seekers would have to carry around piles of documents as thick as telephone directories to be signed, yet another subtle way to discourage people from undertaking the task in the first place.

The proponents had the support of the California Native Plant Society, California Wildlife Foundation, Forests Forever, Forest Unlimited, and Corporate Ethics International, and they felt sure this argument would prevail in San Francisco, but it didn't. The question quickly became how, not if, to approach the California Supreme Court.

To appeal the decision on a point-by-point basis would require a year or more, but the attorneys could go for a quick summary decision, a process usually reserved for emergencies such as stays of execution. They chose this course on grounds that the deadline for getting the initiative onto the 2016 ballot was imminent and there simply wasn't time for a formal appeal, hoping the court would recognize that.

But the justices with the most power in the state didn't consider the issue an emergency, and they declined to overrule the lower courts. This wasn't a ruling on the merits of the case, but it unleashed jubilation within the collective ranks of the opponents. Alfredo Pedroza told the *Napa Valley Register*: "We're glad this is over."

Reading that, Hackett didn't have to wonder about who "we" referred to. The quote was a "tell," he thought, and Pedroza was seemingly unaware that he had constituents who weren't industry leaders and didn't work for them and had added their names to the list of initiative supporters.

Not only had the initiative been kept off the ballot but the ruling had also inadvertently threatened the reputation of the law firm that was the long-established ally of environmentalists and preservationists. The courts had done the industry's work for it, for the moment, and it hadn't cost them a dime.

Not everyone realized—yet—that the court hadn't ruled on the merits, just on the emergency status. Or that opponents were now on record as having formally denied people the right to vote on what many believed was *the* issue. Citizens would continue to have no say in what happened in the hills unless initiative proponents decided to go through to the full appeal process.

In late August, Shute, Mihaly & Weinberger formally filed for a place on the regular appeals docket. The case might not come up for a year, but passion—and animosity—would build behind the scenes meanwhile among thousands of Napans who thought voter suppression was the best description of what had taken place. If the appeals court ruled favorably on the initiative, the Four Horsemen of the Apocalypse would be saddled not only with new limits on what they could do in fragile terrain, but also with a reputation as suppressors of the popular will and therefore of democracy itself.

3.

Mike Hackett decided to remain at the head of Save Rural Angwin, his old leisurely life unlikely to return. He rode on the Vision 2050 float in the Fourth of July parade in Napa that year, with Dan Mufson and others. In the crowd he saw Debra Dommen of Treasury Wine Estates and Jennifer Putnam of the Grapegrowers and heard them screaming, *"1850! 1850! . . ."*

It was a put-down of history as an important element in civic culture and of all opponents of development. It was also typically mean-spirited, he thought. The saddest part was that these women represented for the moment the unlovely, monolithic vintner/grower face in a new and desperate age, one that craved—including its tourists—some recognition of the simplicity and promise of the natural world of two hundred years before. And they didn't even realize it.

The whole initiative experience had drained and humbled Mike. "But this isn't going to die," he told anyone who asked, licking his wounds up on Howell Mountain. "Too many people are in favor. It's not just an initiative anymore, it's a movement."

The attorney sits at a sidewalk table outside Tarla Mediterranean Bar & Grill in the city of Napa, tarrying with a plate of meze and talking about the initiative. If it is eventually revised, the backers will have to get more signatures than before because there will have been many more votes cast in the upcoming 2016 general election. "The proponents'll need a given percentage of those," he says, "and it will be much higher than the last time around." Even if they get the necessary signatures, time will have been gained for new hillside clearing to be undertaken, the industry having adopted a variation of the environmentalists' occasional ploy: "Delay, delay, delay . . ."

The lawyer thoughtfully eats some flatbread weighted with hummus. "The system's broken," he says at last. "Now they're hiring outside lawyers to deny the people the right to vote and using the people's money to pay them. The only answer's to sue the county for refusing to obey the law. That means deposing the supervisors, deposing the lawyers in the county counsel's office, deposing the district attorney. They're all dependent on the wine industry for a social life and a lot more. We'll have to get a justice on the state Supreme Court to disqualify every judge in Napa County and bring in a panel from somewhere else that's capable of ruling fairly.

"It all reminds me of the water wars in Southern California a century ago. Now we have our own little *Chinatown*. To get Napa Valley back to something close to what it originally was will take a long, long time, but it's possible. And at this point the courts are the only way."

VII.

LIFE IN THE ANTHROPOCENE

*Citizens speak out; the future assumes
frightening prospects; and a survivor
turns to the past for inspiration.*

INTERLUDE:

The Plea

He sits at an outdoor table at the Napa Valley Coffee Roasting Company in St. Helena, his eyes, protected from the bright autumn sun by dark glasses, shifting occasionally to note arriving and departing customers. It's September 2016. His V-neck sweater is a throwback to the 1950s, attesting to the advent of cooler weather, and he folds his arms as if in deference to the gravity of what he's about to say.

"Caymus Vineyards paid a million-dollar fine for making many times the amount of wine it was allowed to make. *Many times!*" The winery, he thinks, could have made as much as ten million dollars from it, depriving citizens of tax revenue and adding mightily to pollutants released into the atmosphere. "Do you know how many truckloads of equipment, grapes, waste, bottles, and so on are required to make and move that much wine? It's many thousands. The environmental cost's enormous. Then the county turns around and allows Caymus to extend its visiting hours." He's a longtime member of the vintner class and has held jobs at almost every level in the firmament of fine California wine, including startup, sales, brand development, even for a time working for a white elephant. He knows the valley intimately and is known by it for a steady record of achievement, a lack of hubris, and a goodwill that transcends most political divisions.

He shakes his head. Caymus is more representative than anyone wants to admit, he says. It was formerly owned by old Charlie Wagner, who hired the fledgling Randy Dunn to make his wine for him, way back, and was generally known for fairness and tenacity. Charlie's son, Chuck, inherited his father's success, with all its grandfathered privileges, and turned it into "just another slam-dunk mega-producer." In an extraordinary statement to the *Napa Valley Register*, Chuck Wagner suggested that regulations on wineries are somehow anti-agriculture when, in fact, regulation is the one thing that has so far prevented agriculture's demise in Napa.

The lucky spermer factor seems to have been compounded at Caymus, meaning inherited wealth bestows advantages not enjoyed by most. Charlie Wagner's grandson sold his label Mer Soleil Vineyard in 2014 for a reported $350 million, a brand play with little inventory or anything else other than a reputation for softness on the palate and many fans.

Caymus's overage under Chuck's leadership is nothing exceptional in the valley. Vintners today are a different lot from those in the days of the nascent white elephants. Now they lament the effect of law enforcement, spotty as it is, on their behavior and bottom lines; this is a vintner of another sort, and this one sees more similarity to the big oil companies who, accommodated by the federal government, are well aware of the favoritism they enjoy.

"I went to a meeting of past presidents of the Napa Valley Vintners Association to discuss the enforcement of winery permit regulations. A vote was held on whether or not this was a good idea, and not one hand was raised in favor." He sips his coffee. "The game-changer in all this is citizens' objections. People are finally asking why they should be subsidizing a rich man's hobby.

"As for the vintners, we've met the enemy and he is us."

CHAPTER NINETEEN:

Voices

1. The Assistant

It's all so cynical, and so surprising in a place of such natural beauty. You look up at that view of the Mayacamas, but down here everyone's trying to figure out how to deal with incompetent bosses who hire people just to put them in front of other people in management meetings. Then they fire them two weeks later.

None of the managers of these businesses, whether wineries, restaurants, whatever, have time to actually manage because they're training assistant managers all the time. And they don't last. There's no real connection to anything anymore.

People with real talent and sophistication—mostly women like me—find themselves up against twin barriers: incompetent men, and members of our own sex who don't like the fact that some of us accent our clothes with designer touches and speak three languages.

Meanwhile billionaires drift in and out, innocents in their own ways, thinking everybody welcomes them when in reality they're just part of the wallpaper, exploitable and without intrinsic value. They don't realize that everybody who takes their money laughs at them.

In the 1990s, people would say, "I'm writing a movie script." That was cool. Then a few years passed and people started saying, "I'm writing a book." That was okay. Now you meet some guy who just got here after lucking into millions by selling some sugary label or bizarre phone app. He sidles up, all cozy, and says, "Guess what. I'm making a wine!"

You want to puke. Another wine. It's like these guys—first it was dot-commers, now sports figures, all without a clue—fell out of a crib and saw an empty wine bottle and thought they had gone to heaven.

The multinational effect doesn't help. Paradoxically, the big corporations display the worst parochialism. They refer all decisions, important and otherwise, back to the home office, and impose on the valley the true ineptitude of the corporate citizen. They're disassociated and, in the end, uncaring because caring gets in the way of hard decisions. These always favor the parent company and pave the way for the company's exit from a valley that was too alluring, and then proved to be too difficult.

These companies are accustomed to automatic profits uncomplicated by things like quality, laws, and promises. They have poisoned the well for everyone.

2. The Dot-commer

In this age of digital Darwinism the failure of the wineries to take advantage of the ongoing Internet revolution is amazing. But wineries have succumbed to Hollywood syndrome. Everybody wants to be a part of it, and the vintners know people will work for less money, for glamour. So what if the wineries don't get real talent? This inherent sloth comes from enotourism being so good and so easy.

The wine industry should focus on what people do after they go home, not just on luring them to the wineries. It needs e-commerce, but you don't find these technologies being developed. There's been no game-changer since the 1970s, except the cult wine phenomenon. Money's falling through most vintners' hands. They've begun to focus on this since the recession, when worldwide competition increased as never before. But too many are merely doubling down on enotourism while the digital boom a few miles south of us is transforming the universe.

3. The Investigator

No one knows how much wine the wineries are actually producing. As an investigator for the district attorney I go after tasting violations, but another whole level is the political. We had one investigator leave because she was told not to pursue a winery owned by a well-connected person. And you can't go to the supervisors with something like this and ask for help because the board's so treacherous.

In most counties you can go to Human Resources, too, but Napa's department is very weak and doesn't help with investigations of improper behavior in county government. They should be worried about liability but are afraid to cross the district attorney . . . It's so easy to make things disappear if you're the DA. People who might complain don't because of a spouse working elsewhere who might be fired if they do, or some other retaliation.

I didn't plan on living and working in such a place. The amount of money here is just unreal. Guys who know nothing buy a winery and then go to the DA to make sure they're covered, in case they get into trouble, a practice that's expanding. This is what I have to deal with. What I love about it is being able to help victims get back on the road to a decent life. But that's very hard because of the political situation.

4. The Researcher

I am often questioned about my work, which relates to foreign nationals, foreign banks, and offshore corporations that pose threats to the United States. It isn't focused on the county, only as it relates to projects that should have sought guidance from the Committee on Foreign Investment in the U.S. when foreign nationals are involved, such as Montalcino resort. That project was to develop in the Napa County Airport Specific Zone and by admission of the developer included foreign investors whose money was handled by a Chinese national. The project was rejected in 2001 but revived in 2004. I was astounded by this and appeared to challenge it on public safety grounds. The planning commission rejected the project, but within a month it was reversed again by the board of supervisors. One demonstrated her love of the project, even kissing her fingers and blowing off a kiss. I consider the people who threaten me to be associates of organized crime, for they definitely conspire as well. My position makes me a target of murder threats, stalking, and other unsavory behavior by those I dare to challenge. I am, however, well protected and not discounted by law enforcement when I need to report threats.

I highly recommend public service, particularly to the federal government when one's asked to help, as I was. It's a shame so many have tarnished their own names just to market their wines, or to see that they aren't harmed financially. And I am dismayed by how many people never read local papers, the Wall Street Journal, *or the* New York Times. *They live in their own little worlds, oblivious to the biggest changes this country is experiencing, and behave like sheep.*

5. The Startup

I worked as a sommelier for a while and then moved here and got a harvest job. I started a label with a few barrels of pinot noir in 2001. I got up to eight hundred cases and started a development plan for here in Soda Canyon. The recession was on, and the county was enthusiastic and thought we had the right scope.

We got through most of the hearing before the planning commission, and then a couple of neighbors showed up and objected to everything—traffic, noise, the installation of equipment, fire danger. My wife and I had reached out to the neighbors already, but these wouldn't even look at the plans. One said he'd object permanently, whatever changes we proposed, and that if we built our little winery, "we can't have sex on the deck anymore."

We settled with one by reducing visitation and making sight-line changes, but another one sued. He has a pro bono counsel. Then the planning department started asking for changes in plans already agreed on. We're also fighting on the state level. The Alcohol Beverage Control Board upheld our application, but the discovery demands were vast . . . So far we're allowed twenty visitors a day, six days a week. We can have one party during the Napa Valley wine auction, and two parties a year with up to fifty people, plus some smaller ones.

We were never interested in blowing up a brand to sell to a venture capitalist. We didn't want to get big, but people like us should have a legal pathway forward. We make compromises and agreements, but the ongoing fight's unsettling. We're up to three thousand cases a year and could go up to eight thousand. I'm forty-two years old and have never drawn a salary from the winery. We cobble together a livelihood, the bank coaching us on how to do it without partners.

It still looks like a wine camp in a beautiful place. As an artisan I want to make Rhône-type wines in a quiet environment, to experiment and use big puncheons. It's risky, but we don't plan to get larger. We're willing to pay more for grapes, and have some pinot noir and chardonnay from the Sonoma Coast. Is Napa losing its cachet? Maybe. But whatever happens I believe in Napa—the terroir and the climate.

We have to rediscover some things. We have to be flexible.

6. The Tourist

We tried to get a reservation at the French Laundry in Yountville for years. You have to call exactly one month before the date and callers are already lined up by the time the line opens. Well, we finally get through and the woman turns me down again but then I get a call a few days later. A reservation has opened up! It's more for late afternoon than evening, but would we like this opportunity?

We get there and are surprised by how small the place is. Almost cramped. But it's a very well-oiled operation. They get us to a table next to a stone wall, close to other tables but everybody behaving very well, a kind of hushed appreciation like you get in church. The other diners are middle-aged, too, and it's clear that a lot of them are on an expense account. This guy with a full head of prematurely white hair shows up in a bespoke suit and hands us menus, not the maître d' and not exactly a waiter, either. More like an impresario. He asks, "Would you like a glass of Champagne?"—real champagne, not California—and we say, "Sure."

We toast each other, and open the menus. It's going to be expensive, we know that, but we're ready. My wife orders from the vegetarian side and I order from the meat side—duck breasts—and the impresario asks, "Would you like some more Champagne?" We would, although I can tell that's not the right answer.

He pours, and then this whole train of dishes starts arriving, beautifully conceived and executed bits of stylized food on individual plates. We keep drinking the complimentary Champagne even though by now it's clear the impresario wants us to order something from the huge wine list. Eventually we do order two glasses of French wine because that seems to be mostly what they've got.

My duck breasts are pink and delicious. It doesn't matter so much how small they are because by now we've had all this other little stuff to eat. Then I see a guy in a white apron pushing a trolley among the tables, and on it is a domed serving dish. What I think is the waitress intercepts the trolley and pushes it the final ten feet to our table, and then the impresario appears and grandly lifts the silver cover. And there, in the middle of a cutting board, is what looks like a charred golf ball.

The impresario picks up a little silver hammer and taps the golf ball. The blackened sides fall away, revealing a beautiful little pearly turnip. I can hear someone murmur appreciatively at another table. The impresario takes this one-and-a-half-foot-long carving knife, sharpens it, extends his elbows out to the sides, and meticulously carves, fanning out quarter-size slices on a big plate. He places these in front of my wife and says, very seriously, "This turnip was grown less than one hundred yards from where you're sitting."

Later, as we walk back to the car, we can see the vegetable garden sandwiched between Washington Street and Highway 29. Those must be the most valuable vegetables in Napa Valley. Our bill was seven hundred dollars, but we did drink a lot of free Champagne and were given copies of our menus. And that turnip was really special.

7. The Changeling

I worked for Time *and* Sports Illustrated *in New York, sales and marketing, and pitched the idea for an e-company that failed. I still use the old Luce quote: "You can teach an editor to count, but you can't teach a salesman to write."*

In 2000 I was still having three-martini lunches with journalists on expense account. I read a lot about wine so I wouldn't just be picking Opus One to drink. I wanted to be able to tell a more interesting story and needed educating. Then I got caught up in all the stories.

I got a chance to go to the Wall Street Journal *and put down a deposit on an apartment in Brooklyn. Then I said to myself, "You're going to be working for forty years." So I turned the job down and moved to Sicily. I worked for a wine cooperative and learned to appreciate wine instead of just drinking it. We used wine as a condiment, like salt and pepper, not the way wine's used in the fantasies of Napa wine enthusiasts.*

I returned to New York and worked for a wine importer. I had been one of the "thirty under thirty" in the publishing world, a comer, and it shocked people that now I couldn't get a job in wine sales and marketing. Through a friend I did get one in Napa, in a cellar, where I learned about fermentation and vineyard management, and after four years I started my own wine and wrote my own marketing plan. But I still thought of Sicily where we drank fresh, crisp wines.

Now I'm a cabernet maker by day and a white wine maker by night. I did a field blend using Ribolla Gialla. All wine is intimidating, and most people won't buy a wine they can't pronounce, but white is a cash wine. You pick, make, and sell it, all in the first year, which turned out to be an opportunity. I was up 30 percent after the next year, 400 percent after five.

Doing weird, eccentric wines in cabernet country isn't a good business model. You have to build a platform. But the beauty of Napa Valley is cash flow; the problem is the cost of doing business. One acre isn't enough, you need ten acres and a winery, and a minimum of $8 million, total. It's a lifestyle business.

Now I have a representative who pours my wine at the French Laundry and some chic little places in San Francisco and in bistros from the Bowery to upper Manhattan. I can eat at four-star restaurants and explore more wines of the world. My job has enhanced my life. I can rent a better house, but I still have to work a second job. And I still work my ass off. Someday I may have the American dream and own a winery. I can even sell my dream, but people can't visit it because it's virtual.

We have a boom again in Napa. Without significant resources, it's very hard to even get your foot in the door. All the big icons—Montelena, Mondavi—have been leap-frogged, although the names still carry sales. Brand value, that's all, not quality.

Here the younger generation is saying, "My parents drank cabernet, I'm going to drink a cool wine." It's a DIY economy, everybody following a different dream, wanting their own business but wanting to be famous, too. I'm too old for this. You have to always be representing yourself on social media, and there are all these different groups now—anti-Parker, and the big flavor group. You don't like one critic, or you do. It's no different from the early movements, and a fucking headache, with people fighting what they see as the establishment.

The so-called New Californians isn't a cohesive group, there's no collective, unifying force. Just a bunch of people throwing rocks from different directions.

Napa produces such a small amount of wine, a drop in the global bucket, and we're at a crucial point in the industry and don't know where it's going.

The real question is what's going to happen during a thirty-, fifty-, maybe a hundred-year drought. The one percent of the one percent will still be making wine in 2050 but it'll all be a thousand dollars a bottle and up, and all cabernet. There'll be a lot less of it. Crop yields will fall, the cost of water and farming will go up. And up. Grapes will cost twenty thousand dollars a ton for starters, instead of five, and no one will be planting esoteric varieties.

I joined a climate change task force in 2008. Someone said that the best grapes in 2100 won't be grown in Napa, they'll be grown in the Rockies. The Napa Valley Vintners Association had to fight that, and spent a lot of money trying to refute the argument.

I've been here ten years, and harvest already comes six weeks sooner today. The style of wine has shifted from using vines as sugar-making machines to replanting those that produce better, cleaner, healthier grapes. But I'm too close to it all and I'm trying to isolate a bit. People are beginning to settle down, some have ADD and won't listen to you complain for long, and the older generation, the boomers, doesn't give a shit. You can play with names and political positions over the ages, but nothing really changes. Eventually you just have to say, "Hey, I'm making wine."

CHAPTER TWENTY:

2050

1.

Way back in 1980 a professor named R. W. Butler at the far-distant University of Western Ontario wrote an obscure paper entitled *The Concept of a Tourist Area Cycle of Evolution*. In it he quoted the German geographer Walter Christaller, who had used artists as an example of early discoverers of special places.

If his research had been in Napa, he could as well have used aspiring winemakers instead who

> search out untouched and unusual places . . . Step by step the place develops as a so-called artist colony. Soon a cluster of poets follows . . . then cinema people, gourmets, and the jeunesse dorée [wealthy, trendy young people]. The place becomes fashionable and entrepreneurs take note. The fisherman's cottage, the shelter-huts become converted into boarding houses and hotels come on the scene. Meanwhile the painters have fled . . . Only [those] with a commercial inclination who like

to do well in business remain; they capitalize on the good name of this former painter's corner and on the gullibility of tourists. . . . At last the tourist agencies come . . .

Substitute Yountville, St. Helena, and Calistoga for "untouched and unusual places" which, in the 1950s and 1960s, all had similarities to the model. Butler imagined six stages of tourist evolution: *exploration* (relatively few tourists and no secondary attractions); *involvement* (locals get into the business and pressure government to promote it); *development* (tourist numbers increase; heavy advertising begins; local government control begins to slip away; external businesses move in; natural and cultural attractions are developed and marketed; and residents are increasingly affected against their wishes); *consolidation* (the economy is tied to tourism; major corporations and franchises move in, including resorts, creating defined business districts; discontent and opposition grows among locals); and *stagnation* (carrying capacity exceeded; tourism causes environmental, social, and economic problems; resorts are divorced from the geographic environment; artificial attractions supersede original ones; the area loses fashionability).

Butler's final stage, *decline*, is the most interesting. In it, upscale tourists are replaced by weekenders, then day-trippers, and finally by something even less desirable. Tourism facilities are replaced by other enterprises, and enhanced transportation routes are required. Hotels and resorts are converted to retirement homes and low-income housing. The last long-term residents move away, and the place succumbs, in the worst case, to a tourist slum with seedy venues and warehouses.

Rejuvenation is possible only through a radical change in attractions, Butler concludes, which in Napa Valley's case would likely mean the age-old siren of full-blown real estate development on the valley floor and the hillsides.

With Butler's model and the prospect of increased global warming, it's not hard to imagine a nightmare scenario for a desperate valley lacking sufficient water and stripped of land-use regulations: carnival attractions in what was once countryside, mass-market "tasting rooms" (bars) for wine made elsewhere and anything else that sells, quickly built structures for storing and moving product, and mass entertainment. And adult entertainment theme parks at some wineries require reservations far in advance, calling to mind the waiting time once required for the French Laundry that in this scenario has moved north to Lake County's less populated, still-quasi-rural landscape, while other amenities in Mendocino and Humboldt Counties draw increasing numbers of high-end tourists leaving the hassle and heat of Napa far behind.

Caltrans builds the interstate up the middle of the valley that it has wanted since the 1960s, when the agency designed one and was thwarted only by the concerted efforts of Jack and Jamie Davies and other up-valley socialites. The Wine Train, too, has become a people-mover crowded with commuters to jobs elsewhere and for day-trippers from the East Bay with coupon books for various attractions, including the popular, retro Whack-A-Grape game.

The hard-baked, droughty valley floor is sustaining fewer grapes than it once did, before the aquifer's drawdown and spiking water prices. Some once-stellar resorts have been converted to condos, low-income housing, and a retirement home for animals left annuities by deceased owners. The hotel in south St. Helena built in 2018 has been transformed by 2060 into a minimum-security prison for overflow from the sprawling megalopolis of Napa/American Canyon. A few years later, the Auberge du Soleil is rededicated with fanfare as an isolation ward for sufferers of mysterious new medical conditions as temperatures continue to rise and authorities fear out-of-control epidemics.

In east Napa County, a portion of the unincorporated town of Walt has succumbed to gravity, closing Monticello Road permanently. Some of the ranchettes have been abandoned because of lack of water, while over in St. Helena Bell Canyon Reservoir may still have water but the sediment rushing down after rare winter rainstorms is so prodigious and chemical-laced from development and pesticides and herbicides, and the standing water so algal and now toxic, that authorities don't dare use it.

The valley's most exclusive mega-community, an eight-hundred-acre compound of baronial mansions with show vines west of Yountville, called Promontory, is surrounded by a ten-foot steel palisade fence and its private reservoir patrolled by armed guards. Water impoundment is in effect everywhere, and so competitive and difficult has the search for water become that restrictions on piping it directly from what were public sources to developments, vineyards, and private homes are lifted. An enormous price is charged by corporations that have taken control of most reservoirs and remaining wells, and still paid by a few very wealthy landowners.

Physical conflicts over access to water continue, with gunshots heard constantly in the hills and the entire watershed dangerous for both people and low-flying drones used for surveillance and for fighting microbial vectors with the proliferation of new chemical brews. Less than a quarter of the vines that once thrived in Napa County survive, if barely, and lack the fruity fullness of old. Some quality has been maintained, however, despite the need to remove alcohol and enhance with additives no longer requiring identification on labels.

Wines made from these grapes are more curiosities than classics, but some are highly prized in China, where collectors pay upwards of $75,000 for a single bottle of To Kalon cabernet sauvignon. That heavily guarded vineyard stands as a de facto historic exhibit in the midst of dwellings next to the interstate, its runty grapes clinging like Ozymandian reminders of a forgotten past, gawked at by day-trippers and at night pilfered by armed bootleggers. The long, illicit supply chain is reminiscent of the one during Prohibition, though the percentage of Americans still drinking wine instead of spirits and beer has dropped precipitously with the increasingly heavy use of cannabis and the ever-proliferating variety of designer drugs.

2.

The foregoing is fanciful, some of it preposterous. But all is still possible, increasingly so with time. And none of the industrial groups supposedly overseeing rural Napa's health and prosperity today has looked deeply into this subject. One reason is that honest studies tend to suggest that the only way to survive as a grower and a winemaker is to move farther north, or high into the Sierra or the Rockies. Dwelling on such possibilities is to imperil the sale of wine futures, glamour, and the prospect of eternally growing success that has been the subtext of promotion for more than a century.

The Napa Valley Vintners did look some years ago into the future of the thermal inversion that keeps cool air pumping into the valley from the bay, but nothing much came of it. Neither the Grapegrowers nor the Farm Bureau has done anything similar, and the Winegrowers of Napa County doesn't study. To find informed vocal concern about Napa's future beyond the loose ranks of environmentalists the county must turn, ironically, to a neighbor over in Sonoma County.

High on the windward side of the Mayacamas and east of Santa Rosa is an exemplary scientific redoubt called the Pepperwood Preserve, founded with money from the Bechtel family and dedicated to monitoring the effects of climate change on the biome, wildlife, air, water, even fog. The president, Lisa Micheli, did significant work in Napa on the Rutherford Reach Restoration Project and the lower Napa River's augmented wetlands and has proven herself both knowledgeable and continuously engaged. She's willing to discuss the possible effects of climate change on Napa by midcentury with the proviso that it is simply informed speculation.

The population of California is expected to rise by at least a third in 2050, to sixty million people. Temperatures should be between 4 and 7 percent higher than today. Part of the difficulty of predicting is that the effects of this rise vary according to how much rain falls each year, but a conservative estimate is that water shortages will be severe, and certainly so by contemporary standards.

The effect of climate change on the watershed itself will be more alarming, with sequential tree die-offs due to the increasing heat, and rain deficits. A significant increase in the number and intensity of wildfires will be due to much more fallen, incendiary timber. The scarcity of water will likely hamper firefighting efforts, and most properties will not be judged worth the effort to save them.

As for the river itself, flooding is likely to continue due to rarer but more intense storms, which means that mid-valley the water will continue to inundate vineyards and residential spreads. The city of Napa won't be much affected since a three-foot sea rise could be accommodated by the wetlands to the south. But sedimentation will continue upstream with increased vineyard construction and because both river and streams continue to cut into steep, scoured-out hillsides.

Tree clearing in the hills will mean ever-increasing runoff and sedimentation, and a greater loss of water that would otherwise soak into the ground and replenish pockets of water in the valley's vast subsurface of broken rock which feed the aquifer. Houses and other structures are and will ever be a still-far-worse fate than vineyards, however, because they prevent water from being absorbed by the earth and exacerbate all other environmental problems.

Water will remain the biggest concern. In the end, she says, "It could come down to who gets it—people or grapes?"

CHAPTER TWENTY-ONE

Jefferson's Ghost

1.

The trailer court is off Soscol Avenue, on the northwestern edge of the city of Napa. Single- and double-wides have been cladded to look like real houses, with driveways and even some trees. The cars are clean and bright in the sun, the speed bumps effective, and the small, meticulously kept lawns as devoid of people as those in more affluent subdivisions.

Halfway around the loop a little-noticed lane leads south, then west. Follow it between two long lines of makeshift fencing and suddenly perception is bent and an alternative life appears in the gap between reality and fancy: fruit trees, a couple of middling redwoods, a yellow farmhouse with a tin roof and an old, steep-raftered, swaybacked barn, all suggesting—if you ignore the solar panels—not 2016 but 1904.

Stroll past the old head-trained merlot vineyard where tiny marigolds grow amid native grasses. A narrow-gauge tractor bakes in the sun, near a defunct, one-armed pump for Go Further gas. Beyond the knife-edged shadow of the barn is a spraying tank, stacked rebar, a pile of jacks and plastic cans, a little Caterpillar, and a pastiche of old tools and artifacts rivaling Randy Dunn's.

A pickup pulls in and a slight young man gets out, wearing a T-shirt and jeans but looking decidedly more metrosexual than redneck: short, receding hair, an open if watchful demeanor, blue eyes. His name's Steve Matthiasson and this place has survived largely through inadvertence and discovery by his wife, Jill, while reading the *Napa Valley Register*.

He worked then for a vineyard service company, she ran a nonprofit out of their house in the heart of Napa city, both yearning for a place in the country to which they could move before their two boys were ten years old. They had long searched for what was no longer supposed to exist: an inexpensive remnant of the vanished past affordable to a young couple without inheritance or stock plays. And yet here one apparently was, right on the county line, right in front of everybody's eyes but too shabby to be noticed.

Jill sent Steve to investigate. He couldn't find the house. There wasn't anything in the GPS data bank, but he finally stumbled upon what was clearly a teardown, called the old Bruno Ranch, which had subsisted for a long time on chickens, walnuts, prunes, hay, and merlot before the place went vacant. "They couldn't sell it because of the trailer camp. It had only three electrical plugs, blankets over the windows. Plaster was falling off the walls, and the Wedgewood stove was full of trash."

He brought Jill back to look at it, and she started crying. They made a low-ball offer anyway, and to their surprise it was accepted. So they sold their house in town and bought this misery trove on five hardscrabble acres, too close to a revamped trailer court to ever be chic. Steve's mother, visiting at the time, stripped to her underwear and started spackling, setting the pace for a long-term effort.

To a stranger the place seems to embody both the Jeffersonian ideal of self-sufficiency and the incessant labor of vineyard life that Jefferson questioned later on. Both Jill and Steve still have day jobs, and he has three or four, depending on the number of viticultural clients. Born in Winnipeg, Steve spent time on a family farm in North Dakota and ended up in San Francisco, his biography already dense with the stations of the millennial cross: philosophy student, punk rocker, bike messenger, community gardener, UC Davis student, and a partner committed to a reordering of an old American agricultural dream.

Jill worked for the Community Alliance with Family Farmers and organized field days and community food box deliveries. Steve wanted to make wine, and he saw Napa as "a marquee region equivalent to Bordeaux, Tuscany, Rioja," based on wines he had tasted, all made before the cult wine phenomenon. He thought those of the 1970s and 1980s could be made in that style again, in Napa. Even some of Napa's signature cabernets made in the early 1990s had great appeal. "The Mondavi Reserve blew me away," he recalls, when asked for an example. "I was waiting for the pendulum to swing back again."

He worried about the Napa brand "maintaining relevance." Like Bordeaux, it wasn't as exciting as at an earlier time, yet he found himself defending it. Then he got a job offer in the valley and accepted: "I felt like we were getting out of the bush leagues."

He had given up on buying a farm and began making wine at a custom crusher from purchased grapes, "the most environmentally sound way," leasing small plots owned by people who shared his tastes and farming values. "We found we could pay modestly and farm our own vines on their land. There was so much going on in this valley, much of it under the radar."

With the barter of time and expertise he got advice and the use of others' equipment. "You could figure out how to get things done, and there's always somebody you can borrow from. It was like doing a startup in Silicon Valley." Meet somebody at a school drop-off during harvest who has extra grapes and make a deal. Chat with someone who's not happy with her corks and realize you can help her, all counter to the corporate model.

Then the old Bruno place came along. "It's still a tumultuous time in Napa," he says, "like the 1960s" but far from Aquarian. In fact it's the opposite, instead of drugs and free love "you challenge the system from the inside, and accept hard, cooperative work."

The story evokes memories of early Napa adventures like those at Schramsberg, Stag's Leap, Newton, Forman, Dunn. They all found the valley a relatively unspoiled place where the future of farming was a spiritual pursuit with its own scriptural texts in the Williamson Act and the law establishing the agricultural preserve. Newly arriving inhabitants of white elephants seemed to accept inherent limitations on what they could do and share a concern for overall well-being.

"Eden" is a figurative stretch for what the valley once represented, but all vestiges of that early innocence are lost. The remnant fig leaf kept in place by the wine and hospitality industries grows more tattered every year, revealing more schemes to transform a way of life into a marketable experience as or more valuable than the thing itself. Napa isn't Disneyland, but it is a "destination" for the enjoyment of the "other," farming's savvy cousin out there creating envy in the vineyard.

Steve used stuff he found in the old barn and still does. It's an unreproducible resource as only some implements of former toil can be. In what would now be called a "heritage vineyard" he grafted other vines onto the merlot rootstock and kept making wine. In a few years people started writing about his subtle flavors and low alcohol. Some were made of the usual suspects, like chardonnay, while others were made from grapes few had heard of, including Ribolla.

Then Jon Bonné wrote a piece for the *San Francisco Chronicle*, "and sales really kicked in," Steve remembers. His wines weren't cheap, but neither were they expensive by Napa standards. There's something ineffable there that big, fruity blockbusters lack, not shock and awe, integrity.

The Matthiasson brand fit nicely within the farm-to-table movement, "less about technique, more about impeccable fruit. Young people started seeking out new brands. The old success path was still Parker and the *Spectator*, but we didn't take it." He pauses. "The hundred-point scale's ridiculous—they wouldn't put carrots on it, for instance. A good score still helps, but a 'bad' score doesn't necessarily hurt now."

The *Wine Spectator* gave a Matthiasson wine a mere 88, "and we didn't even hear about it." The wine sold out anyway. "Now there are more young people doing what they care about, with passion," and that includes drinking unhyped wines. "It's coming back to that. We were just a little ahead of the curve, but the market was always there." Media coverage helped, and aided in the fracturing of the old wine industry. "Things went viral—Instagram, Twitter—adding to what is a very exciting time to be making wine, even though there are houses popping up everywhere."

He gestures beyond the little canal toward the broad vista of vineyards in the middle of which houses rise like sleepy mastodons, sheathed in Tyvek. This doesn't bother Steve. "The Farmers Guild's trying to revive the old granges," he says. "Back-to-the-land has swung round again, a worldwide phenomenon. It's all tied to dining, the crafts movement, home cooking, and wine's part of it. Living way in the country isn't as appealing as it once was," a reference to the huge swaths of rural America plagued with joblessness, poverty, and drugs. "The new people moving in here aren't all rich pricks. Some of them care about their vineyards. They take pride in having their names on a bottle."

He's helping them do it. From their perspective, having a recognized viticulturist living in the neighborhood is an asset: He can manage their vineyards, the latter-day, Californian version of Jefferson's Italian vineyardist, Filippo Mazzei, the big difference being that Matthiasson has succeeded where Jefferson and Mazzei failed. Steve thinks his example helps bind newcomers to place through agriculture and the shared mystery of wine, a happier version of the evolved yeoman farmer.

Jefferson's view of the vigneron's life changed radically between the time he first wrote of it as fitting for the Virginia yeoman farmer and his declining years when he saw it as drudgery. As mercurial as anyone, Jefferson's ideals often tumbled in the rough presence of reality.

There's another analogy, unavoidable as the long shadows reach for this little farmstead all the way from the Mayacamas, as if riding breezes under a luminous California sky. The third president of the United States and the dot-commers and other strivers putting up houses out there have something else in common, not just brains and money made far from rudimentary toil, but a consuming love of abode. No American of historical significance ever put more thought, treasure, and time into his own house than did Thomas Jefferson, often foolishly. He may have brought to his house imagination and a Palladian obsession, but he also brought the inability to ever declare it finished.

Included in Jefferson's unfulfilled domestic vision were a producing vineyard and a wine of his own. Now, in this broad, beautiful expanse of valley and hills, stunning views are a matter of course and the afternoon shadows sharp-edged, darkness riding behind. Jefferson's vision of vines as a natural complement to the landscape isn't just aspirational here, where hammer blows ring like distant gunshots and glossy blue-black clusters of cabernet sauvignon hang unperturbed in the soft evening air.

EPILOGUE:

Wildlake Revisited

It's late afternoon when we hoist our mountain bikes off the tailgate of Randy Dunn's Ford pickup and ride down toward the entrance to Wildlake. He's still waiting to hear from Cal Fire about the contested timber removal permit for the land next door, but work there has been delayed until that decision's made, at which time a whole new chapter will begin.

Another vineyard is being developed on the mountainside, farther up, and a haze of dust hangs over it, creating in the distance a blemish like that of a nascent wildfire. It has been a full year since we prepared for the 2015 inferno on Howell Mountain, and this one, too, will be the hottest on record. Stories persist of land subsiding over in the Central Valley, and of dry spigots left by disappearing groundwater. Fish and other living things are threatened with extinction if the drought returns, as it must. El Niño pushed moisture past the North Pacific High out in the Pacific this past winter, but the relief was temporary. Another big fire in Sequoia National Park has filled the southern Sierra Nevada with smoke, and farther south, all the way to Malibu, brush fires keep Los Angeles on edge.

But today is about mountain biking, not firefighting, and we take off, broken clouds coming in from the northwest allowing a shaft of sunlight through now and then. The trip down is fast and, unless a rider's somewhat adept, dangerous. Randy knows the road so well that ruts and exposed rocks have personas all their own, like the changing vistas full of chaparral and big trees.

Randy has the legs and lungs of a younger man. More than once he has taken those half his age down and back up the road from the dense bowl of Wildlake, only to see them vomit in the weeds. Now he wears a ripstop pack in which he carries water, a knife, microchips for the motion-sensor cameras he has mounted along stream banks, and replacement batteries. On every expedition he takes back the used chips and inserts them into his Mac in the office and watches the passage of wildlife: gray foxes, coyotes—sometimes a rabbit with lean jaws, black-tailed deer, and bears great and small that press wet black noses to the lenses.

Only the elegant mountain lion gazes knowingly at the light that comes on automatically at night, piercing the darkness she owns. In the beginning Randy rode with an automatic pistol on his hip, reasoning that if a lion dropped from a tree limb onto his back mid-pedal he might at least have a chance of surviving. But he found that the weapon changed his relationship with everything around him, and he stopped carrying it. He didn't start again after he saw the first gear-laden human torsos on his computer screen—dope growers passing a camera—and started looking for their stash.

We leave the road, drop into low gear, and head up a serpentine game trail above the stream. Dismounting before a barrier of manzanita, we continue on foot, grabbing at roots and tree branches. Randy reported the trespassers to the state's drug enforcement agency and that brought the authorities winging over this stretch of wilderness several times before spotting the cannabis patch below a seep. The agents later paid a visit and found the crop and the telltale black plastic drip line just like those used in the vineyards, but apprehended no one.

Randy has the coordinates and he enters them into his GPS, having decided it's not suicidal to ground-truth the site and see for himself what the growers left behind. But neither does it make for the most comfortable hike. Then we're in the midst of it, the ground torn up by trenching tools, the plants mostly jerked out. A few little spiky cannabis leaves remain, and a plastic line snaking on upslope, into shadow.

He keeps going. At the end is a half-buried blue plastic bin below a spring, the water crystal clear and probably still full of fertilizer brought up on somebody's shoulder. The whole scene is oddly elegiac, no mechanical sound in this fastness, just wind and the call of a red-tail hawk winging determinedly northward. That's the direction from which fiery disaster would have come a year ago. When that fire was over people called me from far away and asked, "Is Napa burning?" No, I told them, Napa isn't burning, but the question stayed with me.

Misfortune seems inherent in every season these days, the future ever more likely to fill with falling embers, and with bulldozers. Vineyard development is legal but leaves more than an imprint on the land and bits of plastic pipe, owing to irremediable transformation. The time has come to say "No more," both on principle and as a practicality, words not just for Napa but also for America. But even as they form on the lips they trigger a savage blowback from the collective harvesters of the last resource.

The hawk screams. From up there the valley to the south appears, as any pilot knows, a green-knit homogenous whole. Its verdancy is shared by vineyard and forest alike, and even human-built structures seem subservient to the natural order. This is an illusion as sure as the distant, hazy shimmer of what seems to be an unpopulated inland shore. That's the San Francisco Bay littoral, home to more than three million people, a number that grows daily, and beyond it live millions more. By century's end they will number eighty million. Many are likely in time to pass through these lovely mountains and will pause as they do now, nature-struck, whether tourists, investors, or refugees, all momentarily stunned by the beauty of the place. Then they'll be off again, as they are today, an inexhaustible, ever-transient source of wealth, conflict, and impossible dreams.

AFTERWORD

In the winter of 2016–17 more rain fell in California than in many years. The Sierra snowpack was formidable and slow to melt, the governor relaxed some restrictions on water usage, and the drought was widely heralded as a thing of the past. But much of that snowpack flowed to the sea. By summer wildfires again became a serious threat all over the state, in part because of all the new growth, and regulators worried about the ongoing availability of water to slake the Golden State's awesome, ever-growing thirst.

The fisheries biologist hired by opponents of development on Howell Mountain found rainbow trout in the upper reaches of Conn Creek, where they were not supposed to be. This small miracle meant that various development plans had to be reworked, or abandoned, and that for a brief moment a few pretty little fingerlings could outshine the brightest lights in the firmament of human endeavor.

Donald Trump was now president, and although Napans voted overwhelmingly for his opponent, many among the vintner and grower classes did not. They were happy with Trump's general opposition to regulation, but increasingly out of step with a county—and a state—desirous of environmental safeguards.

A serendipitous new ally of opponents to development in the valley was the thirty-mile extension of the fault line brought on by the earthquake of 2014 that now extended from the city of Napa to Calistoga, up the west side of Highway 29.

Farmer Andy Beckstoffer finally got a hearing by the county in his challenge to Raymond Vineyards' activities, including the Red Room. Meanwhile Jean-Charles Boisset had bought the winery next door. The supervisors voted three to two not to act on Andy's complaint, including Alfredo Pedroza, who intoned, "This is not Disneyland. . . . This is agriculture in the twenty-first century."

The appeal by backers of the Water, Forest and Oak Woodland Protection Initiative did not prevail in the state supreme court, but proponents vowed to gather signatures again and finally get the issue placed on the 2018 ballot. Few in the county doubted that they would find more signatories than before, or that such an initiative would finally be approved by voters.

Then something unexpected occurred: a spokesperson for the Napa Valley Vintners secretly approached the initiative's proponents and offered to join with them in the renewed effort to pass it. The issue remained so contentious among members of all of the so-called Four Horsemen of the Apocalypse that a confidentiality agreement had to be signed by the negotiators to prevent a revolt before a deal could be done.

By midsummer 2017, several meetings had taken place and a new spirit of trust seemed to prevail. New guidelines were agreed to by environmentalists and members of the Vintners' representatives. In general the terms included greater stream setbacks and woodlands protection, including replacing every oak tree felled for development with three others on the property whose long-term growth was assured, and by 2030 all cutting of oaks would be prohibited.

So, after much acrimony, despair, political maneuvering, spent time and money, and the loss of overall goodwill, the hillsides seemed destined for additional protection. But reaction to the agreement, when revealed to the Vintner's membership, was loudly condemnatory and at the organization withdrew from the agreement. There was simply too much demand for a piece of what was once Edenic, and too much wealth to be denied, though for a moment the possibility of meaningful change had hung in the balance.

Then came the terrible fires in the fall of 2017. Reading and watching the news, I was horrified by their intensity and speed. I had predicted something similar, though further out in time, and felt as if I had somehow helped summon up the disaster. A preamble had been provided two years before on Howell Mountain, and again the fires spared Dunn Vineyards.

But this time more than six hundred structures in the county were damaged, though the percentage of actual destruction of Napa wineries was minuscule, and all the over-all damage small, when compared to what happened in neighboring Sonoma Country. Originally thought to have been set, the fires were nevertheless of human origin, since PG&E lines going down in the winds were the apparent culprits. Those lines were installed to fuel not just the valley's wineries and vineyard operations but also households and three million-plus annual visitors and all the services of a touristic juggernaut.

Developers and professional growers immediately called for new vineyards that would bring the clearing of more forests, claiming that vineyards make good firebreaks. They also mean more water loss, more people, and more activities unrelated to agriculture - houses, roads, service buildings, power lines.

Everyone in the wine industry was making money, ramped-up tourism pushing the county's annual take into the billions. But county officials seemed increasingly uncomfortable with controversial projects. Even Deep Root sounded guardedly optimistic: "The county's climate action plan has been discredited and has to be rewritten. . . . Every millimeter of land will eventually be subject to new laws, which means hundreds of thousands of trees can be saved that might not have been. The system is crumbling from within, people are finally starting to pay attention."

Huntly, Virginia
October 20, 2017

ACKNOWLEDGMENTS

Many people helped with shaping this book with stories, opinions, and facts about the valley and the momentous changes there since *Napa* and *The Far Side of Eden* were published. Others helped immeasurably with criticism of the work itself, foremost among them my friend and agent, Ralph Eubanks, who was there from the beginning with unerring judgment and a steady hand.

I want to thank Ben Loehnen for his fresh perspective and guidance, and everyone at Simon & Schuster for their professionalism and care. My wife, Penny, was an inspiration, as was my daughter, Susanna, who helped me look at the writing in a new way. Likewise, among my friends who made suggestions I am particularly indebted to Ridgeway Hall, John Lang, Meredith Hadaway, Joanne Omang, Mark Borthwick, and Paul Franson. There are many others who helped in various ways and to whom I am immensely grateful. Their names are omitted not by choice but because in Napa feelings run high and friendships sometimes hinge perilously on issues and affiliations.

Lastly, I want to pay fond tribute to Napa County itself, a place like no other. In retrospect it seems as innocent as I was when I first arrived, and even today its beauty and example can, against all odds, still engender hope.

INDEX

About The Author

James Conaway grew up in Memphis, but lived in Europe for several years before moving to Washington, D.C. A former Wallace Stenger fellow at Stanford University, he's the author of thirteen books, including the *New York Times* bestseller, *Napa: The Story of an American Eden*. He divides his time between Washington, D.C., and California.